THE COMPLETE PLANT-BASED DIET COOKBOOK FOR BEGINNERS

1500 Days of Easy and Affordable Recipes to Reduce Your Inflammation. Eat Healthy & Clean to Take Care of Your Health with NO Flavor Sacrifice

Richard Clem

Table of Contents

Introduction...8

Chapter: 1 Plant Based Diet Fundamentals 10

1. 1.1 What is Plant Diet?.............................10

2. 1.2 Benefits of Plant diet.........................10

3. 1.3 Foods to include in your diet.................11

4. 1.4 Foods to Avoid 12

5. 1.5 A One-Week Meal Plan 13

6. 1.6 Latest Research on Plant-based Diets.........13

7. 1.7 What's the bottom line? 14

Chapter: 2 Plant Based Breakfast Options 15

1. Orange French Toast...............................15

2. Baked Mushroom Polenta Bowls.....................15

3. Gluten-free Breakfast Muffin 16

4. Banana Sandwich...................................16

5. Blueberry Lemon French Toast.....................17

6. Antioxidant Blueberry Smoothie 17

7. Chewy Oatmeal Banana Pancakes....................17

8. Banana Baked Oatmeal.............................18

9. Vegan Breakfast Benedict 18

10. Tofu Scramble...................................18

11. Baked Bean Toast 19

12. Gluten-Free Chocolate Chip Pancakes 19

13. Banana Almond Granola 20

14. Chickpea Omelet.................................20

15. Pears and Cranberries...........................21

16. Healthy Oatmeal with Fruit and Nuts 21

17. Egyptian Breakfast Beans........................21

18. Apple-Lemon Breakfast Bowl 22

19. Breakfast Scramble 22

20. Brown Rice Breakfast Pudding 22

21. Chocolate Buttermilk Pancakes...................23

22. Black Bean and Sweet Potato Hash................23

23. Easy Overnight Oats with Chia...................24

24. Apple-Walnut Breakfast Bread 24

25. Garlic-Jalapeño Naan............................24

26. Vegan Kale Caesar Salad.........................25

27. Smokey Tempeh Bacon 26

28. Oil-Free Blueberry Scones 26

29. Country Hash Browns with Sausage Gravy......27

30. Pumpkin Pie Cake................................27

31. Low Fat Cinnamon Nut Granola 28

32. Vegan Yogurt Parfait with Berries & Granola .. 28

33. Easy Breakfast Chia Pudding.....................29

34. Oil-Free Roasted Potatoes.......................29

35. Vegan Huevos Ranchero Case roll.................29

36. Crustless Broccoli Sun-Dried Tomato Quiche .. 30

37. Mint Chocolate Smoothie.........................30

38. Banana Bread with Maple Glaze 31

39. Cornmeal Waffles................................31

40. Blueberry Lemon Bars 32

41. Buckwheat Pancakes 32

42. Oatmeal with Berries and Nuts..................33

43. Carrot Chia Pudding.............................33

44. Sweet Potato Hash Browns........................34

45. Hibiscus Tea 34

46. Lentil Oats Power Porridge 34

47. Baked Pears with Cardamom.......................35

48. Mushroom Veggie Tacos 35

49. Zucchini Cakes..................................35

50. Baked Corn Casserole............................36

51. Yummy Jelly & Peanut Butter Oatmeal 36

52. Sweet Potatoes with a Twist.....................37

53. Fresh Avocado Toast with Pesto 37

54. Crunchy Almond Cereal Breakfast 37

55. Gluten-Free Chocolate Chip Muffins 38

56. Vegan Breakfast Potatoes 38

57. Vegan Whole Wheat Waffles 39

58. Healthy Cinnamon Apples 39

59. Simple Avocado Toast 39

60. Quinoa & Breakfast Patties 40

61. Mixed Berry Bowl 40

62. Pumpkin Griddle Cakes 40

63. Cinnamon Semolina Porridge 41

64. Creamy Porridge with Almonds 41

65. Pineapple and Mango Oatmeal 41

66. Date and Oat Flour Waffles 41

67. Mango Madness 42

68. Sweet Polenta with Pears 42

Chapter: 3 Plant Based Lunch Options 43

69. Butternut Squash and Chickpea Curry 43

70. Cauliflower and Chickpeas Casserole 43

71. Brown Rice with Vegetables and Tofu 44

72. Maple Glazed Tempeh with Quinoa and Kale .. 44

73. Curried Rice 45

74. Grain Dishes Cranberry and Walnut Brown Rice
....45

75. Quinoa Lentil Burger 45

76. Spicy Hummus Quesadillas 46

77. Peanut Soup with Veggies 46

78. Vegetable Stir-fry 46

79. Sweet Oatmeal "Grits" 47

80. Cilantro and Avocado Lime Rice 47

81. Chickpeas and Sweet Potato Curry 48

82. Balsamic Arugula and Beets 48

83. Coconut Rice 48

84. Brown Rice Pilaf 48

85. Coconut Sorghum Porridge 49

86. Barley and Mushrooms with Beans 49

87. Tex-Mex Pita Pizzas 49

88. Full Flour Chock Veggies Chickpea Pizza Crust. 50

89. Lentil Vegetable Soup 50

90. Easy Vegan Corn Chowder 51

91. Creamy Wild Rice Soup 51

92. Quick and Easy Noodle Soup 52

93. "Nacho" Vegan Baked Potato 52

94. Stove-Top Vegan Macaroni and Cheese 52

95. Penne with Tomato-Mushroom Sauce 53

96. "No-Tuna" Salad Sandwich 53

97. Avocado & White Bean Salad Wraps 54

98. Burritos with Spanish Rice and Black Beans 55

99. Black Bean Burgers 55

100. Spinach-Potato Tacos 56

101. Black Bean and Sweet Potato Quesadillas 57

102. Lentil Sloppy Joes 57

103. Corn and Black Bean Cakes 58

104. Taco-Spiced Tortilla Chips 58

105. The Best Oil-Free Hummus 59

106. 8-Ingredient Slow-Cooker Chili 59

107. Sweet Potato Chili with Kale 59

108. Potato-Cauliflower Curry 60

109. Rice Bowls with Kidney Beans, Spinach, and
Mixed Veggies 60

110. No-Fry Fried Rice 61

111. Vegan Mashed Potatoes and Gravy 61

112. Veggie And Apple Slaw 62

113. Potato Salad with Avocado and Dill 62

114. Italian-Style Zucchini and Chickpea Sauté 63

115. Spicy French Fries 63

116. Celeriac, Hazelnut & Truffle Soup 64

117. Squash & Spinach Fusilli with Pecans 64

118. Artichoke & Aubergine Rice 65

119. Guacamole & Mango Salad with Black Beans 65

120. Veggie Olive Wraps with Mustard Vinaigrette 65

121. Black Beans & Avocado on Toast.................66

122. Spinach, Sweet Potato & Lentil Dhal............66

123. Kidney Bean Curry...67

124. Roasted Cauli-Broc Bowl with Tahini Hummus 67

125. Vegan Shepherd's Pie...................................68

126. Easy Healthy Falafels....................................69

127. Lentil Ragu with Courgetti 69

128. Lentil Lasagna 70

129. Sweet Potato & Cauliflower Lentil Bowl 70

130. Smoky Spiced Veggie Rice 71

131. Cauliflower Lentil Bowl 71

132. Sesame Parsnip & Wild Rice Tabbouleh........72

133. Acai Bowl..73

134. Vegan Kebabs with Avocado Dressing 73

135. Cauliflower Steaks with Roasted Red Pepper & Olive Salsa 73

136. Fennel, roast lemon & tomato salad 74

Chapter: 4 Plant Based Diet Dinner Options 75

137. Portobello Burritos 75

138. Plant-Strong Power Bowl 75

139. Millet Fritters 76

140. Satay Tempeh with Cauliflower Rice 76

141. Freekeh Bowl with Dried Figs 76

142. Lentil Vegetable Loaf....................................77

143. Chard Wraps with Millet 77

144. Stuffed Indian Eggplant................................78

145. Sweet Potato Quesadillas.............................78

146. Vegan Curried Rice.......................................79

147. Cauliflower and Potato Curry 79

148. Grilled Eggplant Steaks 80

149. Broccoli and Rice Stir Fry 80

150. Grilled Veggie Kabobs...................................80

151. Grilled Cauliflower Steaks.............................81

152. Vegetable Hash with White Beans 81

153. Broccoli Casserole with Beans and Walnuts .. 82

154. Best Buddha Bowl 82

155. Kimchi Brown Rice Bliss Bowls 82

156. Adzuki Bean Bowls 83

157. Roasted Veggie Grain Bowl...........................83

158. Cauliflower Rice Kimchi Bowls 84

159. Macro Veggie Bowl.......................................85

160. Best Veggie Burger 85

161. Portobello Mushroom Burger 86

162. Crispy Baked Falafel......................................86

163. Vegan Bacon 87

164. Stuffed Acorn Squash 88

165. Twice Baked Sweet Potatoes 88

166. Stuffed Poblano Peppers 89

167. Spaghetti Squash w/ Chickpeas & Kale..........90

168. Sesame Soba Noodles...................................90

169. Maki Sushi Recipe...91

170. Radish Salad 91

171. Kale Salad with Carrot Ginger Dressing 92

172. Healthy Taco Salad 92

173. Butternut Squash Soup.................................93

174. Vegan Broccoli Soup.....................................93

175. Best Lentil Soup..94

176. Easy Coconut Curry.......................................95

177. Easy Vegetarian Chili 95

178. Tomato Basil Soup...96

179. Cream of Mushroom Soup............................96

180. Zucchini Verde Vegan Enchiladas..................97

181. Sushi Salad 97

182. Gingery Noodle Salad 98

183. Twice-Baked Potatoes with Creamy Chive Pesto 99

184. Stuffed Zucchini with Freekeh Pilaf and Currants 99

185. Boiled Potato on Rye Bread, aka Potato Salad on Toast 100

186. Spiced Peanut Sweet Potato Salad 101

187. Spicy Miso Eggplant & Broccoli Salad 101

188. Indian Peanutty Noodles 101

189. Turmeric-Roasted Cauliflower with Pistachio Gremolata 102

190. Crispy Roasted Shallot and Lentil Sheet-Pan Mujadara 103

191. White Bean Soup with Garlic and Parsley 104

192. Vegan Cauliflower Alfredo Bake 104

193. Rutabaga Laksa 105

194. Instant Pot No-Soak Black Bean Soup 106

195. Vegan Chicken Phở 106

196. Bartha 107

197. One-Pot Skinny Pasta Primavera 108

198. Spicy Tuna Poke Bowls 108

199. Spiralized Zucchini, Quinoa and Turkey Sausage Stuffed Peppers 109

200. Vegan Black Bean Burgers 109

201. Vegetable Lasagna with Butternut Squash and Shiitake Mushroom 110

202. Vegetarian Thai Pineapple Forbidden Fried Rice 111

203. Grilled Vegetable Sandwich 112

Chapter: 5 Plant Based Dessert Options 114

204. Easy Vegan Paleo Chocolate Cupcakes 114

205. Banana Split Deluxe 114

206. Date & Coconut Ice Cream 114

207. Healthy Cookie Dough Blizzard Recipe 115

208. Vegan Apple Cider Donuts 115

209. Mind-Blowing Vegan Chocolate Pie 116

210. Easy Healthy Peanut Butter Cups 116

211. Vegan Peanut Butter Cookies 117

212. Vegan Lemon Bars 117

213. Salted Caramel Tahini Cups 118

214. Healthy Almond Pistachio Frozen Yogurt 118

215. Vegan Double Chocolate Cake 119

216. Raspberry Nice Cream 119

217. Gluten-free Blueberry Crisps 120

218. Fudgy Vegan Brownie 120

219. No-Bake Pumpkin Pie 120

220. Chocolate Peanut Butter Shake 121

221. Raw Vegan Chickpea Cookie Dough 121

222. Nutty Cookies 121

223. Pumpkin Spice Shake 122

224. Apple Crisp 122

225. Chocolate and Vanilla 122

226. Peanut Butter Cookies 123

227. Chocolate Vegan Ice-cream 123

228. Tahini no-bake cookies 125

229. Double Chocolate Mug Cakes 125

230. Chocolate Chip Cookies 126

231. Apple Crumble 126

232. Chocolate Pudding 127

233. Banana Blueberry Crumble 127

234. Easy Chocolate Avocado Pudding 128

235. Vegan Snickerdoodles Soft and Chewy 128

236. Dairy Free Chocolate Chip Cookies 129

237. Vegan Cookie Dough Balls 129

238. Chocolate Coconut Date Balls 130

239. Vegan Strawberry Cake 130

240. Vegan Choco-Cakes..................................... 131

241. Pumpkin Mug Cake 131

242. Vanilla Pudding with Fresh Berries 132

243. Chocolate Chia Pudding 132

244. Halloween Graveyards Pudding Cups 133

245. Aquafaba Chocolate Mousse...................... 133

246. Vegan Blondies 134

247. Watermelon Popsicles 134

248. Spinach-Mango Popsicles........................... 135

249. Vegan Pumpkin Brownies........................... 135

250. Lemon sorbet.. 136

251. Rhubarb & Star Anise Sorbet...................... 136

252. Almond Jam Dot Cookies 137

253. No-Bake Cookies.. 137

254. Lemon Cake 138

255. Chocolate Clusters 138

256. Banana Coconut Cookies........................... 138

257. Maple Syrup and Tahini Fudge 139

258. Banana Muffins 139

259. Juicy Brussel Sprouts 140

260. Balsamic Artichokes....................................140

261. Tomato Kebabs 140

262. Parsley Potatoes..141

263. Eggplant and Zucchini Snack......................141

264. Artichokes with Mayo Sauce.......................141

265. Cashew Oat Muffins 142

266. Fried Asparagus...142

267. Carrot Flaxseed Muffins...............................142

268. Chocolate Peanut Fat Bombs.....................143

269. Chocolate Raspberry Brownies 143

Conclusion...144

30-Day Meal Plan..145

Index 147

Introduction

At first glance, it may seem to be a reference to vegetarianism, which may refer to a variety of various things. The most restrictive version is a vegan diet, which consists only of foods derived from plant sources, such as whole grains, vegetables, fruits, soy products, legumes, nuts, and seeds, among other things. However, many vegetarians who self-identify as such are really "lacto-ovo" vegetarians, which means they consume only plant foods, egg yolks and dairy products such as dairy milk, yogurt, and cheese but no animal meat.

There are also people who consider themselves mostly vegetarians, but who also eat fish, poultry on occasion, or who just avoid red meat. However, despite their variations, they all have one thing in common: they are all focused on obtaining the majority of their nutrients from plants.

The Mediterranean Diet and the DASH Diet are two of the most well-known plant-based diets in the world. In addition to recommending substantial increases in fruits and vegetables greater than those both recommend increasing the consumption of whole grains and include plant proteins such as nuts, seeds, and legumes. As for animal protein, both diets urge that it be eaten in moderation, with the Mediterranean Diet preferring seafood over poultry and red meat to be consumed "sparingly." The Omni Heart diet is a plant-based diet that is less well-known outside of the nutrition science community but is highly respected inside it.

In support of the National Institutes of Health, the Omni Heart Diet offers three different options for a cardio-healthy plant-based diet that focuses more on carbohydrates, proteins, or unsaturated fats, depending on one's preferences.

All three Omni Heart patterns, like the Mediterranean and DASH patterns, place a strong emphasis on eating more fruits and vegetables, as well as include plant proteins from nuts, seeds, and legumes.

Phytonutrients (Phyto means plant in Greek) are chemicals found in plant meals that serve as natural antioxidants, anti-inflammatories, and detoxifiers. In addition to being low in calories and high in fiber, vitamins, and minerals, plant foods include hundreds of compounds known as phytonutrients.

These chemicals combine and mix in an infinite number of combinations inside plants to give the advantages described above. Phytonutrients include the orange/red carotenoids found in carrots and tomatoes, polyphenols found in berries, tea, and dark chocolate, and phytoestrogens found in soybeans, among other foods and beverages. Many of these chemicals are responsible for the pigmentation of plants, thus eating a range of fruits and vegetables of different hues, as well as a variety of whole grains, nuts, seeds, and legumes, will naturally alter your phytonutrient intake.

A bioactive chemical is one that has a biological impact inside a human body, tissues, or cells and is expected to have preventative benefits against pathophysiological processes, according to the definition. All compounds or nutrients found in plant-based foods are therefore potentially bioactive in human organisms; however, their protective effect will vary depending on a variety of factors such as the individual's health status or physiological state, the degree to which the food has been processed, the presence of other compounds within the food matrix, and the amount of food consumed.

Plant-based or plant-forward eating habits are characterized by the consumption of meals derived mainly from plants. Nuts, seeds, olive oil, whole grain cereals and legumes are among the foods that fall under this category, as are beans and legumes. It does not imply that you are a vegetarian or vegan who does not consume any meat or dairy products. Rather, you are increasing the percentage of your meals derived from plant sources by a significant margin.

In terms of technical accuracy, all of the interpretations listed above are accurate. Some individuals mistakenly believe that the phrase "plant-based diet" is synonymous with the vegan diet. Others may use the word in a wider sense that encompasses all vegetarian diets, and I've also seen it used to refer to diets that are mostly comprised of plant foods, but not completely so, as in a plant-based diet, for example.

Making plant-based foods the centerpiece of your meals is the primary concept. A plant-based diet places emphasis on foods such as fruits, vegetables, and legumes, while restricting items such as meat, dairy, and eggs. More limitations may be imposed from there, depending on how severe you want to be with your policies. Depending on the individual's perception, it may be necessary to entirely remove items derived from animals or just restrict consumption.

In other words, meat and seafood do not necessarily have to be off-limits; you may just opt to reduce the frequency with which you consume these foods instead. Consider "plant-based" diets to be a wide category of diets that includes a variety of other more specialized diets that come under its umbrella. A plant-based diet, such as the Mediterranean diet, is defined as one that emphasizes plant-based meals above animal-based foods, despite the fact that it includes fish and chicken.

Chapter: 1 Plant Based Diet Fundamentals

Although the plant diet is not strictly a diet, it is more of a way of life. Why? Because people's consumption of plant-based diets may differ significantly depending on the degree to which they incorporate animal foods in their diet. In spite of this, the fundamental concepts of a plant-based diet include the following: The emphasis is on whole foods that have been lightly processed. Limits or avoids the consumption of animal products.

1. 1.1 What is Plant Diet?

Plant diet emphasizes on plants, which include plants, fruits, whole grain products, legumes, seeds, and walnuts, which should account for the bulk of your daily calories. Refined foods such as added sugars, white flour, and processed oils are excluded from the diet. Food quality is given particular emphasis, with many supporters of the plant diet advocating locally produced, organic food wherever feasible. As a result of these factors, this meal is often mistaken with vegan or meatless eating plans. However, despite the fact that they are comparable in some respects, these meals are not quite the same. Instead of relying on plant-based alternatives, vegans refrain from eating animal foods, including dairy, meats, poultry, fish, eggs, and honey. Vegetarians abstain from all forms of meat and poultry, although some vegetarians consume eggs, shellfish, and dairy products. The Plant diet, on the contrary, is more adaptable to individual needs. Followers consume mostly plant-based foods, although they are not prohibited from consuming animal products. While one individual following a WFPB diet may consume no animal foods, another may consume modest quantities of eggs, poultry, fish, meat, and dairy products, depending on their personal preferences.

2. 1.2 Benefits of Plant diet

Following are some of the benefits of plant-based diet:
Assist you in losing weight
Obesity is a public health crisis of pandemic proportions. More than 69 percent of people are overweight and obese. To one's advantage, dietary and lifestyle modifications may aid in weight reduction and have a long-term positive effect on one's health. The use of plant-based diets has been proven to be helpful for weight reduction in many studies. Because of the plant diet's dietary fiber and the absence of processed foods, it is a very effective way to lose extra weight. An analysis of 12 trials involving more than 1,100 individuals showed that those allocated to plant-based diets shed substantially more weight about 4.5 pounds (2 kilograms) over an estimate of 18 weeks than those given to non-vegetarian diets by eating more fruits and vegetables It is possible that following a healthy plant-based diet plan can also help you maintain your weight over time. Those allocated to a plant diet dropped substantially more weight than those assigned to a control diet, and they were able to maintain that weight reduction of 9.25 pounds (4.2kg) during a one-year follow-up period, according to the findings of research conducted on 65 overweight and obese individuals. Furthermore, just avoiding processed items that are not permitted on a plant diet, such as soda, sweets, fast food, and refined grains, may be an effective weight reduction strategy in and of itself.

Beneficial for a Variety of Health Conditions.
Following a whole-foods, plant-based diet not only helps you lose weight, but it may also decrease your chance of developing chronic illnesses and alleviate the symptoms of some of them.

Heart Disease is a medical condition that affects the heart.
Heart health is one of the very well advantages of Plant-Based diets. The quality and kinds of foods included with the diet, on the other hand, are important considerations. Researchers discovered that individuals who had a nutritious plant-based diet high in vegetables and fruits, whole grains, seeds, and nuts had a substantially reduced risk for heart attack than those who consumed a diet heavy in non-vegetarian foods such as red meat poultry, and eggs. Sugary beverages, fruit juices, and cereal grains were shown to be linked with a slightly higher risk for cardiovascular among those who ate poor plant-based diets, according to the findings. When adopting a plant-based diet, it is important to consume the proper types of foods in order to avoid heart disease. This is why following a plant diet is the right approach.

Cancer
There is evidence to indicate that eating a plant-based lifestyle may lower your chance of contracting some kinds of cancer. Based on findings from research of

more than 69,000 individuals, vegetarian diets were shown to be linked with a substantially reduced risk of cancer, particularly for those who adopted a Lacto-ovo vegan lifestyle. Another big research including more than 77,000 individuals found that all those who followed vegetarianism had a 22 percent reduced chance of getting colorectal cancer than those who did not maintain a vegetarian lifestyle. When compared to non-vegetarians, pescatarians (vegetarians who consume fish) showed the highest protection against colorectal cancer, with a 43 percent lower chance of developing the disease

Cognitive Impairment

In some research, it has been suggested that eating a diet high in vegetables and fruits could help delay or prevent mental impairment and Alzheimer's disease in elderly people. Increased plant chemicals and antioxidants are found in plant-based diets, which have been proven to delay the development of Alzheimer's disease and restore cognitive impairments. Increased intake of fruits and veggies has been shown to be significantly linked with a decrease in cognitive decline in a number of studies. After reviewing nine trials with over 31,000 participants, researchers discovered that increasing one's intake of fruits and vegetables resulted in a 20 percent decrease in the chance of acquiring cognitive problems or Alzheimer's

Diabetes

Making the switch to a plant diet may be an efficient way to control or perhaps prevent diabetes from forming in the first place. According to the findings of research, those who maintained a healthy plant-based dietary plan had reduced chance of getting diabetes than those who maintained an unhealthy, non-plant-based eating pattern. eating a plant-based diet (vegan or Lacto-ovo vegetarian) is linked with a roughly 50 percent decrease in the risk of developing type 2 diabetes compared to eating a non-vegetarian diet. In addition, plant-based diets have been found to enhance blood sugar management in individuals with diabetes

Benefits to the Environment

A plant-based diet is beneficial to your health, but it is also beneficial to the environment by reducing greenhouse gas emissions. People who eat a plant-based diet have lower environmental footprints than those who do not. Incorporating environmentally friendly eating habits into one's daily routine may help decrease greenhouse gases, water use, and land devoted to factory farming, all of which contribute to global warming and ecological pollution. A Plant diets comprises the least quantity of animal-based items, such as vegan, vegetarian, and pescatarian, were associated with the greatest environmental advantages. People eating patterns to more ecological, plant-based diet patterns may result in a decrease in greenhouse emissions and land usage and a reduction in water consumption. Furthermore, limiting the amount of animal foods in your diet and buying locally grown, sustainable produce helps stimulate the local economy while decreasing dependence on factory farming, which is an unsustainable form of food production.

3. 1.3 Foods to include in your diet

Animal foods are the centerpiece of many people's meals, from their breakfasts of eggs and bacon to their evening steak dinners. When transitioning to a plant-based diet, the meal should be based mostly on plant-based ingredients. If animal food is eaten, it must be consumed in lesser amounts and with special care to the purity of the food item in question It is preferable to utilize dairy, eggs, poultry, meat, and seafood as a supplement to a plant-based diet rather than as the primary focal point of a meal.

Grocery List

The following fruits are available:

- Berries, citrus fruits such as peaches, pears, bananas, pineapple
- Vegetables such as kale, broccoli, cauliflower, peppers, asparagus, tomatoes, spinach, carrots, and other similar items are available.
- Starchy veggies include butternut squash, sweet potatoes, potatoes, and other root vegetables.
- Whole grains include brown rice, rolled oats, farro, quinoa, barley, brown rice pasta, and similar things.
- Olive oil, avocados, unsweetened coconut, coconut oil and other healthy fats are examples.
- Peas, chickpeas, lentils, peanuts, black beans, and other legumes are examples of legumes.
- Pumpkin seeds, cashews, almonds, tahini, macadamia nuts, sunflower seeds, natural

peanut butter, and other nut butter are examples of seeds, nuts, and nut butter.

- Plant-based milk that is unsweetened: coconut milk, almond milk, cashew milk, and so on.
- Spicy and savory flavors, herbs, and spices such as basil and rosemary; turmeric and curry; black pepper and salt; and so, on
- Mustard, salsa, vinegar, nutritional yeast, soy sauce, lemon juice, and other condiments are examples.
- Plant-based protein sources or powders that do not include any additional sugar or artificial additives include tofu, tempeh, and other plant-based protein sources or powders.
- Beverages include coffee, tea, sparkling water, and other beverages.
- In the event that you must include animal products in your plant-based diet, choose high-quality products from grocery stores or, better yet, buy them directly from local farms.
- When feasible, pasture-raised eggs are used.
- Poultry should be free-range and organic wherever feasible.
- When feasible, pasture-raised, or grass-fed beef and pig are used.
- When feasible, wild-caught seafood from sustainable fisheries is used in the preparation of seafood dishes.
- Organic dairy products from pasture-raised cows are used wherever feasible in the production of dairy products.
- Foods to stay away from or limit on this diet
- The Whole Foods Plant-Based Diet (WFPB) is a style of eating that emphasizes ingesting foods with their most natural shape. This implies that items that have been highly processed are prohibited.
- When shopping for groceries, look for products that are fresh and have the fewest number of components possible.

When buying products with a label, look for those that contain the fewest number of ingredients possible.

4. 1.4 Foods to Avoid

The Whole Foods Plant-Based Diet (WFPB) is a style of eating that emphasizes ingesting foods with their most natural shape. This implies that items that have been highly processed are prohibited. When shopping for groceries, look for products that are fresh and have the fewest number of components possible. When buying products with a label, look for those that contain the fewest number of ingredients possible. Foods to Stay Away From:

- Fast food includes French fries, hamburgers, corn dogs, chicken nuggets, and other such items.
- Refined sugar, cola, juice, pastries, cookies, candies, sweet tea, sugary cereals, and other sweets are examples of added sugars and sweets.
- White bread, white pasta, white rice, bagels, and other refined grains are examples of refined grains.
- Packaged and comfort foods include chips, biscuits, cereal bars, prepared meals, and other things.
- Products made to be vegan-friendly, such as Tofurkey and other plant-based meat alternatives, fake cheese, vegan butter, and so on.
- Synthetic sweeteners, such as Equal, Splenda, Sweet'N Low, and so on.
- Animal goods that have been processed include ham, luncheon meats, sausages, beef jerky, and so on.

Foods to keep to a minimum:

However, although it is possible to incorporate healthful animal foods in a WFPB diet, the consumption of the following items should be limited in all plant-based diets.

- Beef
- Pork
- Sheep
- Game foods are a delicacy.
- Poultry
- Eggs

- Dairy
- Seafood

5. 1.5 A One-Week Meal Plan

It does not need to be difficult to make the switch to a whole-foods, plant-based lifestyle.

The one-week menu that follows may assist you in setting yourself up for success. A limited number of animal foods are included in the diet, but the degree to which you incorporate animal items in your diet is entirely up to you.

Monday

A coconut milk-based oatmeal dish served with berries, coconut, and walnuts for breakfast is a delicious start to the day. For lunch, a large salad with fresh veggies, chickpeas, avocado, pumpkin seeds, and goat cheese. Butternut squash curry can be served for dinner.

Tuesday

Morning snack: Plain, full-fat yogurt served with fresh berries, unsweetened coconut, and pumpkin seeds for breakfast. Chili made without meet for lunch. Tacos are made with sweet potatoes and black beans for dinner.

Wednesday

A smoothie is prepared with pure coconut milk, strawberries, peanut butter, and neutral plant-based protein powder. Hummus and vegetable wrap for lunch. Meal for the evening: Zucchini noodles mixed in pesto served with chicken meatballs.

Thursday

Oatmeal with avocado, salsa, and black beans for breakfast is a delicious option. Salad with quinoa, vegetables, and feta for lunch. Dinner will consist of grilled fish with baked root vegetables and broccoli on the side.

Friday

Breakfast consists of a frittata made with tofu and vegetables. Lunch consists of a large salad
served with grilled shrimp and grilled chicken. Dinner tonight will be roasted portobello fajitas.

Saturday

Breakfast: A smoothie made with blackberries, kale, cashew butter, and coconut protein.

Sushi with vegetables, avocado, and brown rice for lunch, served with a sea salad.

Dinner will consist of cheese-topped eggplant lasagna and a big green salad.

Sunday

Breakfast: An omelet of vegetables prepared with eggs.

Lunch: quinoa dish with roasted vegetables and tahini dressing.

Dinner consists of veggie sandwiches served on a bed of lettuce with sliced avocado on top. According to what you can see, the goal behind a whole-foods, plant-based diet is to eat as little meat and dairy as possible. Many individuals who follow Plant diets, on the other hand, consume more or fewer animal products according to their dietary requirements and preferences.

6. 1.6 Latest Research on Plant-based Diets

The majority of individuals who embrace this style of eating do so because they believe it will improve their health. A plant-based diet, according to some research, may enhance reproductive indicators while simultaneously lowering the chance of acquiring [type 2] diabetes.

Among the findings of a research, diets high in nutritious plant foods (including nuts, whole grains, fruits, vegetables, and oils) were associated with a substantially reduced risk of heart disease.

Following a plant-based diet, according to a study published it can help prevent and treat type 2 diabetes, and it cites research that suggests it may also help reduce the risk of other chronic illnesses, such as cancer, by reducing the intake of animal products. In addition, following a plant-based diet can have a positive impact on emotional and physical well-being, quality of life, and general health in people living with type-2 diabetes, as well as improving physical markers of the condition in this group of individuals.

According to a study in Nutrients, eating a plant-based diet may help decrease the chance of developing heart disease and perhaps cancer among African Americans, who are disproportionately affected by numerous chronic illnesses such as diabetes and obesity.

Additionally, some research has found an association between eating a diet high in plant protein and having an earlier death from any cause. For example, a review of studies that participants whose diets contained the most plant-based protein had a 6 percent lower risk of premature death than participants who consumed less protein overall.

Another study of 135,000 people found a link between increased intake of fruits, vegetables, and legumes and a lower risk of all-cause early death, with participants reaping the greatest health benefits when they consumed three to four servings per day — a number that anyone following a plant-based diet is likely to achieve.

Plant-based foods are divided into the following categories: legumes, fruits, grains, vegetables, nuts, as well as seeds; their processed derived counterparts such as breakfast cereals, pasta, bread, boiled and fermented vegetables and legumes, and fruit purées, juices, and jams; and their derived ingredients including sugars, oleaginous seed-derived oils, herbs, spices, and some spices.

Unlike animal-based meals, they include a high proportion of indigestible fiber, which is made up of indigestible substances such as cellular wall-fibers, hemicellulose, or resistant starch.

Grain products with high carbohydrate, protein, and fat contents are distinguished from other grain products by their high carbohydrate, protein, and lipid levels, respectively. In addition to fiber, plant-based meals include a variety of macronutrients (proteins, fats, and carbs), micronutrients (minerals, trace elements, and vitamins), and phytonutrients (antioxidants and phytochemicals) (e.g., polyphenols and carotenoids). Each one of them contributes to the plant's ability to survive in its environment and reproduce itself.

Despite the fact that plant-based meals may be consumed raw, the majority of the time, they are processed to make them more secure, edible, and/or appealing.

This is particularly true for grain-based foods. Processing may range from very little, such as soaking leguminous seeds, to extremely severe, such as extrusion-cooking white cereal flour and everything in between.

The processing of plant-based meals may also involve the incorporation of other components, such as lipids and cooking agents, into the final product. The potential bundle of bioactive chemicals is clearly altered in various ways, either favorably or adversely, in all of these instances, most notably when cereal goods are refined, which eliminates the majority of the minerals and vitamins present.

7. 1.7 What's the bottom line?

A plant-based diet is a style of eating that emphasizes plant-based meals while avoiding harmful things such as added sugars and processed carbohydrates.

There have been many studies linking plant-based diets to a variety of health advantages, including a lower risk of cardiovascular disease, some malignancies, obesity, type 2 diabetes, and cognitive decline.

Furthermore, shifting towards a more plant-based diet is a wise decision for the environment. Regardless matter the kind of whole foods, plant-based diet you select, following this way of eating will undoubtedly improve your overall health and wellbeing.

Chapter: 2 Plant Based Breakfast Options

Does it happen to you from time to time that you skip breakfast due to a lack of time? We're here to assist you in any way we can! Anything from bagel to eggs has contributed to the fact that the most vital foods have become the most convenient meals of the day. While following the program, you may enjoy deliciously prepared quick breakfast items. A list of a few of them is given further down on this page. One of these quick and simple breakfast recipes. It's worth a chance to see what happens. So, what else are you looking for? Get started now! To satisfy your cravings, grab the necessary items and start cooking. One of these simple Plant-based dishes may be prepared in no time.

1. Orange French Toast

Total time: 30 minutes
Serving: 8 slices
Nutrients per serving: Calories: 300.2, Fats: 9.9 g, Carbohydrates: 20g, Proteins :54g, Sodium:30mg, Calcium:10mg, Iron: 22mg
Ingredients:

- 1 ½ cup of unsweetened plant milk
- 8 whole-grain bread slices
- 1 cup of aquafaba
- 2 tablespoons of pure maple syrup
- ¼ teaspoon of ground cinnamon
- ½ cup of almond flour
- 2 pinches salt (optional
- ½ tablespoon of orange zest
- 8 whole-grain bread slices
- 1 cup of aquafaba

Instructions:

1. Bake at 400 degrees Fahrenheit. Place a cooling rack over a sheet pan and bake for 30 minutes.
2. In a large mixing bowl, whisk the plant milk, aquafaba, maple syrup, salt, cinnamon, and flour until the mixture is smooth and well combined. Transfer to a small pan and set aside. Mix in the orange zest until thoroughly combined.
3. Using a nonstick skillet, cook the ingredients over medium heat. Each bread slice should be dipped into the sauce and let to sit for a few minutes. Turn the pot over and sit for a few more seconds. Place the ingredients in a pan and medium heat for two or three minutes, stirring occasionally. Cook the opposite side for two or three minutes, or until it is golden brown, after carefully turning it over
4. Put the toast on a cooling rack and bake for five to ten minutes, or until it is crisp until golden brown.
5. Blend the applesauce, maple syrup, berries in a blender until the sauce is a chunky consistency, about 30 seconds. Warm the French toast.

2. Baked Mushroom Polenta Bowls

Total time: 1 Hour 30 Minutes
Serving: 4 bowls
Nutrient per serving: Calories :175, Fats:5.1g, Carbohydrates:22g, Proteins:10g, Sodium:201mg, Calcium:20mg, Iron:28 mg
Ingredients:

- 8 Cipollini onions trimmed and peeled
- Freshly ground black pepper, to taste
- 1 15-oz. can no-salt-add white beans, rinsed and drained (1½ cups)
- 1 oz. of dried porcini mushrooms, broken up (1 cup)
- ½ teaspoon of sea salt
- 1 lb. of Brussels sprouts, trimmed and halved
- 5 and ½ cups of no-salt-added vegetable broth
- 1 cup of coarse yellow cornmeal
- 2 tablespoons of white wine vinegar
- 4 Roma of tomatoes
- 2 tablespoons of chopped fresh flat-leaf parsley

Directions:

1. Preheat the oven to 375 degrees Fahrenheit. In a 4-quart Dutch oven,

combine the first main ingredients and stir well (through salt). Over medium-high heat, bring the mixture to a simmer, often stirring to avoid clumping. Transfer the Dutch oven to the oven, leaving the lid ajar. Preheat the oven to 350°F and cook for 1 hour.

2. In the meantime, line a large baking sheet with a rim with parchment paper. Prepare a baking sheet by arranging the Broccoli and onions on it. 1 tablespoon of water should be used to brush the surface. Season with salt to your liking. Place the polenta on a baking sheet next to it in the oven. Oven for about 45 minutes, or until the vegetables are soft. Remove the baking sheet from the oven. Toss in the beans and add a tablespoon of vinegar until everything is well combined.

3. Using tongs, carefully remove the Dutch oven from oven. Using a whisk, smooth up the polenta. Return the Dutch oven to the oven, uncovered. Bake for 10 minutes or until the polenta is rich and creamy, depending on your preference. Remove the baking sheet from the oven. Using a whisk, thoroughly combine the ingredients.

4. In the meantime, grate the tomatoes using the crude side of a cutting board into a large mixing bowl. Add the parsley, the remaining 1 teaspoon vinegar, and salt and pepper to season after mixing everything.

5. Using a large spoon, scoop polenta into shallow dishes. A vegetable mixture should be placed on top. Drizzle the tomato mixture along the outside of the polenta's perimeter. Additional parsley can be added if desired.

3. Gluten-free Breakfast Muffin

Total time: 30 minutes
Serving: 12
Nutrient per serving: Calories:217.8, Fats:13.5 g, Carbohydrates:4.6g, Proteins: 11.3g, Sodium:132 mg, Calcium:24mg, Iron:253 mg

Ingredients:
- ¼ cup of maple syrup
- 1 banana
- 1 apple
- ½ cup of almond milk
- ½ cup of walnuts
- ½ cup of raisins
- ¼ teaspoon of sea salt
- ¼ cup of ground flaxseed
- ½ cup of hot water
- 2 cups of rolled oats
- 2 tablespoons of cinnamon

Directions:
1. Allow 5 minutes for the flaxseed to absorb the water.
2. In a food processor, combine all ingredients (including the flax mixture) until well combined but not smooth (about 30 seconds)
3. In a muffin pan, pour batter into cupcake liners (because this is an oil-free recipe, the cupcake liners are necessary) and bake for 20 minutes at 350°F.
4. Enjoy.

4. Banana Sandwich

Total time: 10 minutes
Serving: 1
Nutrient per serving: Calories: 107.5, Fats: 24g, Carbohydrates: 36g, Proteins: 12g, Sodium: 5.6 mg, Calcium: 25mg, Iron: 45 mg

Ingredients:
- 1 banana, ripe
- 2 slices of whole grain bread
- ¼ cup of raisins
- ¼ cup of water, hot
- 1 tablespoon cinnamon
- 2 teaspoon of cacao powder
- ¼ cup of natural peanut butter

Directions:
1. Combine the raisins, boiling water, cinnamon, and cacao powder in a large mixing bowl.
2. Peanut butter should be spread on whole grain toast.

3. Using a slice of banana, put it over a piece of peanut butter toast.
4. Spread the raisin mixture on the inside of the sandwich.

5. Blueberry Lemon French Toast

Total time: 30 minutes
Serving: 2-3
Nutrient per serving: Calories: 187.5, Fats: 13g, Carbohydrates: 26g, Proteins: 9g, Sodium: 46 mg, Calcium: 98mg, Iron: 22 mg
Ingredients:
- 1/2 of a lemon
- 1 cup of frozen berries
- 1 Tbsp. of maple syrup
- 1/2 teaspoon of nutmeg
- 1 teaspoon of vanilla extract
- 6 slices of whole grain bread
- 1/4 cup of hot water
- 1 teaspoon of cinnamon
- 2 tbs of ground flaxseed
- A pinch of sea salt
- 1 cup of soymilk

Directions:
1. Allow for 5 minutes of resting time after whisking together the flaxseed and hot water.
2. Combine the nutmeg, cinnamon, salt, and vanilla essence in a separate bowl.
3. Add the flax mixture to the plant-based milk and whisk well.
4. Soak whole-grain bread in the batter, then pan-fry in a non-stick pan over low heat till browned on all sides. Cooking without oil requires more effort, so be careful to rotate the toast in the pan every few minutes with a spatula to ensure even cooking.
5. Once the toast is crispy on one side, turn it over and brown the other side.
6. While the bread is cooking, combine the lemon juice, blueberries, and maple syrup in a small bowl and microwave for a few minutes, or heat on the stovetop, until the blueberries are soft.

7. Pour blueberry syrup over the bread and sprinkle with lemon zest from the peel of the lemon when the toast is crispy on all sides.

6. Antioxidant Blueberry Smoothie

Total time: 5 minutes
Serving: 2
Nutrient per serving: Calories: 220, Fats:9g, Carbohydrates: 17g, Proteins: 8g, Sodium: 26 mg, Calcium: 18mg, Iron: 29 mg
Ingredients:
- a small pinch of sea salt
- 1 frozen banana
- 1 cup of frozen blueberries
- 1 cup of unsweetened almond milk, soymilk, or West Soy
- 1 cup of raw spinach
- ½ avocado

Directions:
1. Combine all of the ingredients in a blender until smooth and enjoy.

7. Chewy Oatmeal Banana Pancakes

Total time: 20 minutes
Serving: 8 pancakes
Nutrient per serving: Calories:160, Fats: 10 g, Carbohydrates: 19g, Proteins: 24g, Sodium: 32 mg, Calcium: 11mg, Iron: 13 mg
Ingredients:
- 3 ripe bananas
- 1 teaspoon of cinnamon
- A pinch of sea salt
- 1 and ½ cups of gluten-free oats
- 1 cup of unsweetened non-dairy milk
- 3 tablespoon of chia seeds

Directions:
1. Add the ingredients and mix well.
2. The remainder of the oats, as well as 1 sliced banana
3. In a nonstick frying pan, added pancakes should be cooked on low heat to avoid sticking. Flip just when the bottom side starts to caramelize and develop a deep brown color. If you maintain the pan at a low temperature and use a metal spatula, you will not need to add any oil.

8. Banana Baked Oatmeal

Total time: 30 minutes
Serving: 4
Nutrient per serving: Calories:120, Fats: 10 g, Carbohydrates: 24g, Proteins: 6g, Sodium: 48 mg, Calcium: 88 mg, Iron: 76 mg
Ingredients:
- 1 teaspoon baking powder
- 1 cup of Dairy-free milk
- 1-2 tbs Maple syrup
- Rolled or old-fashioned oats
- 1 Ripe banana:
- Pecan pieces
- Cinnamon,
- Allspice
- Vanilla

Directions:
1. Peanut butter, almond butter, and bananas: Swirl together the almond butter and peanut butter until smooth, then top with slices of banana. Nut-free alternatives include sunflower butter.
2. Maple syrup: A little spray of maple syrup is all that is required to add a little shine.
3. You may prepare the wets and dry oat separately and store them in separate containers (with the wets refrigerated) overnight, combine them in the morning and bake the cake the next day. It will still take 45 minutes to bake the cake. This is the one we favor...
4. Preparing the dough ahead of time: Prepare a pan at night and store it in the refrigerator for use during the week. Leftovers may be stored in the refrigerator for up to 1 week and reheated in a 300-degree oven or microwave. Alternatively, you may eat them straight from the fridge.

9. Vegan Breakfast Benedict

Total time: 30 minutes
Serving: 2
Nutrient per serving: Calories:250, Fats: 10 g, Carbohydrates: 28g, Proteins: 6g, Sodium: 8 mg, Calcium: 9 mg, Iron: 16 mg
Ingredients:
- 4 English whole grain muffins
- 4 slices of tomato
- sliced red onion
- 1 cup of MamaSezz Mac Sauce
- 1 Tablespoon of Dijon mustard
- Black pepper
- 1/2 a teaspoon of turmeric
- 4 slices of tofu
- 1 cup of veggie broth

Directions:
1. First, Combine the vegetable broth, Tamari, and one-half of the turmeric in a mixing bowl. Toss into a nonstick skillet with the tofu. Heat until all of the liquid evaporated.
2. While that's in the oven, Combine the mac sauce, the mustard, and the other half of the turmeric in a large mixing bowl. Add a pinch of ground black pepper to taste. Heat until the sauce is heated, and the sauce has thickened.
3. Stack 2 whole-grain English muffins should be toasted before stacked with tofu, tomato, red onion, and sauce.
4. Finish with a little dusting of paprika and chives, if desired (optional).

10. Tofu Scramble

Total time: 15 minutes
Serving: 4
Nutrient per serving: Calories:210, Fats: 9 g, Carbohydrates: 32g, Proteins: 4g, Sodium: 3 mg, Calcium: 8 mg, Iron: 17 mg
Ingredients:
- ½ cup of diced yellow onion
- 14 ounces extra-firm tofu, crumbled and patted dry
- Sea salt and freshly ground black pepper
- ⅓ cup of almond milk
- 2 tablespoons of nutritional yeast
- 2 garlic cloves, minced
- ½ teaspoon of Dijon mustard
- ¼ teaspoon of ground turmeric
- ¼ teaspoon of ground cumin
- 1 tablespoon of extra virgin olive oil

Directions:

1. In a small mixing bowl, whisk together the garlic, mustard, nutritional yeast, cumin, turmeric, almond milk, and 12 teaspoon salts until well combined and well combined again. Make a mental note to put it away.
2. In a large pan, heat the olive oil over medium to high heat until shimmering. Cook for 5 minutes, or until the onion is tender, adding pinches of pepper with salt along the way.
3. Heat the tofu over medium heat for 3 to 5 minutes until the tofu is fully cooked in a separate pan. Reduce the heat to low and whisk in the almond milk mixture until it is well incorporated.
4. Cook for 3 minutes, stirring periodically until the sauce has thickened. Season with more salt and freshly ground black pepper to taste if desired.
5. Veggies, salsa, and tortillas, if preferred, may be served on the side.

11. Baked Bean Toast

Total time: 10 minutes
Serving: 1
Nutrient per serving: Calories:200, Fats: 8g, Carbohydrates: 12g, Proteins: 9g, Sodium: 2 mg, Calcium: 10 mg, Iron: 21 mg
Ingredients:
- 1/2 an avocado
- 1 cup of Baked Beans, heated
- 2 slices of whole grain toasted bread

Directi0ns:
1. Using a quarter of an avocado, spread it on each piece of whole-grain bread.
2. Spread 1/2 cup of hot Baked Beans on top of each piece of bread.
3. Take pleasure in your filling, nutritious, and delicious breakfast.

12. Gluten-Free Chocolate Chip Pancakes

Total time: 30 minutes
Serving: 8
Nutrient per serving: Calories:100, Fats: 9g, Carbohydrates: 10g, Proteins: 8g, Sodium: 4 mg, Calcium: 9 mg, Iron: 16 mg

Ingredients:
- 1 teaspoon of pure vanilla extract
- ⅓ cup of gluten-free vegan mini chocolate chips
- 1 large, sliced banana
- 1 tablespoon of flaxseed meal
- 1¼ cups of buckwheat flour
- ¼ cup of certified gluten-free rolled oats
- ½ cup of unsweetened applesauce
- ¼ cup of pure maple syrup
- 2 tablespoons of unsweetened coconut flakes
- 1 tablespoon of sodium-free baking powder

Directions:
1. In a small saucepan, mix the flaxseed meal with 12 cup water until well combined. Heat over medium heat for 3 to 4 minutes, or until the mixture drips off a spoon with a stringy appearance. Pour the contents into a glass measuring cup as soon as possible. Solids should be discarded.
2. In a large mixing bowl, whisk together the following five ingredients until well combined through salt. Combine the milk, applesauce, maple syrup, vanilla extract and 2 tablespoons of the flaxseed liquid in a medium-sized mixing bowl. Add the milk mixture to the flour mixture and whisk until well combined. The batter will be very thick. Add in the chocolate chips and mix well.
3. Using a large nonstick griddle or pan, heat the ingredients over medium heat. Pour 1 1/3 cup batter each pancake onto the griddle and spread lightly with a spatula. Cook for 6 to 8 minutes, or until the pancakes seem somewhat dry on top and are lightly browned on the bottom, and they release easily off the griddle, depending on your preference. Cook for another 5 minutes after flipping the pancakes. Transfer to a serving dish and cover with foil to keep warm.

4. Repeat the process with the remaining batter, wiping the griddle clean between each batch. Warm pancakes are served with banana slices on the side. Alternatively, sprinkle with more maple syrup if desired.

13. Banana Almond Granola

Total time: 75 minutes
Serving: 16
Nutrient per serving: Calories:250, Fats: 8g, Carbohydrates: 20g, Proteins: 6g, Sodium: 2 mg, Calcium: 13 mg, Iron: 19 mg
Ingredients:
- 1 teaspoon of salt
- 1 cup of slivered toasted almonds
- 8 cups of rolled oats
- 2 cups of pitted and chopped dates
- 2 ripe, peeled and chopped bananas
- 1 teaspoon of almond extract

Directions:
1. Preheat the oven to 275 degrees Fahrenheit.
2. In a large mixing bowl, combine the oats and set them aside. Prepare two baking sheets measuring 13 x 18 inches with parchment paper.
3. Bring 1 cup of water to a boil in a medium saucepan with the dates and bring to a simmer. Cook for 10 minutes on a medium heat setting. If necessary, add more water to prevent the dates from sticking to the pan.
4. Remove the pan from the heat and combine the mixture with the bananas, almond extract, and salt in a blender until smooth. Process until the mixture is smooth and creamy.
5. Combine the oats and the date mixture in a large mixing bowl. Divide the granola between the two baking sheets that have been prepped and spread out evenly.
6. Stir every 10 minutes for 40 to 50 minutes, or until the granola is crisp and golden brown. Removing the pan from the oven and cool completely before adding the

slivered almonds. As the cereal cools, it will become even crisper.
7. Keep the granola in an airtight container to prevent it from drying out.

14. Chickpea Omelet

Total time: 30 minutes
Serving: 3-6
Nutrient per serving: Calories:201, Fats: 10g, Carbohydrates: 7.8g, Proteins: 8.9g, Sodium: 2.1 mg, Calcium: 8.6 mg, Iron: 14mg
Ingredients:
- 1/3 cup of nutritional yeast
- ½ teaspoon of baking soda
- 3 white and green parts of green onions, chopped
- 4 ounces sautéed mushrooms
- 1 cup of chickpea flour
- ½ teaspoon of onion powder
- ½ teaspoon of garlic powder
- ¼ teaspoon of white pepper
- ¼ teaspoon of black pepper

Directions:
1. In a small mixing bowl, whisk the chickpea flour, onion powder, garlic powder, white pepper, black pepper, nutritional yeast, and baking soda until well combined and smooth. 1 cup water should be added and stirred in until the batter is smooth.
2. Using a frying pan, cook the ingredients over medium heat. Pour the batter onto the pan in the same manner as if you were cooking pancakes. As the omelets are cooking, sprinkle 1 to 2 teaspoons of the green onions and mushrooms into the batter for each omelet. Toss the omelet on the other side. Cook for about a minute on the opposite side after flipping the omelet after browned on the underside.
3. Alternatively, top your heart-healthy Chickpea Omelet with tomato slices and spinach or salsa and spicy sauce, or whatever heart-healthy, plant-perfect toppings you like.

15. Pears and Cranberries

Total time: 15 minutes
Serving: 4
Nutrient per serving: Calories:300, Fats: 6g, Carbohydrates: 32g, Proteins: 3g, Sodium: 10 mg, Calcium: 19 mg, Iron: 12 mg
Ingredients:

- 1 teaspoon of ground cinnamon
- 1 batch warm basic Polenta
- 1/4 cup of brown rice syrup
- 2 peeled, cored, and diced pears
- 1 cup of cranberries

Directions:

1. In a medium saucepan, bring the brown rice syrup to a boil and add the pears. Cook, occasionally stirring, until the pears are soft, approximately 10 minutes. Remove from the heat and mix in the cranberries and cinnamon.
2. To assemble, divide the polenta into four separate dishes and top with the pear compote before serving.

16. Healthy Oatmeal with Fruit and Nuts

Total time: 15 minutes
Serving: 1
Nutrient per serving: Calories:280, Fats: 9g, Carbohydrates: 42g, Proteins: 3g, Sodium: 4.5 mg, Calcium: 4.6 mg, Iron: 13 mg
Ingredients:

- Apricots
- Maple syrup
- Ripe sliced banana
- 2 tablespoons of chopped nuts, such as walnuts, pecans, or cashews
- 2 tablespoons of dried and chopped fruit
- ¾ cup of rolled oats
- ¼ teaspoon of ground cinnamon
- 1 Pinch of sea salt
- ¼ cup of fresh berries

Directions:

1. In a small saucepan, combine the oats and 112 cups water and bring to a boil. Using high heat, bring the mixture to a boil. Reduce the heat to medium-low and cook for another 5 minutes, or until the water has been completely absorbed.
2. Combine the cinnamon and salt in a separate bowl. Depending on your preference, garnish with berries, banana, almonds, and dried fruit. Pour a little amount of maple syrup on top if desired. Serve when still heated.

17. Egyptian Breakfast Beans

Total time: 2 hours 15 minutes
Serving: 4
Nutrient per serving: Calories:100, Fats: 2g, Carbohydrates: 12g, Proteins: 16g, Sodium: 17 mg, Calcium: 13.5 mg, Iron: 11.5 mg
Ingredients:

- Sea salt
- 1 lemon
- 1½ pounds of dried fava beans
- 1 medium peeled and diced small yellow onion
- 1 teaspoon ground cumin
- Zest and juice of 1 lemon
- 4, peeled and minced cloves garlic

Directions:

1. Drain and rinse the beans, then place them in a large saucepan with the rest of the ingredients. Bring the pot to a boil over high heat, covering it with 4 inches of water. Cover and simmer until the beans are soft, 112 to 2 hours, depending on the size of the beans.
2. The onion should be sautéed in a medium skillet or saucepan over medium heat for 8 to 10 minutes, or until it is soft and beginning to brown, while the beans are cooking. Cook for a further 5 minutes after adding the garlic, cumin, lemon zest, and lemon juice. Make a mental note to put it away.
3. When the beans are completely cooked, remove all but 12 cups of the liquid from the saucepan and stir in the onion mixture until the beans are well coated. Season with salt to taste after mixing well. Garnish with the lemon quarters before serving.

18. Apple-Lemon Breakfast Bowl

Total time: 15 minutes
Serving: 1-2
Nutrient per serving: Calories: 605, Fats: 9g, Carbohydrates: 10g, Proteins: 18g, Sodium: 5 mg, Calcium: 6mg, Iron: 11.5 mg
Ingredients:
- 2 tablespoons of walnuts
- ¼ teaspoon of ground cinnamon
- 4 to 5 medium apples
- 5 to 6 pitted dates
- 3 tablespoons of lemon juice

Directions:
1. Apples should be cored and sliced into big pieces.
2. In the food processor bowl, combine the dates, half of the lemon juice, walnuts, cinnamon, and three-quarters of the apple. Process until smooth. Blend until the ingredients are finely ground, scraping down the edges of the bowl as necessary.
3. Process until the apples are shredded, and the date mixture is uniformly spread, then add the remaining apples and lemon juice and pulse until combined.

19. Breakfast Scramble

Total time: 30 minutes
Serving: 6
Nutrient per serving: Calories: 505, Fats: 9g, Carbohydrates: 15g, Proteins: 20g, Sodium: 8mg, Calcium: 6mg, Iron: 11 mg
Ingredients:
- 3 peeled and minced cloves of garlic
- 1 to 2 tablespoons of low-sodium soy sauce
- ¼ cup of nutritional yeast
- 1 peeled red onion
- 1 seeded red bell pepper
- 2 cups of sliced mushrooms
- 1 large head cauliflower
- Sea salt
- ½ teaspoon of freshly ground black pepper
- ¼ teaspoon of cayenne pepper
- 1 and ½ teaspoons of turmeric

Directions:
1. In a medium skillet or saucepan, combine the onion, red and green peppers, and mushrooms and cook, often stirring, for 7 to 8 minutes, or until the onion is transparent. Add 1 to 2 teaspoons of water at a time, constantly stirring, to prevent the veggies from sticking to the pan.
2. Cook for 5 to 6 minutes, or until the cauliflower florets are soft, depending on how big your cauliflower is.
3. Season with salt and pepper to taste, then add the cayenne pepper, garlic, soy sauce, turmeric, and nutritional yeast to the pan and simmer for another 5 minutes, or until the mixture is hot and aromatic.

20. Brown Rice Breakfast Pudding

Total time: 15 minutes
Serving: 4
Nutrient per serving: Calories: 703, Fats: 11g, Carbohydrates: 30g, Proteins: 35g, Sodium: 7mg, Calcium: 4mg, Iron: 22 mg
Ingredients:
- Salt to taste
- ¼ cup of slivered toasted almonds
- 3 cups of cooked brown rice
- 2 cups of unsweetened almond milk
- 1 tart cored and chopped apple
- ¼ pf cup raisins
- 1 cinnamon stick
- ⅛ to ¼ of ground cloves, to taste
- 1 cup, pitted and chopped dates

Directions:
1. Whisk periodically while cooking the rice over medium-low heat for 12 minutes or until the mixture thickens. Remove from the heat and stir in the almond milk and cinnamon stick until the mixture is smooth.
2. Remove the cinnamon stick from the pan. Combine the apple, raisins, and salt in a large mixing bowl
3. Garnish with the toasted almonds before serving.

21. Chocolate Buttermilk Pancakes

Total time: 30 minutes
Serving: 12
Nutrient per serving: Calories: 208, Fats: 10g, Carbohydrates: 28.7g, Proteins: 69g, Sodium: 9mg, Calcium: 32mg, Iron: 90 mg
Ingredients:

- 1 tablespoon of apple cider vinegar
- ¼ cup of unsweetened applesauce
- 1¼ cups of whole-grain gluten-free flour
- 2 tablespoons of unsweetened cocoa powder
- 1 tablespoon of pure maple syrup
- 1 teaspoon of vanilla extract
- 1 tablespoon of baking powder
- 1 tablespoon of ground flaxseed
- ¼ teaspoon of sea salt
- 1 tablespoon of vegan mini chocolate chips

Directions:

1. In a medium-sized mixing bowl, whisk the dry ingredients (flour, cocoa powder, baking powder, flax, chocolate chips, and salt). Whisk until the ingredients are completely mixed.
2. In a small mixing bowl, combine the wet ingredients (almond milk, maple syrup, vanilla extract, and vinegar) and stir well. This will result in vegan buttermilk that you can use to make pancakes.
3. Add the vegan buttermilk and applesauce to the flour mixture and whisk just until the batter is just mixed for about 30 seconds.
4. Allow the batter to rest for 10 minutes to rise and thicken as the flaxseeds soak up the liquid; it may almost double in size during this time.
5. To prepare the pan, heat it over medium heat and spritz it with a little amount of nonstick spray, if preferred, before adding the ingredients. You can make many pancakes at the same time if you have a big skillet. Scoop the batter into 3-inch circles using a pastry scoop. Cook for 2 to 3 minutes, or until the bubbles in each of the pancakes have popped and the tops begin to look dry. Cook for another 1 to 2 minutes after flipping the pancakes. You should be able to obtain a total of 12 pancakes.

22. Black Bean and Sweet Potato Hash

Total time: 30 minutes
Serving: 4
Nutrient per serving: Calories: 118, Fats: 9g, Carbohydrates: 23.4g, Proteins: 89g, Sodium: 12mg, Calcium: 62mg, Iron: 80 mg
Ingredients:

- 2 cups of chopped peeled sweet potatoes
- Splash of hot sauce
- Chopped cilantro
- 1 cup of chopped onion
- 1 to 2 cloves of minced garlic
- 1 cup of cooked black beans
- ¼ cup of chopped scallions
- 2 teaspoons of hot chili powder
- ⅓ cup of low-sodium vegetable broth

Directions:

1. Place the onions in a nonstick pan and cook, turning periodically, for 2 to 3 minutes over medium heat, until soft. Stir in the garlic until it is well-combined.
2. Stir in the sweet potatoes and chili powder until the veggies are well coated with the chili powder. 3. Stir in the broth until it is well-combined. Cook for another 12 minutes, stirring periodically until the potatoes are tender and the liquid has evaporated. Cook the veggies in a little amount of liquid, 1 to 2 tablespoons at a time, until they are tender.
3. Combine the black beans, scallions, and salt in a large mixing bowl. Continue to cook for another 1 or 2 minutes, or until the beans are well heated.
4. Add in the spicy sauce (if using) and mix well to combine. Season with salt and pepper to taste. Garnish with chopped cilantro before serving.

23. Easy Overnight Oats with Chia

Total time: 10 minutes
Serving: 1
Nutrient per serving: Calories: 300, Fats: 9g, Carbohydrates: 23g, Proteins: 89.4g, Sodium: 18mg, Calcium: 60mg, Iron: 123 mg
Ingredients:

- 1 heaping tablespoon of chia seeds
- Dash of powdered vanilla bean powder or extract
- Fruit of choice
- ¾ cup of gluten-free rolled oats
- ¼ cup of plant milk
- ½-1 tablespoon of maple syrup
- ¼ teaspoon of cinnamon
- ½ cup of water

Directions:

1. In a 16-ounce mason jar or another container of your choosing, combine the oats, liquid, chia seeds, maple syrup, cinnamon, and vanilla extract. Make a thorough mix. Place the jar in the refrigerator overnight once it has been sealed.
2. In the morning, combine the ingredients once again and top with anything you want, such as fresh fruit, more chia seeds, or chocolate nibs.

24. Apple-Walnut Breakfast Bread

Total time: 60 minutes
Serving: 8
Nutrient per serving: Calories: 120, Fats: 9g, Carbohydrates: 20g, Proteins: 88g, Sodium: 10mg, Calcium: 90mg, Iron: 173 mg
Ingredients:

- 2 cups of whole wheat flour
- 1 teaspoon of ground cinnamon
- ½ cup of chopped walnuts
- 1½ cups of unsweetened applesauce
- ¾ cup of packed light brown sugar
- ½ teaspoon of baking powder
- 1 teaspoon of salt
- ⅓ cup of plain unsweetened plant milk
- 1 tablespoon of ground flax seeds mixed with 2 tablespoons of warm water
- 1 teaspoon of baking soda

Directions:

1. Preheat the oven to 375 degrees Fahrenheit.
2. Applesauce, brown sugar, almond milk, and flax mixture should be combined in a big mixing bowl and whisk until smooth and thoroughly combined. Make a mental note to put it away.
3. Separately, whisk the flour, baking soda, baking powder, salt, and cinnamon in a large mixing bowl. In a small bowl, whisk together the dry and liquid ingredients until they are well combined. Combine all ingredients in a large mixing bowl, then transfer to a 9x5-inch loaf pan, spreading evenly and smoothing the top.
4. Bake for 25 to 30 minutes, or until the top is golden brown and a toothpick inserted in the middle comes out clean. Allow for approximately 20 minutes of cooking time in the pan before removing it and allowing it to cool fully on a wire rack.

25. Garlic-Jalapeño Naan

Total time: 2 hours
Serving: 16
Nutrient per serving: Calories: 500, Fats: 13g, Carbohydrates: 50g, Proteins: 68g, Sodium: 40mg, Calcium: 20mg, Iron: 143 mg
Ingredients:

- 1 teaspoon of sea salt
- ½ cup of chopped fresh cilantro
- 1 teaspoon of lemon juice
- 2 and ½ cups of unsweetened, unflavored plant-based milk
- 1 tablespoon of date paste or pure cane sugar
- 4 minced cloves of garlic
- 1 tablespoon of finely chopped jalapeño pepper
- 2 teaspoons of active dry yeast
- 3 and ½ cups + 2 tablespoons of whole wheat flour
- ½ cup of sliced onion

Directions:

1. 2½ cups of milk should be heated to a high but not boiling temperature (120°F to 130°F). Pour boiling milk into the bowl of a food processor equipped with a dough blade or the bowl of a stand mixer fitted with a dough hook and pulse until smooth. Stir in the date paste and yeast until everything is well-combined. 2 tablespoons of the flour should be sprinkled over the milk mixture. Refrigerate for at least 10 minutes or until bubbly, after which remove from heat and put aside.

2. In a large mixing bowl, whisk the remaining 312 cups of flour and the salt until smooth. Combine the flour mixture with the milk mixture in a food processor or mixer on low speed for 2 to 3 minutes, or until a dough starts to come together. Half of the onion, garlic, and jalapeno should be added now. Continue to process or mix for another 2 to 3 minutes, or until the dough begins to pull away from the edges of the bowl and is no longer sticky.

3. Cover the dough with a clean, moist towel once it has been transferred to the bowl. Refrigerate for 45 to 60 minutes or until the dough has doubled in size around 45 to 60 minutes.

4. Preheat the oven to 525 degrees Fahrenheit. On the top rack of the oven, place a pizza stone or an upside-down baking sheet to bake on. Prepare three baking sheets by lining them with parchment paper and generously dusting them with flour.

5. Transfer the dough to a work surface that has been lightly floured. Dividing the dough into 16 equal pieces, roll each portion into a ball. Roll the balls into 6x4-inch ovals using a rolling pin and transfer to the baking sheets prepared. Cover loosely with wet towels and put aside in a warm area for 10 minutes to allow the temperature to increase.

6. In a medium-sized mixing bowl, combine the remaining 14 cups of milk, onion, garlic, jalapeno, cilantro, and lemon juice until well combined. Flour a pizza peel, a plate, or an upside-down baking sheet before starting.

7. Place two dough ovals on a pizza peel and press them together. Apply a little coating of the milk mixture to each. Transfer the ovals to the heated pizza stone or baking sheet in the oven as quickly as possible. Alternatively, bake for 90 seconds or until the naans bubble up and exhibit a little browning on top. Stack them on a plate lined with a clean kitchen towel and cover them with a clean kitchen towel to keep them warm. Then repeat the process with the rest of the dough and the milk mixture. Warm the dish before serving.

26. Vegan Kale Caesar Salad

Total time: 30 minutes
Serving: 10 cups
Nutrient per serving: Calories: 510, Fats: 5g, Carbohydrates: 50g, Proteins: 68g, Sodium: 40mg, Calcium: 20mg, Iron: 143 mg
Ingredients:
- 1 teaspoon of Sea salt
- 1 teaspoon Freshly ground black pepper
- ⅓ cup of quinoa
- 2 slices of whole-grain bread
- 1⅓ tablespoons of Dijon mustard
- 2 cloves of garlic
- 1 (15-oz.) can chickpeas
- 6 oz. baby kale
- ⅓ cup white wine vinegar
- ⅓ cup plant-based milk
- 6 oz. cherry tomatoes

Directions:
1. Preheat the oven to 375 degrees Fahrenheit. Cook the quinoa and 2/3 cup water in a saucepan over high heat until the quinoa is tender. Reduce the heat to low, cover, and let It simmer for 20 minutes, stirring occasionally. Remove from heat and set aside to cool before fluffing with a fork.

2. Cashews should be soaked in extremely hot water for 15 minutes in a dish. Remove the nuts from the water and rinse them.

3. Preheat the oven to 350°F and bake the breadcrumbs on a baking sheet for 8 to 10 minutes, until crisp. Remove from the heat and set aside to cool.

4. Chickpeas, cooked quinoa, kale, and tomatoes are mixed in a large mixing bowl.

5. Using an immersion blender (or food processor), mix the soaked cashews, vinegar, plant milk, Dijon mustard, and garlic until smooth. Process until the mixture is smooth. Taste and season with salt and pepper to your liking. Toss the kale salad with approximately half of the Caesar dressing until it is well coated. Serve with the leftover dressing on the side and the croutons on top of the salad.

27. Smokey Tempeh Bacon

Total time: 1hour and 10 minutes
Serving: 2
Nutrient per serving: Calories: 90, Fats: 9g, Carbohydrates: 50g, Proteins: 58g, Sodium: 47mg, Calcium: 29mg, Iron: 140 mg
Ingredients:

- 1 teaspoon of onion powder
- 1/4 cup of low-sodium tamari
- 2 tablespoons of date syrup
- 1/2 teaspoon of garlic powder
- 1/8 teaspoon of freshly ground black pepper
- 1 tablespoon of molasses
- 2 teaspoons of liquid smoke

Directions:

1. Preheat the oven to 375 degrees Fahrenheit. Prepare a baking sheet by lining it with parchment paper.

2. Using a sharp knife, cut the tempeh into 1/4-inch strips, approximately 24 slices total.

3. Optional: Boil the piece of tempeh for twenty minutes in a covered outdoor pot over medium heat, covered with a lid. Remove from the oven and set aside until cool enough to handle. After that, you may start slicing.

4. In a container or watertight container bag big enough to hold the tempeh slices, whisk together all of the marinade ingredients. Place the tempeh in the marinade and let it sit for a few minutes, 30 minutes, but preferably up to overnight.

5. Remove the tempeh from the marinade and arrange it in a single layer on a baking sheet lined with parchment paper. Bake for 15 minutes, turning halfway through, or until they're crispy and lightly browned, depending on your oven. Overcooking will result in them becoming dry. Instead, cook the tempeh in a nonstick pan over moderate medium heat on each side until it is golden brown. Keep an eye on them to make sure they don't burn.

6. Leftovers may be kept in the fridge for seven days if they are stored in an airtight container.

28. Oil-Free Blueberry Scones

Total time: 1 hour 10 minutes
Serving: 8
Nutrient per serving: Calories: 780, Fats: 8g, Carbohydrates: 40g, Proteins: 88g, Sodium: 27mg, Calcium: 79mg, Iron: 130 mg
Ingredients:

- 1 tablespoon of baking powder
- 2 tablespoons of chia seeds
- 1 teaspoon of pure vanilla extract
- 1 cup of blueberries
- 1 tablespoon of flax meal
- 2 tablespoons of water
- 3 tablespoons of maple syrup
- 1 tablespoon of lemon juice
- 1 and 1/4 cups of oat flour
- 1 and 1/4 cups of blanched almond flour
- 1/2 teaspoon of salt
- 1/4 cup of unsweetened plant milk

Directions:

1. Preheat the oven to 400 degrees Fahrenheit. Prepare a baking sheet by lining it with parchment paper.
2. Combine the flax meal and water in a separate bowl and leave aside.
3. Combine the almond flour, baking powder, oat flour, chia seeds, and salt in a large mixing bowl.
4. Combine the flax mixture with the soymilk, maple syrup, lemon juice, and vanilla extract and mix well before adding to the dry mixture. Mix just until the ingredients are barely mixed. The dough is quite thick and sticky when it is finished. It's possible that you'll have to use your hands to put it back together. If the mixture is too dry, add a tablespoon or more plant milk.
5. Stir in the blueberries with a light hand.
6. Form the scones mixture into a 7-inch circle on a floured surface using a rolling pin. Placing them on a baking sheet and carefully pulling them apart so that there is at least an inch between them could ensure they cook evenly.
7. Bake for 15-20 minutes on the center rack, or until the top is gently golden brown. Because every oven is different, check them at 15 minutes to see whether they are golden brown.
8. To decorate the top with an icing sugar drizzle, combine 1/2 cup loosely packed icing sugar and 1 tablespoon plant milk in a mixing bowl and blend well. Drizzle over the top of each scone.
9. If you have leftovers, store them in a container in the fridge for up to 7 days or freeze them for 3 months.

29. Country Hash Browns with Sausage Gravy

Total time: 1 hours 20 minutes
Serving: 4
Nutrient per serving: Calories: 100, Fats: 1g, Carbohydrates: 30g, Proteins: 8g, Sodium: 73mg, Calcium: 3mg, Iron: 150 mg
Ingredients:
- 2 teaspoon of low sodium tamari
- sea salt and pepper
- 1/3 lb. vegan breakfast sausage cut into small pieces
- 3 tablespoons of whole wheat or unbleached flour
- 1 cup of low-sodium vegetable broth
- 1 cup of unsweetened non-dairy milk
- 1/2 teaspoon of onion powder
- 2 tablespoons of nutritional yeast

Direction:
1. Gravy Made in Minutes. Over medium heat, brown the vegan sausages in a medium nonstick pan until it is cooked through. Season the sausage with onion powder, nutritional yeast, salt, and pepper after sprinkling the flour over it.
2. Stir in the soup, non-dairy milk, and tamari or soy sauce with a whisk until everything is well combined. Continue to whisk constantly over medium heat until the sauce begins to thicken. Reduce the heat to maintain a comfortable temperature.
3. Using a large nonstick skillet, cook the ingredients over medium heat. Distribute the premade hash browns evenly across the pan and cook for 6-10 minutes, occasionally stirring, before flipping and cooking for another 5 minutes or until they are beginning to brown.
4. Stir in the diced onion, garlic, and bell pepper until everything is well combined. Once again, flatten the potato and veggies into a uniform layer, and allow them to rest until they begin to brown. Repeat the process of turning over and browning the potato wedges until they reach the crispiness you want.
5. Serve the hash with a drizzle of breakfast gravy and chives on top for garnish.

30. Pumpkin Pie Cake

Total time: 40 minutes
Serving: 1
Nutrient per serving: Calories: 140, Fats: 84g, Carbohydrates: 54g, Proteins: 13g, Sodium: 37.3mg, Calcium: 30.0mg, Iron: 10 mg

Ingredients:

- 2 teaspoon of apple cider vinegar
- 1/4 cup of date sugar
- 3/4 cup of pumpkin puree
- 1/4 cup of non-dairy milk
- 1 teaspoon of vanilla extract
- 1/3 cup of maple syrup

Directions:

1. Preheat the oven to 350 degrees Fahrenheit (180C). Prepare an 8 × 8-inch baking dish by lining it with parchment paper. Tip: Crumble the parchment first, and then smooth it out with your hands. It will conform much more easily to the dish. Alternatively, gently spray with cooking spray.
2. In a large mixing bowl, whisk together all of the wet ingredients until well mixed.
3. In a separate dish, combine the dry ingredients and stir them into the liquid ingredients. Stir just until the ingredients are evenly distributed.
4. Pour the batter into the baking tray and spread it out evenly.
5. Bake for 30 minutes, or until a tester or sharp knife inserted into the center of the cake comes out clean. Depending on your oven, it may take a few extra minutes to bake.

31. Low Fat Cinnamon Nut Granola

Total time: 1 hour 20 minutes
Serving: 4
Nutrient per serving: Calories: 190, Fats: 36g, Carbohydrates: 2.6g, Proteins: 9.8g, Sodium: 2mg, Calcium: 7mg, Iron: 35 mg
Ingredients:

- 3/4 cup of unsweetened dried cranberries
- 1/2 cup of unsweetened apple sauce dash sea salt
- 1/2 cup of shredded coconut
- 2 cups of whole oats
- 2 cups of puffed corn
- 2 teaspoon of Ceylon cinnamon
- 1 teaspoon of vanilla extract
- 2 cups of puffed millet

- 1/2 cup of sliced almonds

Directions:

1. Preheat oven to 300 Fahrenheit.
2. In a large mixing bowl, combine the oats, puffed corn, and millet; stir in the nuts.
3. In a second small mixing bowl, combine the maple syrup, applesauce, cinnamon, vanilla, and sea salt until well combined.
4. Mix the cereals with the liquid ingredients until everything is well combined.
5. Distribute the mixture on two baking sheets lining with parchment paper.
6. Bake for 30-40 minutes, turning the pan every 10 minutes, or until the top is gently browned.
7. Stir in the dried fruit.

32. Vegan Yogurt Parfait with Berries & Granola

Total time: 5 minutes
Serving: 2
Nutrient per serving: Calories: 68, Fats: 10g, Carbohydrates: 17g, Proteins: 105g, Sodium: 13.5mg, Calcium: 65mg, Iron: 125 mg
Ingredients:

- 1/3 cup of homemade granola
- 1 Tbsp. of Trader Joe's Ancient Grains
- 1 teaspoon of maple syrup
- 1 cup of unsweetened homemade yogurt
- 3/4 cup of berries

Directions:

1. 1/3 of the fruit should be placed in the bottom of a glass container.
2. On top of the fruit, spread half of the retail location carton or approximately 1/4 cup homemade yogurt, if desired. Adding approximately 1/2 teaspoon maple syrup can make it a bit sweeter if you want.
3. If using, sprinkle 1/2 of the oats and a dusting of Ancient Grains on top of the salad.
4. Repeat the layers of yogurt, fruit, and granola until all of the ingredients are used.

33. Easy Breakfast Chia Pudding

Total time: 2 hours and 10 minutes
Serving: 4
Nutrient per serving: Calories: 163, Fats: 1.2g, Carbohydrates: 110g, Proteins: 19g, Sodium: 27mg, Calcium: 9.2mg, Iron: 200mg

Ingredients:
- 1/4 cup of homemade granola
- 1/2 cup of unsweetened homemade yogurt
- 2 cups of homemade almond milk
- 6 tablespoons of chia seeds
- 3 tablespoons of date syrup or maple syrup
- 1 teaspoons of vanilla extract non-alcoholic

Directions:
1. Pour the non-dairy milk into a mixing bowl.
2. Pour the milk into a separate bowl and mix the chia seeds, maple syrup or date syrup, and vanilla extract.
3. Place in the refrigerator and let chill for several hours, mixing at minimum once after approximately 30 minutes to ensure that the seeds are evenly distributed.
4. Fill individual bowls with the yogurt mixture and sprinkle with fruit and granola.

34. Oil-Free Roasted Potatoes

Total time: 1 hour 10 minutes
Serving: 4
Nutrient per serving: Calories: 350, Fats: 15g, Carbohydrates:10g, Proteins: 19g, Sodium: 5.9mg, Calcium: 9.2mg, Iron: 110 m

Ingredients:
- 1 large red onion
- 2-3 tablespoon of whole wheat flour
- 2 large russet peeled potatoes
- 2 large yams
- 1 large pepper

Directions:
1. Preheat oven to 450 °F
2. Set aside in a big nonstick skillet with a little water until the water comes to a boil. Once it does, steam for approximately 5 minutes, or until the potatoes are crunchy and the onions are translucent.
3. After draining the cooked veggies, please keep them in the pot and sprinkle with flour, tossing well.
4. After putting the cap back on the pan, shake it gently for a couple of seconds to release the steam. You are denting the edges of the potatoes, which will aid in the crispiness of the potatoes when they are cooked later.
5. Using a baking sheet lightly coated with oil or a Silpat, spread the potatoes out in a thin layer, don't cram the potatoes, or the edges will not become crispy. Taste and sprinkle with salt and pepper to your liking.
6. Grill for 30-45 minutes at 450 °F, rotating halfway through but keeping an eye on them to ensure they don't burn.

35. Vegan Huevos Ranchero Case roll

Total time: 45 minutes
Serving: 6
Nutrient per serving: Calories: 294, Fats: 102g, Carbohydrates: 50g, Proteins: 18.3g, Sodium: 18.2mg, Calcium: 18mg, Iron: 16.0mg

Ingredients:
- 2 large avocados
- 1/2 6 oz can of low salt black olives
- 1 package of corn tortillas
- 2 15 oz. cans of black beans
- 1 Jalapeño

Directions:
1. Spread a little quantity of ranchero sauce over the base of your baking sheet using the back of a spoon to cover the whole bottom. Add another layer of tortillas, splitting them up to cover the pan, then drizzle with a bit of extra sauce on top.
2. Place half of the black beans on atop of the tortillas and fold the tortillas in half.
3. Place half of the tofu scramble on top of the tortillas, followed with ranchero sauce and another covering of tortillas.

4. More ranchero salsa, beans, scrambled eggs, sauce, and a last layer of tortillas are placed on top of the tortillas. Pour sauce on top to completely cover the tortillas and prevent them from being too crunchy in the oven.

5. Cover with aluminum foil and bake for 30 minutes at 350 degrees. Remove the lid and look inside the pan for any liquid. If there is a significant amount, return the dish to the oven for around 5 min.

6. Serve with sliced olives and green onions on the side. Optional jalapenos and sliced avocado are also included.

36. Crustless Broccoli Sun-Dried Tomato Quiche

Total time: 1 hour 20 minutes
Serving: 4
Nutrient per serving: Calories: 35, Fats: 112g, Carbohydrates: 30.1g, Proteins: 8g, Sodium: 18mg, Calcium: 1 mg, Iron: 54 mg
Ingredients:

- ⅔ cup sun-dried tomatoes
- ½ cup artichoke hearts chopped
- 12.3-oz. box of dried extra firm Silken tofu
- 2 leeks cleaned and sliced
- 1 ½ cup of broccoli chopped
- 1/2 teaspoon of turmeric
- 3-4 dashes of Tabasco sauce
- ½-1 teaspoon of sea salt
- 2 tablespoon of low sodium vegetable broth
- 2 cloves of garlic chopped
- 3 tablespoons of nutritional yeast
- 2 teaspoons of yellow mustard
- 1 teaspoon of lemon juiced
- 1 tablespoon of tahini
- 1/4 cup of old-fashioned oats
- 1 tablespoon of cornstarch

Directions:
1. Preheat the oven to 375 degrees.
2. Prepare a 9-inch pie dish or cheesecake pan by coating it with baking parchment or spraying it with some oil before starting.

3. Using your hands or a spoon, combine all of the onions and broccoli on a baking sheet with a little vegetable stock, salt, pepper, or a water-soy sauce combination, and toss well. Season with salt and pepper. Preheat the oven to 200 degrees for 20-30 minutes.

4. In the meanwhile, combine the tofu, garlic, yeast, mustard, lemon, tahini, 1/8 cups oats, cornmeal, a few dashes of Tabasco, and salt in a food processor and process until smooth and creamy. Serve immediately. Blend until everything is well-combined and smooth. A little amount of oats may be added if the mixture becomes too runny while baking. Taste for taste and heat and adjust the amount as necessary.

5. Place the cooked veggies, artichoke hearts, and sun-dried tomatoes in a large mixing bowl. Toss to combine. Scrape the tofu slurry from the processor bowl into the bowl of the stand mixer.

6. Make sure that all of the veggies are evenly distributed throughout the mixture. If the mixture seems too dry, a little amount of vegetable broth or water may be added.

7. Fill the pie plate, cheesecake pan, or cupcake tins with the mixture and smooth it out evenly.

8. Bake for 30-35 minutes, or until the top is just beginning to brown.

9. Allow to cool completely before cutting into wedges. It may be served warm, or it can be refrigerated and served cold.

37. Mint Chocolate Smoothie

Total time: 5 minutes
Serving: 2
Nutrient per serving: Calories: 710, Fats: 22g, Carbohydrates:10g, Proteins: 32g, Sodium: 10mg, Calcium: 30mg, Iron: 20 mg
Ingredients:

- 1/2 cup of lightly packed fresh mint
- 1/2 teaspoon mint extract
- 2 handfuls spinach

- 1 tablespoon of ground flaxseeds
- 2-3 tablespoons of cacao nibs
- 1/2 cup of old-fashioned oats
- 4 medium frozen bananas
- 1/2 cup of non-dairy milk

Directions:
1. Fill the base of a high-powered mixer halfway with the extra oats, ground flax, and cacao nib.
2. Combine the bananas, greens, and non-dairy milk in a large mixing bowl.
3. If you wish to add additional pieces of cacao, set them aside and add them afterward after the mixture has been mixed a little.
4. Begin by blending at a low speed and increasing it gradually. If the batter is too thick, add a little more non-dairy milk.

38. Banana Bread with Maple Glaze

Total time: 55 minutes
Serving: 10
Nutrient per serving: Calories:110, Fats: 26g, Carbohydrates:18g, Proteins: 72g, Sodium: 8.7mg, Calcium: 20mg, Iron: 50 mg
Ingredients:
- ½ teaspoon of sea salt
- ½ teaspoon of Ceylon cinnamon
- ⅓ cup of maple syrup
- ½ cup of oats
- ½ teaspoon of baking soda
- ½ cup of mini vegan chocolate chips
- ¼ cup of chopped walnuts
- ½ cup + 2 tablespoon of non-dairy milk
- 1 teaspoon apple of cider vinegar
- 3 tablespoons of almond butter
- ¾ cup of unbleached all-purpose flour
- 1 and ½ teaspoon of non-aluminum baking powder
- ½ cup of mashed banana
- 3 teaspoons of vanilla extract

Directions:
1. Preheat the oven to 350 degrees Fahrenheit (177 degrees Celsius).
2. In a small mixing bowl, whisk together the non-dairy milk and apple cider vinegar

until well combined. Allow at least five min for the non-dairy milk to curdle before serving.
3. Combine the almond butter, mashed banana, vanilla extract, maple syrup, cinnamon, and salt in a large mixing bowl until well combined.
4. A large mixing bowl, mix oats, all-purpose flour, baking powder, and baking soda until well combined.
5. Pour the non-dairy milk mixture in to mixing bowl with the wet ingredients, whisking constantly.
6. In a separate bowl, mix the wet ingredients with the dry components by stirring well.
7. Combine the white chocolate and walnuts in a separate bowl.
8. Pour the sauce into a lightly greased bread pan and line the bottom part with parchment paper long enough to hang over the edges of the pan. Oven for about 25 minutes, or until a toothpick inserted into the center comes out clean.

39. Cornmeal Waffles

Total time: 30 minutes
Serving: 4
Nutrient per serving: Calories:mm110, Fats: 26g, Carbohydrates:18g, Proteins: 72g, Sodium: 8.7mg, Calcium: 20mg, Iron: 50 mg
Ingredients:
- 1 Tbsp. of maple syrup
- 1 Tbsp. of coconut oil
- ½ teaspoon of vanilla extract
- 1 cup of cornmeal
- ½ cup of oats
- 2/3 cup of whole wheat flour
- 1 cup of blueberries
- 2/3 cup of chopped walnuts
- ½ teaspoon of baking powder
- ½ teaspoon of sea salt
- ½ cup of soy milk or other plant milk
- 1/3 cup of applesauce
- 1 teaspoon of Ceylon cinnamon

Directions:

1. Combine the wet ingredients in a large mixing bowl (milk, applesauce, syrup, and vanilla extract).
2. In a separate bowl, combine the dry ingredients: corn, oats, wheat, baking powder, salt, and cinnamon. Pour the batter into the baking dish.
3. Pour the flour mixture into the wet components and gently mix them.
4. Cook the waffles in your waffle cooker according to the manufacturer's instructions.
5. To create blueberries syrup, put a little amount of maple syrup over a cup of berries and microwave for a few seconds to warm the blueberries.
6. Add a spoonful of applesauce, a drizzle of blueberry/maple syrup, and a few walnuts on the top of each waffle.

40. Blueberry Lemon Bars

Total time: 1 hour
Serving: 16
Nutrient per serving: Calories: 140, Fats: 96g, Carbohydrates: 39g, Proteins: 42g, Sodium: 3.7mg, Calcium: 80mg, Iron: 10mg
Ingredients:
- 2/3 cup of applesauce
- 1/4 cup of vegetable oil
- 1/3 cup of maple syrup
- 6 Tbsp. of fresh lemon juice
- 3 Tbsp. of chia seeds
- 1 1/2 cups of old-fashioned oats
- 1/2 teaspoon of sea salt
- 1/2 cup of walnuts chopped
- 1 cup of blueberries
- 1/2 cup of old-fashioned oats

Directions:
1. The oven should be preheated at 350 degrees, and you should line a baking dish with baking parchment.
2. In a small dish, whisk together the chia seeds and lemon juice until well combined. Set down to thicken.
3. In a large mixing bowl, combine the dry ingredients (oat wheat, oats, coconut,

bicarbonate of soda, salt) with the nuts and blueberries until well combined.
4. In a separate bowl, combine the wet ingredients, including the apple sauce, cooking oil (or applesauce), maple syrup, and soaked chia seeds.
5. Put the flour mixture into the wet ingredients and mix until everything is well blended. You may want to use your arms to make sure everything is well mixed. Because of this, the bread will be very dry.
6. Using your spoon, level the top of the dough into the pan that you have already prepared.
7. Bake for about 30 minutes or until the edges are brown in your preheated oven.
8. Allow to cool completely before extracting from the pan. Make squares out of the leftovers.

41. Buckwheat Pancakes

Total time: 30 minutes
Serving: 4
Nutrient per serving: Calories: 340, Fats: 18g, Carbohydrates:20g, Proteins: 62g, Sodium: 2.7mg, Calcium: 60mg, Iron: 40 mg
Ingredients:
- 1 teaspoon of Ceylon cinnamon
- 1-1 1/2 cup of non-dairy milk
- 1 tablespoon of maple syrup
- 1/2 cup of chopped walnuts
- 1 cup of blueberries
- 1 cup of buckwheat flour
- 1/4 cup of cornmeal
- 1/2 cup of oatmeal
- 1 large banana frozen
- 1/2 cup of applesauce
- 1 tablespoon of baking powder
- 1/4 teaspoon of sea salt

Directions:
1. Buckwheat through cinnamon should be combined with the dry ingredients.
2. If you're using raw, ripe banana, smash it up with a spoon in a mixing dish before proceeding. After that, combine it with the remainder of the wet components, ranging

from non-dairy milk to maple syrup. First, thaw the frozen banana in the oven for a few seconds.

3. Put the milk mixture into the dry ingredients and stir just until everything is mixed. Allow for a little moment of contemplation. The batter will be very thick, but you may think it down with a bit more non-dairy milk if it becomes too thick.

4. Preheat a nonstick pan over medium heat. If you're using a metal pan, spray it with nonstick cooking spray beforehand. Using about 2 big spoonsful of batter, drop them onto the pan. Spread them evenly using the back of a spoon due to the thick consistency of the batter. When the edges seem to be dry, flip the pan.

5. Don't overcook the food. Dryness may result as a result of this.

6. Using tongs, transfer to a serving dish and top with blueberries, sliced banana, maple syrup (or more applesauce), and almonds.

42. Oatmeal with Berries and Nuts

Total time: 15 minutes
Serving: 2
Nutrient per serving: Calories: 140, Fats: 12g, Carbohydrates:30g, Proteins: 42g, Sodium: 2.1mg, Calcium: 30mg, Iron: 10 mg
Ingredients:
- 1 Tbsp. of chia seeds
- 1/4 teaspoon of sea salt
- 1 cup of organic berries I often used frozen
- 1/4 cup of walnuts or mixed nuts
- 3/4 cup of old-fashioned organic oats
- 1 1/2 cups of water
- 2 Tbsp. of ground flaxseeds

Directions:
1. Put 1 1/2 cups water, the oatmeal, the crushed flax, the chia seeds, and the salt to a boil in a small saucepan.

2. Reduce the heat to low and continue to cook for 7-10 minutes, or until the water has disappeared and the oatmeal is mushy.

3. Chop the berries into bite-size pieces before serving.

4. Toss the porridge with the blueberries and nuts before serving it with soy yogurt or almond milk

43. Carrot Chia Pudding

Total time: 1 hour 10 minutes
Serving: 6
Nutrient per serving: Calories: 840, Fats: 9g, Carbohydrates:90g, Proteins: 62g, Sodium: 2.8mg, Calcium: 70mg, Iron: 109 mg
Ingredients:
- 1 cup of light canned coconut milk split
- 3/4 teaspoon of coconut extract mixed
- 1 of cup non-dairy milk
- 1/2 cup of chia seeds
- 1/4 teaspoon of ground ginger
- 1/2 teaspoon of Ceylon cinnamon
- 1/4 teaspoon of ground cloves
- 5-6 carrots peeled and shredded
- 1 1/2 cups of homemade almond milk
- 1/4 cup of maple syrup
- 1 teaspoon of vanilla extract
- 1/3 teaspoon of ground cardamom

Directions:
1. Simmer the shredded carrots, 1/2 cup almond milk, and 1/2 cup soy milk in a medium-sized pot until the carrots are tender. Boil until the carrots are soft, approximately 20 minutes, after which add in the seasonings. Set aside for several minutes to allow the mixture to cool.

2. As soon as the carrots have been allowed to cool somewhat, transfer them to a blender along with the cooking liquid and mix thoroughly, adding more almond milk if the mixture becomes too thick.

3. Blend in a slower, more deliberate motion to include the remaining milk and sugar.

4. Put into a large mixing bowl and stir in the chia seeds until thoroughly combined.

5. Place the bowl in the refrigerator to chill, stirring every 15 minutes to ensure that the chia seeds are well distributed

throughout the mixture. Allow to cool until the chocolate has set.

6. Serve in separate bowls garnished with berries, cinnamon, chopped walnuts, pumpkin seeds, or tiny chocolate chips.

44. Sweet Potato Hash Browns

Total time: 35 minutes
Serving: 4
Nutrient per serving: Calories: 65, Fats: 48g, Carbohydrates: 76g, Proteins: 43g, Sodium: 2.8mg, Calcium: 33.8mg, Iron: 54mg
Ingredients:
- 1/2 teaspoon of smoky paprika optional
- sea salt & pepper
- 2 large chopped sweet potatoes or yams
- 1 large onion
- 1 large red or green pepper

Directions:
1. Pre-heat a big nonstick skillet over medium heat and put the onions in the pan. Cook until they begin to brown a little on the edges.
2. Continue to simmer, often stirring so that the potatoes do not burn, until the peppers and spices are tender. If necessary, add a little water and cover the pan to speed up the cooking process; however, before serving, uncover the pan and allow the water to evaporate.
3. Season with salt and pepper

45. Hibiscus Tea

Total time: 20 minutes
Serving: 4
Nutrient per serving: Calories:32, Fats: 0.9g, Carbohydrates:9g, Proteins: 2g, Sodium: 2.8mg, Calcium: 30mg, Iron: 19 mg
Ingredients:
- 1/2 cup of dried hibiscus flowers
- 4 cups of filtered water
- 10-20 drops of liquid stevia

Directions:
1. Prepare a 15-minute tea by steeping 1/2 cup dried flowers in 4 cups boiling water for 10-15 min.

2. Pour in your sugar replacement and serve immediately, either hot or cooled over crushed ice. If you want to use dates syrup, begin with a little quantity, such as a few teaspoons, and gradually increase the amount until you get the desired sweetness.
3. Alternatively, you may use pomegranate juice to reduce the acidity of the dish.
4. Drink no more than 1 quart of water each day.

46. Lentil Oats Power Porridge

Total time: 1 hour 10 minutes
Serving: 4
Nutrient per serving: Calories:142, Fats: 8g, Carbohydrates:7g, Proteins: 0.2g, Sodium: 5.8mg, Calcium: 10mg, Iron: 29 mg
Ingredients:
- 2 Tbsp. of oat bran
- 1 Tbsp. of Kasha
- 1 Tbsp. of ground flaxseeds
- 1 Tbsp. of chia seeds
- 4 large dates rough chopped
- 1 Tbsp. of raisins
- frozen berries and bananas
- 2 cups of unsweetened soy, almond or oat milk
- 1 Tbsp. of lentils
- 2 Tbsp. of steel cut oat

Directions:
1. Bring the non-dairy milk to a boil, then add the lentils, grains, seeds, and oats, stirring constantly. Reduce the heat to a simmer, stirring periodically. Bring the lentils to a boil for approximately fifteen minutes or until they are soft. It is possible that you will need to pour more almond milk to maintain the consistency creamy.
2. Stir in the walnuts and dried fruit, then reduce the heat to low and cook just until the fruits are warmed through. Fresh fruit should be cut and placed on top.

47. Baked Pears with Cardamom

Total time: 45 minutes
Serving: 4
Nutrient per serving: Calories:14, Fats: 72g, Carbohydrates: 7g, Proteins: 2g, Sodium: 43mg, Calcium: 1mg, Iron: 66mg

Ingredients:
- 1 teaspoon of vanilla extract
- 3 firm ripe pears halved and seeded
- 1 1/2 Tbsp. of lemon juice
- 2 Tbsp. of sugar
- 1/4 cup of white wine
- 1/2 teaspoon of ground cardamom

Directions:
1. Preheat the oven to 400 Fahrenheit. In an 8-inch square baking dish, combine the wine, cardamom, and vanilla.
2. In a baking dish, arrange the pears cut side up and drizzle with lemon juice. Sugar should be sprinkled on top.
3. Bake for thirty min, or until the vegetables are soft, after covering the pan with aluminum foil and placing it on the center rack of the oven.
4. Remove the foil and place the pan on the top rack. 5 minutes in the broiler, or until golden brown. Keep a close eye on everything.
5. Transfer the pear to a serving plate and sprinkle with the liquid from the pan to finish the dish.

48. Mushroom Veggie Tacos

Total time: 30 minutes
Serving: 3
Nutrient per serving: Calories 360, Fats: 14 g, Carbohydrates:0.7, Proteins: 0.2g, Sodium: 5.8mg, Calcium: 10mg, Iron: 29 mg

Ingredients:
- 1/2 teaspoon of chili powder
- 1/4 teaspoon of cumin
- 1 large avocado diced
- 1/3 cup of hummus
- 1/3 cup of salsa
- 6 corn tortillas
- 1/2 large red onion
- 4 oz of mushrooms
- 1/4 teaspoon of garlic powder
- 1/2 teaspoon of sea salt and pepper
- 3 leaves of lettuce
- 1/2 large, diced bell pepper
- 1 large, diced tomato
- 1/2 cup of canned tomatoes

Directions:
1. In a sauté pan, add the red onion, mushrooms, and bell pepper, along with a little water. Cook until the vegetables are soft.
2. Combine the drained fresh tomatoes, spices, and salt and pepper in a large mixing bowl.
3. Corn tortillas should be toasted in a kitchen until crisp but still flexible.
4. Place about one-quarter cup or so of hummus on one half of the corn tortilla and fold it in half. Fill the taco halfway with the vegetable mixture and close it up.
5. Add the tomatoes, lettuce, avocado, and salsa to the top of the dish.

49. Zucchini Cakes

Total time: 1 hour 10 minutes
Serving: 4
Nutrient per serving: Calories 30, Fats: 14g, Carbohydrates: 7g, Proteins: 13g, Sodium: 5.8mg, Calcium: 10mg, Iron: 30 mg

Ingredients:
- 2 tablespoons of red onion grated
- 1/4 cup of cornmeal
- 1 teaspoon of baking powder
- 1/2 teaspoon of sea salt
- mango salsa
- 1 tablespoon of ground flaxseeds
- 3 tablespoons of fresh water
- 2 medium zucchinis grated
- 1/3 15-oz of can chickpeas

Directions:
1. In a small mixing dish, mix the flaxseed meal and 2 tablespoon water and set aside for approximately 10 minutes to rest.
2. In a large mixing bowl, combine the zucchini, chickpeas, and red onion.

3. Combine the corn, flour, baking powder, flax blend, and salt in a large bowl. Mix until everything is well-combined.
4. Spray a baking pan with the spray bottle and add approximately 2-3 teaspoons of the mixture, smoothing it to make it even with the surface.
5. Cook for approximately 2 minutes on each side.

Serving suggestions: Serve with relish or mango salsa, with a squeeze of lemon on the side, if desired

50. Baked Corn Casserole

Total time: 1 hour 20 minutes
Serving: 6
Nutrient per serving: Calories: 500, Fats: 14 g, Carbohydrates: 87.1g, Proteins: 2g, Sodium: 21mg, Calcium: 10.7mg, Iron: 44 mg
Ingredients:
- 1/2 teaspoon of cumin
- 1 teaspoon of sea salt and pepper
- 1/2 teaspoon of cayenne pepper
- 1 14-16 oz. of block firm organic tofu
- 1 1/4 cup of cornmeal
- 1 1/2 cup of water
- 3/4 cup of non-dairy unsweetened milk like soy
- 1 10 oz package of frozen spinach thawed
- 2 4 oz cans of diced mild chilies
- 3 cloves of garlic minced
- 2 ears of fresh corn taken off of cob
- 10 oz package of frozen thawed
- 1 teaspoon of baking powder

Directions:
1. Preheat the oven to 400 Fahrenheit. Using a spray bottle, lightly coat a 9x12 or 13" baking sheet with oil or line the dish with parchment paper for an oil-free option.
2. Prepare the corn by heating 1 1/2 cups water in a pan over medium heat with 1/2 cup of the soy yogurt until it is nearly boiling, then straining the mixture. Gradually mix in the cornmeal and continue to swirl continuously until the mixture thickens somewhat. Transfer the mixture to a large mixing bowl.

3. Add garlic, soy, 1 cup corn, and the other 1/4 cup milk substitute to a stick blender and blend until smooth. Process until the mixture is smooth. In a large mixing bowl, combine the cooked cornmeal and the buttermilk.
4. Combine the spinach, remaining whole corn, chopped chilies, baking powder, spices, salt, and pepper in a large mixing bowl until everything is thoroughly combined. This may require some extra effort.
5. Pour the mixture into your casserole tray and bake for 60-70 minutes, or until the edges are crispy and hard. The center will be a little wobbly for a little longer. Allow for 20-30 minutes of resting time before serving.
6. Prepare the dish and cover it with chutney or enchilada sauce.

51. Yummy Jelly & Peanut Butter Oatmeal

"**Preparation time:** 2 minutes"
"**Cooking time:** 5 minutes"
"**Servings:** 1"
"**Ingredients:**"
- "½ cup gluten-free oats"
- "1 mashed banana"
- "1 tablespoon peanut butter"
- "1 tablespoon raspberry jelly"
- "½ teaspoon ground cinnamon"
- "½ cup with 1 tablespoon unsweetened vanilla almond milk"
- "1 tablespoon ground flax seed"

Directions:
1. "Put oats, ½ cup almond milk, cinnamon, and mashed banana in a small-sized saucepan."
2. "Turn the heat on to medium flame and stir for 3-5 minutes."
3. "Within a few minutes, the oats will thicken, and the milk will evaporate."
4. "After the milk has evaporated, add 1 tablespoon of almond milk."
5. "Stir until the almond milk has also evaporated."

6. Transfer the oats to a bowl after taking them off the stove.
7. Serve with peanut butter and jelly.

Per serving: Calories: 354kcal; Fat: 16g; Carbs: 49g; Protein: 10g

52. Sweet Potatoes with a Twist

"**Preparation time:** 5 minutes"
"**Cooking time:** 10 minutes"
"**Servings:** 2"
"**Ingredients:**"

- "2 tablespoons plain vegan yogurt"
- "2 medium-sized sweet potatoes"
- "2 tablespoons almond butter"
- "2 tablespoons maple syrup"
- "½ cup homemade or store-bought granola"

Directions:

1. Add all Clean the sweet potatoes thoroughly and poke holes in them with a fork.
2. Microwave them for 2 minutes, turn them over, and microwave again. When done, it should be easy to pierce with a fork.
3. Let them cool.
4. Cut from the middle, ensure the insides are facing upward, and slightly mash the insides with a fork until a small mouth forms.
5. Fill it with almond butter, yogurt, maple syrup, and granola.
6. Serve hot.

Per serving: Calories: 410kcal; Fat: 16g; Carbs: 62g; Protein: 9g

53. Fresh Avocado Toast with Pesto

"**Preparation time:** 15 minutes"
"**Cooking time:** 15 minutes"
"**Servings:** 1"
"**Ingredients:**"

- "1 slice of gluten-free bread"
- "⅓-¼ ripe and peeled large avocado"
- "½ slices tomato"
- "2 cups fresh stemless basil"
- "1 tablespoon lemon juice"
- "1 tablespoon extra-virgin olive oil"
- "2-3 large & peeled garlic cloves"
- "1 tablespoon nutritional yeast"
- "¼ teaspoon sea salt and as needed"
- "1 tablespoon water"
- "1 pinch of red chili flakes"

"**Directions:**"

1. Put some garlic, nutritional yeast, lemon juice, and sea salt inside a mixer, then include some basil leaves. This is the first step in preparing pesto. Blend till somewhat loose paste develops.
2. To the mixture, include some olive oil and water. Ensure a paste-like consistency is reached by scraping the edges of the bowl with a spoon.
3. Take your slice of bread and toast it in the toaster.
4. Apply the avocado to the toast by mashing it first.
5. Serve with 2 tablespoons of pesto and fresh tomatoes on top of the avocado.
6. Sprinkle red chili flakes and sea salt as per taste.
7. The leftover pesto can be refrigerated for 1 week.

Per serving: Calories: 221kcal; Fat: 11.4g; Carbs: 23g; Protein: 9.1g

54. Crunchy Almond Cereal Breakfast

"**Preparation time:** 5 minutes"
"**Cooking time:** 15 minutes"
"**Servings:** 8"
"**Ingredients:**"

- "1 cup organic oats"
- "1 cup organic spelt flakes"
- "¼ cup date syrup"
- "1 ½ cups roughly chopped almonds"
- "7 tablespoons melted coconut oil"
- "Any plant-based milk"

"**Directions:**"

1. "Get your microwave up to temperature by preheating it to 330 degrees."
2. "Butter paper should be used to line the baking sheet."
3. "Put all of the components into a sizable container and combine them using a rubber spatula."

4. "It is important that the components adhere to one another like granola bars."
5. "Evenly distribute the mix across the baking sheet."
6. "Bake them for fifteen mins, or till they reach the desired level of crunchiness."
7. Let it cool, and then break it into cereal-like pieces.
8. Serve with almond milk or any of your choice.

Per serving: Calories: 286kcal; Fat: 14.7g; Carbs: 34.4g; Protein: 6.6g

55. Gluten-Free Chocolate Chip Muffins

"**Preparation time:** 15 minutes"
"**Cooking time:** 28 minutes"
"**Servings:** 10"
"**Ingredients:**"
- "¾ cup applesauce"
- "⅓ cup coconut sugar"
- "¼ cup maple syrup"
- "1 teaspoon baking powder"
- "¼ teaspoon sea salt"
- "¼ melted coconut oil"
- "¼ cup unsweetened almond milk"
- "½ cup unsweetened cocoa powder"
- "1 ½ teaspoon baking soda"
- "¾ cup gluten-free flour blend"
- "⅓ cup almond flour"
- "¼ cup ground rolled oat flour"
- "⅓ cup dairy-free semi-sweet chocolate chips"
- "2 batches of flaxseed egg (14grams flaxseed meal mixed into 75ml water and let it rest for 5 minutes)"

"**Directions:**"
1. "Put the microwave temperature to 375 degrees."
2. "If you have a muffin tin, you may use cupcake liners to line it, or you can just brush it using oil."
3. "Add maple syrup, applesauce, baking powder, baking soda, and sea salt to the flax eggs and stir."

4. Using the whisk, add almond milk and melted coconut oil.
5. Add all the flour and cocoa powder. Whisk it together to create a batter.
6. The batter should have a scoopable consistency.
7. Fill the muffin tray with the batter.
8. "Bake for twenty to twenty-eight mins, or till a toothpick placed in the center comes out clean."
9. "After allowing them to cool, place them on a cooling rack."
10. Enjoy them with any plant-based milk.

Per serving: Calories: 232kcal; Fat: 11.7g; Carbs: 31.4g; Protein: 3.7g

56. Vegan Breakfast Potatoes

"**Preparation time:** 10 minutes"
"**Cooking time:** 35 minutes"
"**Servings:** 1"
"**Ingredients:**"
- "1 tablespoon extra-virgin olive oil"
- "1 teaspoon garlic powder"
- "1 pound of potatoes, washed, dried, and cut"
- "½ teaspoon sea salt or as needed"
- "Fresh cracked pepper as needed"
- "½ teaspoon paprika"

"**Directions:**"
1. Turn the microwave temperature up to 425 degrees Fahrenheit and cover a sheet pan using butter paper.
2. Place potatoes that have been cut into cubes that are a half-inch large in the center of the cookie sheet. Top the potatoes with olive oil, paprika, sea salt, garlic powder, and pepper.
3. After the potatoes have been thoroughly combined, put them out on the baking tray.
4. Put them in the microwave and cook them for twenty-five mins.
5. After you have given them a spin, return them to the oven for another ten mins, or till the sides are golden brown.
6. Serve hot, and enjoy!

Per serving: Calories: 127kcal; Fat: 2.5g; Carbs: 24.2g; Protein: 2.7g

57. Vegan Whole Wheat Waffles

"**Preparation time:** 5 minutes"
"**Cooking time:** 10 minutes"
"**Servings:**"
"**Ingredients:**"
- "2 tablespoons coconut sugar"
- "2 cups gluten-free flour blend"
- "1 tablespoon baking powder"
- "¼ cup extra-virgin olive oil"
- "Pinch of sea salt"
- "1 ¾ cup of unsweetened vanilla almond milk"

"**Directions:**"
1. "Have a look at the waffle manufacturer's cooking directions and adjust the temperature appropriately."
2. "Put the flour, baking powder, sugar, and milk into a container and mix in the olive oil."
3. Mix until no lumps remain
4. If you are not using a non-stick waffle maker, spray on some oil first.
5. "Take some of the batter, and using a scoop, place it in the middle of the waffle plate."
6. Shut the lid and cook following the manufacturer's instructions.
7. Open the lid once it's done and place them over a wire tray with the help of a bamboo stick or wooden spoon.
8. Serve hot with any plant-based milk or fruits.

Per serving: Calories: 277kcal; Fat: 10.6g; Carbs: 44.1g; Protein: 6.9g

58. Healthy Cinnamon Apples

"**Preparation time:** 10 minutes"
"**Cooking time:** 10 minutes"
"**Servings:** 4"
"**Ingredients:**"
- "1 tablespoon coconut oil"
- "1 teaspoon vanilla extract"
- "4 large peeled, cored, and ¼-inch sliced apples"
- "1 teaspoon cinnamon"
- "1 teaspoon cornstarch"
- "½ cup cold water"
- "3 tablespoons brown organic sugar"

"**Directions:**"
1. Cook the apples inside a saucepan for about six mins over a flame setting of moderate. Be sure to have the oil hot before you do anything else.
2. Make a cornstarch mixture by mixing cornstarch in water. Leave it to rest.
3. Add cinnamon, sugar, vanilla, and cornstarch to the apples, stirring well.
4. Keep stirring until it starts simmering and the apples become tender.
5. Let it cool before serving with yogurt or oatmeal.

Per serving: Calories: 126kcal; Fat: 1.9g; Carbs: 27.3g; Protein: 0.4g

59. Simple Avocado Toast

"**Preparation time:** 2 minutes"
"**Cooking time:** 5 minutes"
"**Servings:** 2"
"**Ingredients:**"
- "1 slice whole grain bread"
- "¼ medium avocado"
- "1 pinch of sea salt"
- "2 teaspoons bagel seasoning (you can make your own as well)"

Directions:
1. Toast the slice of bread in a toaster.
2. Mash the avocado and spread it on the toast.
3. Sprinkle it with the seasoning and sea salt.
4. "Prepare to be served with the non-dairy milk alternative of your choosing."

"**Per serving:** Calories: 172kcal; Fat: 9.8g; Carbs: 17.8g; Protein: 5.4g"

60. Quinoa & Breakfast Patties

"**Preparation time:** 3 minutes"
"**Cooking time:** 6 minutes"
"**Servings:** 4"
"**Ingredients:**"

- "2 flax eggs (water and flaxseed meal)"
- "1 cup cooked quinoa"
- "½ cup shredded carrots"
- "2 teaspoons parsley"
- "½ cup shredded broccoli florets"
- "1 ½ teaspoon garlic powder"
- "1 ½ teaspoon onion powder"
- "¼ teaspoon black pepper"
- "⅓ teaspoon salt"
- "2 cloves of minced garlic"
- "2 tablespoons coconut oil"
- "½ gluten-free breadcrumbs"

Directions:

1. "Except for the oil, include all of the components to a big basin and mix them up thoroughly."
2. "Make the mix into patties using your hands."
3. "Oil should be heated in a saucepan or skillet set at a moderate flame."
4. After the pan is heated, lay your formed patties on it and allow them to cool for two to three mins per side, or till they are golden brown.
5. Serve immediately with your favorite sides.

Per serving: Calories: 229.6kcal; Fat: 11.1g; Carbs: 27.7g; Protein: 9.3g

61. Mixed Berry Bowl

"**Preparation time:** 10 minutes"
"**Cooking time:** 0 minutes"
"**Servings:** 2"
"**Ingredients:**"

- "1 ½ cups coconut milk"
- "2 small-sized bananas"
- "1 cup mixed berries, frozen"
- "2 tablespoons almond butter"
- "1 tablespoon chia seeds"
- "2 tablespoons granola"

Directions:

1. Add coconut milk, bananas, berries, almond butter, and chia seeds.
2. Puree until creamy, uniform, and smooth.
3. The combined concoction should then be distributed among the serving containers, and granola should be sprinkled on top. Instantly distribute after cooking.

"**Per serving:** Calories: 533kcal; Fat: 42g; Carbs: 43g; Protein: 6.9g"

62. Pumpkin Griddle Cakes

"**Preparation time:** 20 minutes"
"**Cooking time:** 10 minutes"
"**Servings:** 4"
"**Ingredients:**"

- "½ cup oat flour"
- "½ cup whole-wheat white flour"
- "1 teaspoon baking powder"
- "¼ teaspoon Himalayan salt"
- "1 teaspoon sugar"
- "½ teaspoon ground allspice"
- "½ teaspoon ground cinnamon"
- "½ teaspoon crystallized ginger"
- "1 teaspoon lemon juice, freshly squeezed"
- "½ cup almond milk"
- "½ cup pumpkin puree"
- "2 tablespoons coconut oil"

Directions:

1. In a large mixing container, carefully incorporate all of the ingredients: flour, baking powder, salt, sugar, and spices. Include the lemon juice, milk, and pumpkin puree to the bowl in a slow and steady stream.
2. Heat an electric griddle on medium and lightly slick it with coconut oil.
3. Bake your cake for about three mins, or till bubbles begin to appear, then toss it and continue cooking it for another three mins, or till the bottom is golden.
4. Continue the procedure with the remainder batter and oil. If preferred, offer powdered using cinnamon sugar before eating. Enjoy!

Per serving: Calories: 198kcal; Fat: 9.4g; Carbs: 24.5g; Protein: 5.27g

63. Cinnamon Semolina Porridge

"**Preparation time:** 5 minutes"
"**Cooking time:** 10 minutes"
"**Servings:** 3"
"**Ingredients:**"
- "3 cups almond milk"
- "3 tablespoons maple syrup"
- "3 teaspoons coconut oil"
- "¼ teaspoon kosher salt"
- "½ teaspoon ground cinnamon"
- "1 ¼ cups semolina"

Directions:
1. In a pan, bring the almond milk, maple syrup, coconut oil, salt, and cinnamon to a simmer over medium heat.
2. As soon as it is heated, start adding the semolina flour while stirring constantly. Reduce the flame to maintain the bubbles, and keep cooking the porridge for the amount of time necessary for it to acquire the firmness you desire.
3. "Serve hot, garnished with the toppings you like best, and enjoy! Bon appétit!"

"**Per serving:** Calories: 491kcal; Fat: 13.22g; Carbs: 76g; Protein: 16.6g"

64. Creamy Porridge with Almonds

"**Preparation time:** 2 minutes"
"**Cooking time:** 25 minutes"
"**Servings:** 4"
"**Ingredients:**"
- "2 ½ cups vegetable broth"
- "2 ½ cups unsweetened almond milk"
- "½ cup steel-cut oats"
- "½ cup slivered almonds"
- "1 tablespoon farro"
- "¼ cup nutritional yeast"
- "2 cups old-fashioned rolled oats"
- "½ teaspoon salt (optional)"

"**Directions:**"
1. "Place the almond milk and vegetable broth inside a big pot, and then bring the mixture up to a boil."

2. Cook the steel-cut oats, almonds, and farro with the nutritional yeast in a pan at moderate flame for approximately twenty mins while mixing often.
3. After the wrapped oats have been added, give everything a good stir. Continue to cook the oats for another five mins, or till they reach the desired consistency of being thick and creamy.
4. "If you like salt, sprinkle some on top. Wait eight mins after the porridge has cooled prior to serving."

"**Per serving:** Calories: 209kcal; Fat: 8g; Carbs: 22g; Protein: 14.2g"

65. Pineapple and Mango Oatmeal

"**Preparation time:** 5 minutes"
"**Cooking time:** 0 minutes"
"**Servings:** 2"
"**Ingredients:**"
- "2 cups unsweetened almond milk"
- "2 cups rolled oats"
- "½ cup pineapple chunks, thawed if frozen"
- "½ cup diced mango, thawed if frozen"
- "1 banana, sliced"
- "1 tablespoon chia seeds"
- "1 tablespoon maple syrup"

Directions:
1. Stir the almond milk, oats, pineapple, mango, banana, chia seeds, and maple syrup in a large bowl until you see no clumps.
2. "Cover and refrigerate to chill for at least 4 hours, preferably overnight."
3. Serve chilled with your favorite toppings.

Per serving: Calories: 512kcal; Fat: 22.1g; Carbs: 13.1g; Protein: 14.1g

66. Date and Oat Flour Waffles

"**Preparation time:** 10 minutes"
"**Cooking time:** 8 to 10 minutes"
"**Servings:** 12"
"**Ingredients:**"
- "4 cups rolled oats"
- "¼ cup chopped dates or raisins"
- "⅓ cup whole-wheat flour"

- "½ teaspoon salt (optional)"
- "5 cups water"

"**Directions:**"

1. "In a large bowl, thoroughly combine the oats, dates, flour, and salt (if desired)."
2. After adding the water, give it a good swirl till it's completely mixed. After pouring the batter into a mixing bowl, pulsing it for a few minutes will bring it to an uniform smoothness.
3. "Cook on High for 8 to 10 minutes in a waffle iron until done. Serve hot."

Per serving: Calories: 169kcal; Fat: 2.4g; Carbs: 30.6g; Protein: 6.8g

67. Mango Madness

"**Preparation time:** 5 minutes"
"**Cooking time:** 0 minutes"
"**Servings:** 4 cups"
"**Ingredients:**"

- "1 banana"
- "1 cup chopped mango (frozen or fresh)"
- "1 cup chopped peach (frozen or fresh)"
- "1 cup strawberries"
- "1 carrot, peeled and chopped (optional)"
- "1 cup water"

Directions:

1. Preparing the ingredients:

2. "Purée everything in a blender until smooth, adding more water if needed."
3. If you can't find frozen peaches, and fresh ones aren't in season, just use extra mango or strawberries, or try cantaloupe.

Per serving: Calories: 376kcal; Fat: 2g; Carbs: 95g; Protein: 5g

68. Sweet Polenta with Pears

"**Preparation time:** 5 minutes"
"**Cooking time:** 10 minutes"
"**Servings:** 3"
"**Ingredients:**"

- "¼ cup brown rice syrup"
- "2 large pears, peeled, cored, and diced"
- "1 cup fresh cranberries"
- "1 teaspoon cinnamon, ground"
- "1 batch polenta, warm"

Directions:

1. Pour the rice syrup into a moderate pan. "Include the cranberries, pears, and cinnamon. Cook for ten mins, mixing regularly."
2. "Once the pears are tender, remove and pour on the polenta."
3. Enjoy.

Per serving: Calories: 226kcal; Fat: 7g; Carbs: 12g; Protein: 17.9

Chapter: 3 Plant Based Lunch Options

While adopting a healthy lifestyle might be difficult, taking little measures can assist you get started on the right track. Almost everything you'll need may be found at your neighborhood grocery shop or grocery store chain. All you really need to know is what ingredients to buy in order to prepare nutritious meals. Eating healthful meals and engaging in regular physical activity frequent way may aid you, if you're on a plant-based diet here are some suggestions, a few delectable dishes to prepare and savor

69. Butternut Squash and Chickpea Curry

"**Preparation time:** 20 minutes"
"**Cooking time:** 6 hours"
"**Servings:** 8"
"**Ingredients:**"
- "1 ½ cup shelled peas"
- "1 ½ cup chickpeas, uncooked and rinsed"
- "2 ½ cup diced butternut squash"
- "12 ounces chopped spinach"
- "2 large tomatoes, diced"
- "1 small white onion, peeled and chopped"
- "1 teaspoon minced garlic"
- "1 teaspoon salt"
- "3 tablespoons curry powder"
- "14 ounces coconut milk"
- "3 cups vegetable broth"
- "¼ cup chopped cilantro"

Directions:
1. Put all of the components, with the exception of the spinach and peas, into a slow cooker that has a capacity of six quarts.
2. Close the pot, power in the slow cooker, set the timer for six hrs of cooking, and simmer the chickpeas on high flame for as long as necessary for them to become soft.
3. After that, put the peas and spinach in the slow cooker and continue cooking for an additional half an hour.
4. Test the consistency of the sauce by stirring it, and if it is too thin, add one spoonful of cornstarch that has been

blended using two tbsps. of water. Distribute with rice that has been prepared.
Per serving: Calories: 774kcal; Fat: 83.25g; Carbs: 12.64g; Protein: 3.71g

70. Cauliflower and Chickpeas Casserole

"**Preparation time:** 10 minutes"
"**Cooking time:** 60 minutes"
"**Servings:** 4 to 6"
"**Ingredients:**"
- "3 garlic cloves, minced"
- "2 cups vegetable broth"
- "1 cup brown rice"
- "¼ cup nutritional yeast"
- "1 celery rib, sliced finely"
- "½ cup buffalo hot sauce"
- "½ cauliflower head, medium and chopped"
- "1 teaspoon onion powder"
- "2 cups chickpeas, cooked"

"**Directions:**"
1. Turn the oven up to 400 degrees Fahrenheit. The next step is to combine the onion powder, broth, nutritional yeast, and hot sauce inside a saucepan of moderate length and bring the combination up to a temperature of moderate-high.
2. Allow the mixture to boil. In the meantime, spoon the chickpeas into a casserole dish. Then, top it first with the cauliflower pieces, then the celery, and finally the brown rice.
3. As soon as the liquid combination reaches boiling, take it off the stove and add the garlic in a spoonful at a time. The subsequent step is to evenly distribute the mix across the surface of the casserole dish.
4. After placing the dish on the center rack of the oven and covering it using foil, roast it for fifty-five to sixty mins. It is best served hot.

Per serving: Calories: 413kcal; Fat: 5.3g; Carbs: 74.1g; Protein: 19.3g

"**Per serving:** Calories: 410kcal; Fat: 13.2g; Carbs: 60g; Protein: 14.3g"

71. Brown Rice with Vegetables and Tofu

"**Preparation time:** 12 minutes"
"**Cooking time:** 33 minutes"
"**Servings:** 4"
"**Ingredients:**"

- "4 teaspoons of sesame seeds"
- "2 spring garlic stalks, minced"
- "1 cup spring onions, chopped"
- "1 carrot, trimmed and sliced"
- "1 celery rib, sliced"
- "¼ cup dry white wine"
- "10 ounces tofu, cubed"
- "1 ½ cups long-grain brown rice, rinsed thoroughly"
- "2 tablespoons soy sauce"
- "2 tablespoons tahini"
- "1 tablespoon lemon juice"

"**Directions:**"

1. Warm up two tsps. worth of the sesame oil above a burner that is moderate-high in a griddle or a big skillet. To assure that the garlic, onion, carrot, and celery cook evenly, mix them occasionally while they are in the pan for the next three mins.
2. While the wine is being added to the saucepan in order to "deglaze" it, the veggies should be moved to 1 edge of the griddle. Sauté the tofu for eight mins with the remainder amount of sesame oil, making sure to mix it regularly.
3. At moderate-high flame, raise two and a half water cups to a rolling boil. After the rice has been cooked for around half an hour, or till it is soft, smooth it and mix it using the tahini and soy sauce. The rice can be served immediately.
4. Mix the veggies and tofu into the hot rice, then sprinkle over a couple tablespoons of fresh lemon juice and offer the dish while it is still warm. Serve and enjoy!

72. Maple Glazed Tempeh with Quinoa and Kale

"**Preparation time:** 15 minutes"
"**Cooking time:** 30 minutes"
"**Servings:** 5"
"**Ingredients:**"

- "1 cup quinoa"
- "1 ½ cups vegetable stock"
- "8 ounces tempeh, cubed"
- "2 tablespoons pure maple syrup"
- "3 tablespoons dried cranberries"
- "1 tablespoon fresh chopped thyme"
- "1 tablespoon fresh chopped rosemary"
- "1 tablespoon olive oil"
- "Juice 1 orange"
- "1 clove of garlic, minced"
- "4 ounces baby kale, chopped"

"**Directions:**"

1. Prepare a baking sheet by lining it with cookie sheet and preheating the microwave to 400 degrees Fahrenheit. Place the broth in a pot and put it on the stove above a heat setting of medium. Bring the liquid to a boil, then stir in the quinoa.
2. Reduce the temperature to low, wrap, and stew for fifteen mins, or till the meat is done. Put the tempeh in a moderate container, sprinkle the maple syrup over it, and give it a good toss till everything is incorporated.
3. When that is happening, get a huge container and pour the remaining components into it. To blend, give it a good swirl.
4. In a large bowl, combine the quinoa, cooked tempeh, and a generous amount of salt and pepper. Offer, and have fun with it!

"**Per serving:** Calories: 321kcal; Fat: 12g; Carbs: 35g; Protein: 16g"

73. Curried Rice

"**Preparation time:** 5 minutes"
"**Cooking time:** 25 minutes"
"**Servings:** 4"
"**Ingredients:**"

- "1 tablespoon olive oil"
- "1 broccoli, chopped"
- "2 teaspoons ginger"
- "1 cup spinach, chopped"
- "1 tablespoon water"
- "1 teaspoon curry powder"
- "1 cup brown rice"
- "2 garlic cloves, minced"
- "Salt to taste"
- "2 carrots, chopped"
- "Pepper to taste"

Directions:

1. Whether you use this recipe as a base or a side, it will surely offer a kick to any dish served! To save time, you should prepare all the vegetables ahead of time.
2. Once you're ready to start cooking the dish, prepare a saucepan to a heat slightly higher than medium, then combine the ginger, garlic, and oil in the saucepan. Once you can smell these ingredients, you can add the broccoli and carrot pieces. At this point, you should stir the ingredients and season to your fancy.
3. Next, flash steam the vegetables.
4. You can complete this task by placing one tablespoon of water into the bottom of the skillet and placing a lid over the top for one minute.
5. Add your cooked brown rice and the curry powder when that is set. Be sure to toss everything and coat the ingredients well.
6. If the rice is seasoned to your fancy, let it cool off slightly, and then serve.

Per serving: Calories: 250kcal; Fat: 5g; Carbs: 45g; Protein: 10g

74. Grain Dishes Cranberry and Walnut Brown Rice

"**Preparation time:** 10 minutes"
"**Cooking time:** 15 minutes"
"**Servings:** 5"
"**Ingredients:**"

- "¼ cup water"
- "¼ cup dried cranberries"
- "14 ounces of vegetable broth"
- "¾ cup brown rice"
- "¼ cup chopped walnuts"
- "⅛ teaspoon ground cinnamon"
- "Salt to taste"

"**Directions:**"

1. To begin this recipe, you should first cook your brown rice in the vegetable broth according to the directions on the package.
2. "Once this is done, allow the rice to cool slightly before adding it to a mixing bowl."
3. With the rice in place, add the walnuts and cranberries. Begin to season with salt and ground cinnamon.
4. Once everything is in place, toss the flavors together, and your dish is set.

Per serving: Calories: 150kcal; Fat: 5g; Carbs: 25g; Protein: 5g

75. Quinoa Lentil Burger

"**Preparation time:** 5 minutes"
"**Cooking time:** 25 minutes"
"**Servings:** 4"
"**Ingredients:**"

- "1 tablespoon + 2 teaspoons olive oil"
- "¼ cup red onion, diced"
- "1 cup quinoa, cooked"
- "1 cup cooked drained brown lentils"
- "1 x 4 ounces green chilies, diced"
- "⅓ cup oats rolled"
- "¼ cup flour"
- "2 teaspoons corn starch"
- "¼ cup panko breadcrumbs, whole-wheat"
- "¼ teaspoon garlic powder"
- "½ teaspoon cumin"
- "1 teaspoon Paprika"
- "Salt and pepper"

- "2 tablespoons Dijon mustard"
- "3 teaspoons honey"

Directions:

1. Your pan should be preheated to moderate, and then two tsps. of olive oil should be added. After adding the onion, continue to fry it for another five mins till it becomes tender. After that, get a small container and put the honey and the Dijon mustard inside of it.
2. Find a huge container, include the components for the burger, and give it a good mix. Make four individual patties using your hands. In the saucepan that you are using, add one tbsp. of oil and warm it at moderate temperature.
3. Fry the patties for ten mins per side after adding them to the pan. Relish with some honey mustard that you've drizzled on top!

Per serving: Calories: 268kcal; Fat: 8g; Carbs: 33g; Protein: 10g

76. Spicy Hummus Quesadillas

"**Preparation time:** 5 minutes"
"**Cooking time:** 15 minutes"
"**Servings:** 4"
"**Ingredients:**"

- "4 x 8-inch whole grain tortilla"
- "1 cup hummus"
- "Your choice fillings: spinach, sundried tomatoes, olives, etc."
- "Extra-virgin olive oil for brushing"

"To serve:"

- "Extra hummus"
- "Hot sauce"
- "Pesto"

Directions:

1. Put your tortillas on a flat surface and cover each with hummus. Add the fillings, then fold over to form a half-moon shape.
2. Place a pan on the stove at moderate flame and pour a little bit of oil to it. Once the undersides are cooked, rotate the quesadillas over. After you have finished with the rest of the quesadillas, offer them up and have fun!

"**Per serving:** Calories: 256kcal; Fat: 12g; Carbs: 25g; Protein: 7g"

77. Peanut Soup with Veggies

"**Preparation time:** 10 minutes"
"**Cooking time:** 25 minutes"
"**Servings:** 3"
"**Ingredients:**"

- "2 tablespoons soy sauce"
- "1 cup brown rice"
- "1 garlic clove, minced"
- "½ red onion, chopped"
- "4 tablespoons peanut butter"
- "1 carrot, small and chopped"
- "3 tablespoons tomato paste"
- "½ courgette, medium and chopped"
- "3 cups vegetable broth"
- "½ tablespoons ginger, grated"
- "2 tablespoons peanuts"
- "Dash hot sauce"

Directions:

1. In order to get things started, bring the stock to a simmer in a big pan set at moderate flame. Let it come to a boil. Prepare the rice during this time by adhering to the directions that are included on the package.
2. After that, add the onion, carrot, and zucchini to the skillet and mix them together. Combine thoroughly. After that, add the ginger and garlic to the mix using a spatula.
3. Include the peanuts, tomato paste, and peanut butter to the pan. Combine. Taste for seasoning, then put soy sauce to it. Now, allow it to simmer until the rice gets cooked. Serve it hot.

Per serving: Calories: 488kcal; Fat: 15g; Carbs: 76g; Protein: 15g

78. Vegetable Stir-fry

"**Preparation time:** 10 minutes"
"**Cooking time:** 40 minutes"
"**Servings:** 3"
"**Ingredients:**"

- "2 tablespoon olive oil"

- "½ zucchini"
- "½ red bell pepper"
- "4 garlic cloves"
- "½ broccoli"
- "1 cup cabbage"
- "½ cup brown rice"
- "2 tablespoons tamari sauce"
- "1 red chili pepper"
- "1 teaspoon cayenne powder"
- "1 parsley"
- "Optional: sesame seeds"

Directions:

1. First, cook your brown rice according to the directions provided on the package.
2. As the rice cooks, remove your frying pan and place some water at the bottom. Once it is boiling, add all the diced vegetables from the list above. Once in place, be sure the water covers the ingredients, and then cook everything for two minutes under high heat. Once done, drain the vegetables and place them to the side.
3. After that, include some garlic, cayenne pepper, and parsley to the skillet along with some olive oil. After this has cooked for a minute or so, add the vegetables back, along with the tamari sauce and your rice.
4. Cook everything here for an additional two minutes before removing it from heat.
5. When it is ready, add some sesame seeds as garnish.

Per serving: Calories: 280kcal; Fat: 10g; Carbs: 35g; Protein: 10g

79. Sweet Oatmeal "Grits"

"**Preparation time:** 5 minutes"
"**Cooking time:** 15 minutes"
"**Servings:** 4"
"**Ingredients:**"

- "1 ½ cups steel-cut oats, soaked overnight"
- "1 cup almond milk"
- "2 cups water"
- "A pinch of grated nutmeg"
- "A pinch of ground cloves"
- "A pinch of sea salt"
- "4 tablespoons almonds, slivered"
- "6 dates, pitted and chopped"
- "6 prunes, chopped"

Directions:

1. "Bring the steel-cut oats, almond milk, and water to a boil in a deep saucepan."
2. To the mixture, include the cloves, nutmeg, and salt. As soon as you can, reduce the flame to a boil, cap the pan, and cook the vegetables for almost fifteen mins, or till they have become more tender.
3. "Then, spoon the grits into four serving bowls; top them with the almonds, dates, and prunes. Bon appétit!"

Per serving: Calories: 380kcal; Fat: 11.1g; Carbs: 59g; Protein: 14.4g

80. Cilantro and Avocado Lime Rice

"**Preparation time:** 5 minutes"
"**Cooking time:** 20 minutes"
"**Servings:** 4"
"**Ingredients:**"

- "2 avocados, sliced"
- "5 cups brown rice, cooked"
- "½ teaspoon cumin"
- "¼ cup cilantro, chopped"
- "2 tablespoon lime juice"
- "1 garlic clove, minced"
- "Salt to taste"

"**Directions:**"

1. For a rice recipe with a twist, you need to try this recipe! Begin by taking out a mixing bowl and mashing down the avocado pieces until they are perfectly smooth.
2. Once the avocado is set, add in your seasonings and cilantro, and squeeze in the lime juice.
3. Finally, stir in your brown rice that has already been cooked and blend well before serving.

Per serving: Calories: 450kcal; Fat: 15g; Carbs: 60g; Protein: 5g

81. Chickpeas and Sweet Potato Curry

"**Preparation time:** 15 minutes"
"**Cooking time:** 55 minutes"
"**Servings:** 2"
"**Ingredients:**"

- "1 teaspoon olive oil"
- "1 small onion, chopped"
- "2 garlic cloves, chopped finely"
- "2 cups tomatoes, chopped finely"
- "1 teaspoon curry powder"
- "½ teaspoon red chili powder"
- "Salt and ground black pepper to taste"
- "1 small sweet potato, peeled and cubed"
- "1 (14 ounces) can of chickpeas, drained and rinsed"
- "7 ounces of full-fat coconut milk"

Directions:

1. "Heat-up olive oil in a saucepan over medium heat and sauté the onion and garlic for about 4–5 minutes."
2. Sauté for around two to three mins, mashing the tomatoes using the side of the spatula while you do so, after which you should include the tomatoes, spices, salt, and black pepper.
3. Boil the sweet potato for around one to two mins after stirring it in. Chickpeas and coconut milk should be combined, and then the dish should be brought to a simmer at high temperature.
4. "Now, adjust the heat to medium-low and simmer, partially covered, for about 35–40 minutes. Serve hot."

Per serving: Calories: 480kcal; Fat: 23.8g; Carbs: 547g; Protein: 13.8g

82. Balsamic Arugula and Beets

"**Preparation time:** 10 minutes"
"**Cooking time:** 0 minutes"
"**Servings:** 4"
"**Ingredients:**"

- "2 cups baby arugula"
- "1 tablespoon balsamic vinegar"
- "1 teaspoon olive oil"
- "2 red beets, baked, peeled, and cubed"
- "1 avocado, peeled, pitted, and cubed"
- "1 teaspoon garam masala"
- "½ teaspoon salt"
- "½ teaspoon cayenne pepper"

"**Directions:**"

1. "Mix the arugula with the beets and the other ingredients in a bowl, toss, and serve."

"**Per serving:** Calories: 151kcal; Fat: 1.4g; Carbs: 4.1g; Protein: 5.9g"

83. Coconut Rice

"**Preparation time:** 10 minutes"
"**Cooking time:** 25 minutes"
"**Servings:** 7"
"**Ingredients:**"

- "2 ½ cups white rice"
- "⅛ teaspoon salt"
- "40 ounces coconut milk, unsweetened"

"**Directions:**"

1. Put all of the components into a big pot, put it on the stove at moderate flame, and whisk constantly till everything is combined.
2. Bring the mix to a boil, then reduce the temperature to moderate-low and continue to cook the rice for another twenty-five mins, till it reaches the desired texture and every drop of fluid has been consumed. Serve straight away.

Per serving: Calories: 535kcal; Fat: 33.2g; Carbs: 57g; Protein: 8.1g

84. Brown Rice Pilaf

"**Preparation time:** 5 minutes"
"**Cooking time:** 25 minutes"
"**Servings:** 4"
"**Ingredients:**"

- "1 cup cooked chickpeas"
- "¾ cup brown rice, cooked"
- "¼ cup chopped cashews"
- "2 cups sliced mushrooms"
- "2 carrots, sliced"
- "½ teaspoon minced garlic"
- "1 ½ cups chopped white onion"
- "3 tablespoons vegan butter"

- "½ teaspoon salt"
- "¼ teaspoon ground black pepper"
- "¼ cup chopped parsley"

Directions:

1. To prepare the onions, use a big saucepan, put it across moderate flame, include butter, and once it has melted, include the onions. Fry the onions for five mins, or till they have become tender.
2. After browning the mushrooms, include the carrots and garlic, and then simmer them for a further ten mins. Finally, include the chickpeas and continue to cook them for one more min.
3. After the cooking is complete, take the skillet off the temperature, include the nuts, parsley, salt, and black pepper, and then stir everything together till it is well combined. Serve straight away.

Per serving: Calories: 409kcal; Fat: 17.1g; Carbs: 54g; Protein: 12.5g

85. Coconut Sorghum Porridge

"**Preparation time:** 10 minutes"
"**Cooking time:** 15 minutes"
"**Servings:** 2"
"**Ingredients:**"

- "½ cup sorghum"
- "1 cup water"
- "½ cup coconut milk"
- "¼ teaspoon grated nutmeg"
- "¼ teaspoon ground cloves"
- "½ teaspoons ground cinnamon"
- "Kosher salt, to taste"
- "2 tablespoons agave syrup"
- "2 tablespoons coconut flakes"

Directions:

1. In a skillet, combine the sorghum, water, milk, nutmeg, cloves, and cinnamon, and season with kosher salt. Boil the mixture over low heat for approximately fifteen mins.
2. Spoon the porridge inside serving bowls. Top with agave syrup and coconut flakes. Bon appétit!

Per serving: Calories: 289kcal; Fat: 5.1g; Carbs: 57.8g; Protein: 7.3g

86. Barley and Mushrooms with Beans

"**Preparation time:** 5 minutes"
"**Cooking time:** 15 minutes"
"**Servings:** 6"
"**Ingredients:**"

- "½ cup uncooked barley"
- "15 ½ ounces of white beans"
- "½ cup chopped celery"
- "3 cups sliced mushrooms"
- "1 cup chopped white onion"
- "1 teaspoon minced garlic"
- "1 teaspoon olive oil"
- "3 cups vegetable broth"

"**Directions:**"

1. "Put oil in your saucepan at medium heat, and when hot, add vegetables and cook for 5 mins until soft."
2. "Pour in broth, stir in barley, bring the mixture to boil, and then simmer for 50 minutes until tender."
3. When everything is finished, include the beans towards the combination of barley, toss till everything is combined, and then cook for an additional five mins till everything is heated. Offer immediately after cooking.

Per serving: Calories: 202kcal; Fat: 2.1g; Carbs: 39g; Protein: 9.1g

87. Tex-Mex Pita Pizzas

Total time: 30 minutes
Serving: 6
Nutrient per serving: Calories: 500, Fats: 17g, Carbohydrates: 32.1g, Proteins: 4g, Sodium: 8mg, Calcium: 0.9mg, Iron: 29.8mg

Ingredients:

- ½ teaspoon of ground cumin
- 1 15-ounce of can black beans
- 1 cup of chopped avocado
- 1 cup of oil-free salsa
- 2 tablespoons sf nipped fresh cilantro
- 1 cup of chopped onion
- 1 cup of chopped bell pepper

- 2 cloves of garlic
- 1 cup of fresh corn kernels
- 6 6- to 7-inch of whole wheat pita rounds

Directions:

1. Preheat the oven to 350 degrees Fahrenheit. Prepare two baking sheets by lining them with parchment paper.
2. Boil 14 cups of water in a big pot on the stovetop. Continue cooking for 10 minutes, or until the onion is soft, stirring periodically and adding more water, 1 to 2 tablespoons at a time, if required, to keep the pan from sticking, until the onion is cooked but not brown. Combine the soybeans and corn in a large mixing bowl.
3. Pour in the beans and corn and cook for another 5 minutes, stirring periodically, until the flavors are combined, and the beans are cooked through.
4. In the meanwhile, arrange the pita circles on the baking sheets that have been prepared. Oven for 10 to 15 minutes, or until the bread is gently browned and toasted.
5. Using a fork, mash the avocado. Avocado and bean combinations should be spread over pita rounds. Sprinkle with salsa and a sprinkling of cilantro, if desired.

88. Full Flour Chock Veggies Chickpea Pizza Crust

Total time: 1 hour 40 minutes
Serving: 4
Nutrient per serving: Calories: 440, Fats: 12 g, Carbohydrates: 7g, Proteins: 2g, Sodium: 8mg, Calcium: 1mg, Iron: 9 mg
Ingredients:

- 1 tablespoon of tahini
- ¼ teaspoon of sea salt
- Ground black pepper
- 1 cup of chickpea flour
- 1 tablespoon of apple cider vinegar
- ¼ teaspoon of baking powder
- 1 cup of unflavored, unsweetened plant-based milk

Directions:

1. Put in a blender following ingredients, mix the vinegar, chickpeas flour, baking powder, tahini, plant milk, pepper, and salt until well combined. Make a smooth and creamy batter by blending all of the ingredients.
2. Preheat a nonstick skillet with a 10-inch diameter. Add the batter into a pan, then cook over medium to high heat for twenty minutes, or until the batter has set. Using a broad spatula, lift the crust and turn it over to the other side. Cook for a total of 10 minutes. To cool fully, move to a wire rack to cool and set for approximately 10 minutes.
3. Preheat the oven to 350 degrees Fahrenheit. Prepare a baking sheet by lining it with parchment paper.
4. Mix the first four veggies from your selected toppings combination in a separate pan and cook until tender. Cook the veggies for 5 to 7 minutes over medium-low heat, or until the vegetables are gently done and the spinach has wilted. If necessary, add 1 tablespoon of water to prevent the veggies from sticking together.
5. Marinara sauce, sautéed veggies, and nutritional yeast should be spread on top of the crust. Preheat the oven to 150°F or 200°F.
6. Remove the pizza from the oven and add the garnishes. Serve with basil or chopped pepper Serve as soon as possible.

89. Lentil Vegetable Soup

Total time: 2 hours
Serving: 6
Nutrient per serving: Calories: 60, Fats: 4 g, Carbohydrates: 6g, Proteins: 0.2g, Sodium: 5mg, Calcium: 1mg, Iron: 2 mg
Ingredients:

- 6 small white potatoes
- 1 16-ounce bag of brown lentils
- 1-2 cups of finely chopped spinach
- salt and pepper

- 2 small onions, chopped
- 2 carrots, chopped
- 1 15.5-ounce of can fire roasted tomatoes,
- 8 cups of vegetable broth
- 8 cups of water

Directions:

1. Boil on low for 2 hours, occasionally stirring, using all of the ingredients except the spinach. Approximately 5 minutes just before the soup is complete, add the spinach. Salt and black pepper to your liking.

90. Easy Vegan Corn Chowder

Total time: 50 minutes
Serving: 10
Nutrient per serving: Calories 360, Fats: 14 g, Carbohydrates:0.7, Proteins: 0.2g, Sodium: 76mg, Calcium: 10mg, Iron: 29 mg

Ingredients:

- 1 large russet potato
- 1 medium red bell pepper, cored, seeded
- ⅓ cup of almond flour
- Sea salt
- freshly ground black pepper
- 1 small onion
- 6 small garlic cloves, minced
- 1 teaspoon of finely chopped fresh parsley
- 1 teaspoon of finely chopped fresh thyme
- 6 to 7 cups of Vegetable Stock
- 6 cups of fresh or frozen corn

Directions:

1. Put the onion, garlic, and 1½ cups of the Vegetable Stock in a big stew pot or Dutch oven and bring to a boil. Bring the saucepan to a cook over high heat, covering it with a lid. Reduce heat to low and cook, covered, for approximately 10 minutes, or until the onion is transparent.
2. Combine the corn, potato, and 412 cups of the remaining stock in a large mixing bowl. Bring to the boil over medium heat, stirring constantly. Reduce the heat to low and cook for 10 to 15 minutes, or until the potato is tender.

3. 1/2 of the mixture should be transferred to a mixer and blended until smooth. Return the pot to its original position. If required, use approximately 1 cup stock to thin down the sauce and make it creamier.
4. Combine the bell pepper, parsley, and herbs in a large mixing bowl. Simmer for just another 10 minutes, or until the flavors have melded together and the pepper is fork tender.
5. Between now and then, flour mixture and 1/3 cup water in a blender and mix until completely smooth. In a separate bowl, whisk together the almond cream and the chowder. Taste and sprinkle with salt to your liking. Serve when still heated.

Storage: Allow the soup to cool fully before transferring it to a sealed jar. Refrigerate for 4 days or freeze for up to one month before serving.

91. Creamy Wild Rice Soup

Total time: 1 hour 15 minutes
Serving: 6
Nutrient per serving: Calories: 455, Fats: 14 g, Carbohydrates:0.7, Proteins: 0.2g, Sodium: 11mg, Calcium: 10mg, Iron: 29 mg

Ingredients:

- ½ cup of chopped carrot
- ¼ teaspoon of sea salt
- 1 tablespoon of snipped fresh thyme
- 1 tablespoon of white wine vinegar
- 4 cups of vegetable stock
- 1 package button mushrooms
- ¼ cup of almond flour
- ¼ cup of chickpea flour
- ¾ cup of uncooked wild rice
- ½ cup of thinly sliced leek, white part
- 4 cloves of garlic, minced
- 1 cup of chopped red bell pepper

Directions:

1. In a 5-quart Dutch oven or soup pot, mix the stock, mushroom, wild rice, leek, and garlic and bring to a boil. Bring to the boil over high heat, then lower the heat to medium-low to keep the sauce from boiling over. Cover the pan and cook for 45

to 50 minutes, or until the rice is cooked through, kernels will start to pop open. Combine the peppers, carrots, and salt in a large mixing bowl. Cover and continue to cook for another 8 minutes.

2. Mix the almonds and chickpea flour; whisk in 1/4 cups water until well combined. In a separate bowl, whisk together the ingredients for the soup. Cook for 1 to 2 minutes, stirring continuously, or until the sauce is thick and bubbling. Add up to 1/2 cups of additional water at a time until the required consistency is reached. Combine the herbs and vinegar in a separate bowl.

92. Quick and Easy Noodle Soup

Total time: 50 minutes
Serving: 10
Nutrient per serving: Calories: 990, Fats: 87g, Carbohydrates: 65g, Proteins: 0.2g, Sodium: 11.3mg, Calcium: 17mg, Iron: 44mg
Ingredients:
- 1 cup of chopped carrots
- 6 cups of vegetable stock
- Freshly ground black pepper
- 3 cups of dried brown rice fettuccine noodles
- 1 cup of chopped onion
- 1 cup of chopped celery
- ½ teaspoon of crushed dried sage
- ¼ teaspoon of crushed, dried thyme
- 1 teaspoon of low-sodium tamari or soy sauce
- ½ teaspoon of crushed dried marjoram

Directions:
1. In a 4-quart Dutch oven, mix the onions, celery, carrot, broth, tamari, marjoram, sage, herbs, and pepper and cook until the vegetables are tender. Using high heat, bring the mixture to a boil. Lower heat to medium-low and cover for 20 minutes to let flavors blend.
2. Bring the pot back to a boil after adding the noodles. Cook for a further 10 minutes, or until the noodles are cooked.

93. "Nacho" Vegan Baked Potato

Total time: 50 minutes
Serving: 2
Nutrient per serving: Calories: 335, Fats: 20 g, Carbohydrates:37, Proteins: 12g, Sodium: 8mg, Calcium: 70mg, Iron: 29 mg
Ingredients:
- Cilantro for garnish
- Lime wedges for garnish
- 1 large baking potato
- 1½ teaspoons of nutritional yeast
- ¼ to ½ avocado
- Salt and black pepper
- ½ cup of black beans
- ¼ cup of salsa of your choice

Directions:
1. If you are baking the potato, preheat oven to 450°F (230°C) (rather than microwaving it).
2. Pierce the potato a few times with a knife to let the steam escape, if necessary. Depending on the size of the potato, bake it for 40 minutes in the oven or microwave it for 4–6 minutes on high power in the microwave. Check the potatoes with a knife or knife to see whether it is mushy and cooked all the way through before serving.
3. As soon as the potato is through cooking, split it open and toss on the healthy yeast if you want.
4. Place the black beans, sauce, and avocado on top of the tortillas. Sprinkle with salt, if desired, and serve with coriander and lime wedges on the side.
5. Take pleasure in your delicious and nutritious dinner!

94. Stove-Top Vegan Macaroni and Cheese

Total time: 45 minutes
Serving: 2
Nutrient per serving: Calories 360, Fats: 14g, Carbohydrates: 3.8g, Proteins: 0.2g, Sodium: 7.1mg, Calcium: 22mg, Iron: 31mg
Ingredients:
- 3 cloves of garlic

- 4 ounces of dried whole-wheat pasta
- Freshly ground black pepper
- 1 large russet potato
- 1 cup of chopped carrots
- ½ cup of nutritional yeast
- 1 teaspoon of sea salt
- ½ cup of chopped yellow onion
- 1 teaspoon of ground turmeric
- ½ cup of raw cashews

Directions:

1. Cook the potatoes, carrots, onion, turmeric, and garlic in a medium saucepan with 2 cups of water until the potatoes are tender. Using high heat, bring the mixture to a boil. Reduce the heat to low and cook, covered, for twenty minutes until vegetables are tender.
2. Put the cashew in a small pan and fill it with enough water to completely submerge the nuts. Drain after soaking for at least ten min.
3. In the meanwhile, boil the macaroni in a large pot according to the package instructions, draining after each batch. Drain well after rinsing with cold water. Bring the pot back to a boil.
4. Move the potatoes mix to a blender and process until smooth. Combine the cashews, nutritious yeast, salt, and 1/2 cup of water in a mixing bowl. Blend on high for 2 minutes, or until the mixture is smooth and creamy.
5. Toss the macaroni with the appropriate quantity of sauce once it has been topped with it. Season with freshly ground pepper.

95. Penne with Tomato-Mushroom Sauce

Total time: 20 minutes
Serving: 11
Nutrient per serving: Calories:280, Fats: 6 g, Carbohydrates:8 g, Proteins: 0.7g, Sodium: 9.6 mg, Calcium: 18mg, Iron: 19 mg
Ingredients:

- 1 cup of chopped fresh basil
- Sea salt and freshly ground black pepper
- 12 ounces of whole-grain penne pasta

- 1 medium yellow onion, diced
- 1 can of San Marzano crushed tomatoes
- 1 cup of unsweetened plant milk
- 1-pound mushrooms
- 4 cloves of garlic
- 2 teaspoons of dried thyme

Directions:

1. Prepare a big saucepan of water by bringing it to a boil. Boil the linguine according to the directions on the box. Drain the water well in a strainer and put it aside.
2. To prepare the onions and mushrooms in the meanwhile, sauté them in a large pan over medium heat, turning periodically until the onions begin to color and become translucent for about 7 to 8 minutes. Pour in 1–2 tablespoons of water at a time, as required, to prevent the veggies from adhering to the pan while cooking.
3. Cook for 1 minute after you've added the garlic and thyme. Cook for 10 minutes, stir periodically until the tomatoes are mashed and the liquid has been absorbed. Mix in the plant milk, cooked pasta, and basil until everything is evenly covered. Sprinkle with salt and pepper and serve immediately. Season with salt and pepper to taste. Cook for approximately 1 minute or until the mixture is well heated. Serve when still heated.

96. "No-Tuna" Salad Sandwich

Total time: 10 minutes
Serving: 4
Nutrient per serving: Calories: 228, Fats: 65g, Carbohydrates: 76g, Proteins: 18.4g, Sodium: 43mg, Calcium: 73mg, Iron: 27.1mg
Ingredients:

- ¼ cup of diced red onion
- ¼ cup of diced celery
- 1 can of chickpeas
- 3 tablespoons of tahini
- pinch of sea salt
- pinch of black pepper

- 1 tablespoon of roasted unsalted sunflower seeds
- 1 teaspoon of Dijon or spicy brown mustard
- 1 tablespoon of maple syrup
- ¼ cup of diced pickle
- 1 teaspoon of capers

Directions:

1. Place chickpeas in a mixing bowl or dish and smash them with a fork, reserving just a few whole beans.
2. Combine the maple syrup, tahini, red onion, mustard, and celery in a mixing bowl, along with the pickle, caper, salt and pepper, and sunflower seeds (if using). To integrate, stir the ingredients together. Season with salt and pepper to taste and season with salt as required.
3. Toast the bread if required, then prepare any additional sandwich toppings that may be requested (such as lettuce, tomato, and onion).
4. Piece the bread in half and spread a generous quantity of the chickpea paste approximately 1/2 cup over one layer. Top with preferred toppings and cover with the other slice of bread. Repeat the process with the remaining sandwiches.

97. Avocado & White Bean Salad Wraps

Total time: 25 minutes
Serving: 2
Nutrient per serving: Calories: 266, Fats: 36g, Carbohydrates: 63g, Proteins: 59g, Sodium: 20mg, Calcium: 10mg, Iron: 41mg
Ingredients:

- 1 teaspoon of smoked paprika
- ½ teaspoon of onion powder
- 1 to 2 Roma tomatoes
- 2 large handfuls of baby spinach
- 1½ cups of cooked great northern beans
- 1 tablespoon of liquid aminos
- Freshly ground black pepper
- 2 lavash wraps
- 2 large wheat tortillas
- 1 tablespoon of white balsamic vinegar

- 2 small avocados
- ½ teaspoon of onion powder
- Pinch of Sea salt
- 1 tablespoon of diced canned green chiles
- 1 teaspoon of garlic powder
- 2 tablespoons of fresh lime juice
- 2 tablespoons of fresh parsley or cilantro

Directions:

1. Toss the soybeans in a large skillet with a little olive oil and cook for 2 minutes, or until they are heated. Cook, stirring periodically until the liquid aminos have completely evaporated, about 5 minutes. Boil, turning once or twice a minute until the vinegar has completely evaporated and the liquid is no longer visible. Remove the pan from the heat and smash the soybeans with a spoon until well combined.
2. Scrape the avocado's skin into a large mixing bowl and mash it when there are no more pieces of avocado left. In a large mixing bowl, combine the smashed beans, lemon zest, parsley, green bell peppers, garlic powder, paprika, and onion powder until well combined. Combine until everything is well-combined. Taste and season with salt and pepper to your liking.
3. Half of the avocado's mixture should be spread over one tortilla. Across the narrower width of the wrap, about an inch or so from one side, arrange a row of tomato slices, followed by a row of spinach, followed by some other row of tomatoes, followed by another row of spinach. The wrap should be wrapped over the first line of tomatoes, and this should be done until the wrap is fully rolled up. Section the meat into three to four pieces.
4. Repeat the process with the next wrap and the remaining ingredients, and then plate and serve. You may keep it in the fridge for up to 3 days if you use an airtight container.

Note: You may use chickpeas in place of the white beans if you like. Serve the filling with tortilla chips as a dip!

98. Burritos with Spanish Rice and Black Beans

Total time: 35 minutes
Serving: 8
Nutrient per serving: Calories: 63, Fats: 52g, Carbohydrates: 51g, Proteins: 2g, Sodium: 8.8mg, Calcium: 17mg, Iron: 75mg
Ingredients:

- 2 cloves of garlic
- Salt and freshly ground black pepper
- 8 7- to 8-inch of whole grain tortillas
- 1 medium onion
- 1 yellow or green pepper
- ½ teaspoon of chipotle chili powder
- ½ teaspoon of smoked paprika
- ½ –1 jalapeño Chile
- 2 cloves of garlic
- 1 teaspoon of ground cumin
- 1 teaspoon of ancho chili powder
- 4 cups of cooked brown rice
- 1½ cup of diced tomatoes

Directions:

1. Using a deep nonstick skillet, cook the ingredients over medium heat. Cook the onion, stirring constantly, until it starts to color a little.
2. Boil for the next 2 minutes, trying to take care not to scorch the garlic, after which you may add the pepper, jalapeno, and garlic cloves.
3. Cook for approximately 15 minutes, stirring regularly, after which add the other ingredients and mix again. If it gets too dry, a little amount of vegetable broth or the leftover tomato juice may be added.
4. Taste the dish and season with salt and other spices to your liking.
5. Fry tortillas one at a time In a dry nonstick pan over medium heat for 40 seconds, or until warm and malleable, flipping once, until heated through. To stay warm, wrap the area with a wet towel.

6. Spread approximately 1 cup of the bean-and-vegetable mixture over each tortilla just under the center, leaving a border around the edges. Fold the lower portion of each tortilla over the contents to enclose it. Fold in the opposite edges of the tortilla and wrap it up. Place the burritos on a plate with the seams facing up. Warm the dish before serving. Hot pepper sauce may be served on the side if requested.

99. Black Bean Burgers

Total time: 30 minutes
Serving: 6
Nutrient per serving: Calories: 274, Fats: 343g, Carbohydrates: 43.1g, Proteins: 90g, Sodium: 8.52mg, Calcium: 41mg, Iron: 29mg
Ingredients:

- ¼ cup cornmeal
- 2 tablespoons salsa
- 1 cup of cooked brown rice
- 1 15-ounce can of black beans
- 1 teaspoon of garlic powder
- ¼ teaspoon of chili powder
- ½ onion
- ¼ cup of corn
- 1 teaspoon of cumin

Directions:

1. To cook the brown rice, place 1/2 cup of rice and 1 cup of water in a saucepan and heat to a rolling boil. Once the water is boiling, lower the heat to a simmer. Once the water has been absorbed, check the rice to determine whether it is completely cooked. If this is the case, add a bit more water and continue to cook until it is done. Cook dried beans until mushy, or rinse canned beans before using. Put the beans in a medium-sized mixing bowl and mash them up with your hands, a potato masher, or a fork until they are smooth.
2. Preheat the oven to 350 degrees Fahrenheit. Prepare a sheet pan by lining it with parchment paper.

3. In a sauté pan, sweat the onion until translucent. Sweating indicates that the moisture originates from the vegetables, and thus no oil is required. Remember to keep the pan covered at all times. If the onions begin to cling to the pan, add a little amount of water. As soon as the onions are transparent, add the corn and seasonings. Heat for another few minutes if necessary.

4. To assemble the bean bowl, combine the cornmeal, salsa, vegetables, and rice. Combine all of the ingredients until they have a uniform consistency. Feel free to use your hands to complete this task. After that, shape the mixture into patties. It is recommended that the thickness be about 12 inches and the diameter be approximately 3 inches.

5. Place the patties on a baking sheet lined with baking parchment and heat for fifteen min at 350oF. Bake for a further 15 minutes after flipping the patties. Serve on a bed of lettuce leaves with tomatoes, onions, ketchup, and mustard on the side for dipping. Alternatively, you could serve the burger on a bed of fresh spinach rather than on a bun...delicious!

100. Spinach-Potato Tacos

Total time: 50 minutes
Serving: 6
Nutrient per serving: Calories: 988, Fats: 141g, Carbohydrates: 117g, Proteins: 4.9g, Sodium: 11.8mg, Calcium: 0.9mg, Iron: 11mg
Ingredients:
- 2 cloves of garlic
- 12 corn tortillas
- ½ cup of chopped fresh cilantro
- 2 large Yukon gold potatoes
- 1 (10-ounce) package of frozen spinach
- 3 tablespoons of nutritional yeast
- Sea salt
- freshly ground black pepper
- 1 large onion
- 1 medium poblano pepper

- 2 teaspoons of ground cumin
- 1 cup of unsweetened plant milk

Directions:
1. Put the potato in a medium pot and cover with enough water to cover them. Toss the ingredients together and bring to a boil, then lower the heat to moderate and simmer, covered, for 10 to 12 minutes, just until the potato is soft when pierced with a sharp knife. Drain the water well and put it aside.

2. In the meanwhile, spread a clean kitchen roll or several sheets of towel on the countertop and arrange the defrosted spinach at the base of one short end of the towel or sheet. When you have the spinach wrapped in a towel, hold it over a sink and twist each side of the roll to press out the liquid as much as you can from the spinach. Unroll the paper and put it aside.

3. Boil the onion and jalapeno pepper in a large pan over medium heat, turning periodically and adding more water 1–2 tablespoons at a time as required to prevent the veggies from sticking, for 7 to 8 minutes, or until the vegetables are tender and translucent. Cook for approximately 1 minute, constantly stirring, until the onion and cumin are fragrant.

4. Combine the greens and potatoes that have been set aside with both the plant milk and healthy yeast. Season with salt and black pepper to taste, then simmer for 2 to 3 minutes, or until the vegetables are cooked through. Take the pan off the heat and put it aside.

5. In the meanwhile, heat a big nonstick pan over medium heat until it is hot. Cook for a few minutes until the corn tortillas are heated throughout, adding as many as fit in a single layer to the pan as needed. Remove them from the pan and place them in a warm place, covered with a clean kitchen towel to maintain their heat.

Repeat the process with the remaining tortillas to make a stack.

6. Using individual serving plates or a big platter, arrange the tortillas on a serving plate and divide the potato mixture among them, spooning it into the middle of each tortilla. Serve with a sprinkle of cilantro on top.

101. Black Bean and Sweet Potato Quesadillas

Total time: 1 hour
Serving: 4
Nutrient per serving: Calories: 621, Fats: 69g, Carbohydrates: 63.7g, Proteins: 82g, Sodium: 54mg, Calcium: 1.81mg, Iron: 41mg
Ingredients:
- 1 cup of fresh spinach
- 1 jalapeño pepper
- 6-8 whole-wheat tortillas
- 1 large, sweet potato
- 1 cup of brown rice, cooked
- ¼ teaspoon of chili powder
- ¼ teaspoon of cumin
- 8 ounces vegetarian beans
- 1 cup of salsa
- 8 ounces of black beans
- ¼ teaspoon of onion powder

Directions:
1. Preheat the oven to 375 degrees Fahrenheit. Preparing a sheet baking sheet with parchment paper is a good idea.
2. Cut and slice the sweet potatoes about an hour earlier you intend to eat the meal.
3. Sweet potatoes should be baked in the oven for 40 minutes to an hour, or until they are tender.
4. In the meanwhile, prepare the rice according to package directions, either in a pressure cooker or on the stovetop.
5. Take the sweet potatoes out of the oven and place them in a large mixing bowl. Sweet potatoes should be mashed with the salsa, rice, and fresh spinach.
6. In a saucepan, combine the sweet potato mash with the black beans and fried beans,

stirring constantly over medium heat until the mixture is completely heated. Stir in the onion powder, chili powder, and cumin until well combined.

7. Using a deep fryer on medium heat, warm a tortilla and spread the sweet potato and beans mixture on the side that will be visible when the tortilla is finished. If desired, garnish with jalapenos.
8. Place a second whole grain tortilla on top of the first. For about 3 minutes, press down on the top tortilla with a spatula while the pan is on medium heat. Cook again for three minutes after flipping using a spatula.
9. Voila! Section the cake into the appropriate number of pieces. Serve with a dollop of salsa on top.

Tip: You may also use black-eyed peas for the black beans, or any other preferred beans, in this recipe.

102. Lentil Sloppy Joes

Total time: 1.5 hours
Serving: 6
Nutrient per serving: Calories: 385, Fats: 52.1g, Carbohydrates: 53g, Proteins: 50g, Sodium: 5mg, Calcium: 7.1mg, Iron: 65.1mg
Ingredients:
- 1 ½ cups of dried brown lentils
- 1 15-ounce can have diced fire roasted tomatoes
- 1 teaspoon of vegetarian Worcestershire sauce
- salt to taste
- 3 ⅓ cups of water or low-sodium vegetable stock
- 1 onion
- 2 tablespoons of brown sugar
- 1 teaspoon of rice vinegar
- 1 red bell pepper
- 1 tablespoon of chill powder
- 2 tablespoons of soy sauce
- 2 tablespoons of Dijon mustard

Directions:
1. Put 1 cup of water or broth in a big saucepan and bring to a boil.

2. Toss in the scallions and red pepper and simmer for 5 minutes, turning periodically, until the onions are softened somewhat but not completely.

3. Mix in the chili powder until it is completely incorporated. In a large mixing bowl, combine the remaining water, lentils, vegetables, and the remainder of the spices. In a large saucepan, combine all of the ingredients and bring to a boil. Reduce heat to low and simmer for one hour, mixing periodically.

4. As a side dish, serve the meat on whole wheat buns or freshly baked bread with the toppings of your choice.

103. Corn and Black Bean Cakes

Total time: 35 minutes
Serving: 10
Nutrient per serving: Calories: 511, Fats: 85g, Carbohydrates: 5.4g, Proteins: 62.9g, Sodium: 5mg, Calcium: 1.0mg, Iron: 2.7mg
Ingredients:
- 1/4 cup of unsweetened applesauce
- Tomato Salsa
- Sour "Cream" for serving
- chopped fresh cilantro
- 1½ cups of whole wheat pastry flour
- ½ cup of cornmeal
- 1 tablespoon of aluminum-free baking powder
- 1 cup of black beans, rinsed and drained
- 6 green onions
- ½ teaspoon of sea salt
- 1½ cups of unsweetened, unflavored plant milk
- 1 medium red bell pepper
- 1 (10-ounce) package of frozen corn kernels

Directions:
1. Preheat the oven to 250 degrees Fahrenheit.
2. A big mixing bowl is ideal for combining all of the ingredients. Whisk in the flour until it is well mixed. Toss the plant milk, applesauce, red pepper, corn, black beans,

and spring onions into a well in the middle of the flour mixture and stir to incorporate. To combine the ingredients, gently fold them together until they are well integrated. Don't overmix the ingredients.

3. Cook over medium heat, occasionally stirring, until a few drops of water placed into the pan leap and sizzle.

4. Pour 12 cup mixture for each pancake onto the pan, ensuring they don't touch one other and continue to do so until there is no more room. Allow 4 minutes for the undersides to brown and the pancake to be easily flipped without coming apart before removing from the heat. Flip the pancakes over with a spatula and continue cooking until another side is nicely browned and crisp, approximately 4 minutes. Heat a heatproof plate in the oven to make the pancakes warm while you prepare the rest of the meal. Toss the remaining batter in a separate bowl and repeat the process.

5. Serve the pancakes with salsa, sour "cream," and chopped cilantro on the side to garnish

104. Taco-Spiced Tortilla Chips

Total time: 1 hour 15 minutes
Serving: 5
Nutrient per serving: Calories: 141, Fats: 7.9g, Carbohydrates: 62.1g, Proteins: 2g, Sodium: 51mg, Calcium: 47mg, Iron: 61mg
Ingredients:
- ½ teaspoon of paprika
- ½ teaspoon of ground coriander
- ¼ teaspoon of sea salt
- 5 oil-free corn tortillas
- 1 tablespoon of nutritional yeast
- 1 tablespoon of lemon juice
- ½ teaspoon of ground cumin
- ¼ teaspoon of Chile de árbol or chipotle Chile powder
- ½ teaspoon of garlic powder
- ½ teaspoon of onion powder

Directions:

1. Preheat the oven to 300 degrees Fahrenheit. Prepare a baking sheet by lining it with parchment paper.
2. In a large mixing bowl, combine the nine ingredients (through the salt) and 1 tablespoon water. Toss gently to coat the tortilla triangles in the dressing.
3. Spread the tortillas out on the baking sheet that has been prepared. Bake for 1 hour, or until the potatoes are crispy. Allow the chips to cool fully on the pan. Store in the refrigerator to avoid contamination.

105. The Best Oil-Free Hummus

Total time: 10 minutes
Serving: 1
Nutrient per serving: Calories: 752, Fats: 19g, Carbohydrates: 87g, Proteins: 20g, Sodium: 8.4mg, Calcium: 41mg, Iron: 7.3mg
Ingredients:

- Juice of 1 lemon
- 2 teaspoons of ground cumin
- 2 teaspoons of Bragg Liquid Aminos
- ¼ cup of water or vegetable broth
- 2 cans of chickpeas
- 3 cloves of garlic

Directions:

1. Combine all of the ingredients to form a thick paste. You may also make this dish more individualized by combining one or all of the following ingredients: 1 cup of green olives, 1 bundle of green mint, 1 cup raw spinach, 1 cup of roasted eggplant.

106. 8-Ingredient Slow-Cooker Chili

Total time: 4 hours 20 minute
Serving: 6
Nutrient per serving: Calories: 113, Fats: 51g, Carbohydrates: 65g, Proteins: 62g, Sodium: 1.2mg, Calcium: 10.4mg, Iron: 13.8mg
Ingredients:

- 2 cups of water
- 1 cup of fresh or frozen whole kernel corn
- 2 cups of dried pinto beans
- 1 14.5-ounce can have diced tomatoes

- 6 cloves of garlic
- 4 cups of unsalted vegetable stock
- 1 cup of chopped red onion
- 1 1-ounce packet of vegetarian chili seasoning

Directions:

1. Cooking in a 5-quart crockpot for 4 to 5 hours on low heat will result in tender and flavorful beans. Combine the broth and water in a mixing bowl.
2. Boil at high temperature for 4 hours, occasionally stirring, until the vegetables are tender. Add the maize for the final 15 minutes of cooking. Toss with desired toppings and serve.

107. Sweet Potato Chili with Kale

Total time: 45 minutes
Serving: 6
Nutrient per serving: Calories: 380, Fats: 15g, Carbohydrates: 36g, Proteins: 91.2g, Sodium: 41.4mg, Calcium: 0.9mg, Iron: 4mg
Ingredients:

- 2 pounds fresh tomatoes
- 1 tablespoon of salt-free chili powder
- 2 cups of lacinato kale
- 3 cups of orange juice
- 2 medium sweet potatoes
- 1 large red onion
- 2 teaspoons of smoked paprika
- ¼ teaspoon of chipotle powder
- 2 15-ounce cans of salt-free kidney beans
- 2 red bell peppers

Directions:

1. For 8-10 minutes, cook the onion and green pepper in 1/2 of the oranges in a big saucepan until the onion is tender and translucent.
2. With the exception of the kale, combine all of the other ingredients.
3. After bringing the saucepan to a boil, lower the heat to a low level and continue to cook for 25-30 minutes, just until the potatoes are tender but not mushy.
4. Remove pan from heat and toss in kale until it is wilted, then serve.

5. Prepare in a pressure cooker by placing all ingredients in the pot and cooking on elevated heat for 6 minutes before releasing the pressure.

108. Potato-Cauliflower Curry

Total time: 1 hour
Serving: 5
Nutrient per serving: Calories: 523, Fats: 51g, Carbohydrates: 62g, Proteins: 78g, Sodium: 51mg, Calcium: 40mg, Iron: 2mg
Ingredients:
- cups cooked brown rice
- 1 tablespoon of finely snipped fresh cilantro
- 4 cups of 2-inch cauliflower florets
- 2 cups of 1½-inch potato pieces
- Pinch of Cayenne pepper
- Pinch of Sea salt
- 1 cup of onion wedges
- ¼ cup of tomato paste
- ¼ cup of raw cashews, finely ground
- 2 tablespoons of lime juice
- 1 tablespoon of mild curry powder
- 1½ teaspoon of grated fresh ginger
- 1 teaspoon of cumin seeds
- 1 clove of garlic

Directions:
1. In a big pot or deep skillet, place the cauliflower in a crockpot and steam until tender. Fill the basket with water until it is just below the rim. Bring the water to a boil. Cover the pan with a lid and steam for 5 minutes, or until the cauliflower is crisp and tender. Transfer the cauliflower to a large mixing bowl.
2. Set aside fifteen minutes or till potatoes are soft in a steamer basket, covered with a pan of water. Drain the water from the pan and add it to the cauliflower in the bowl.
3. To make the sauce, place the shallot wedges, tomatoes paste, chili powder, onion, coriander seeds, and garlic in a blender and mix until smooth. 1 tablespoon of water should be added.

Cover with plastic wrap and mix until smooth. Transfer the sauce to a pan and add 1 additional cup of water, stirring constantly. Bring the sauce to a boil, then lower the heat to medium-high and continue to simmer for 5 to 7 minutes. Reduce the heat to medium-low and simmer for another 10 minutes, or until the sauce has darkened in color.

4. To make the sauce, combine the cooked cauliflower and potato, beans, walnuts, lemon zest, and cayenne pepper in a large mixing bowl. Continually whisk and add more water as required to get the desired consistency for 5 to 7 minutes, or until the veggies have absorbed the sauce; remove from heat. Season with salt to taste. Serve the veggie combination over the rice garnished with cilantro and enjoy!

109. Rice Bowls with Kidney Beans, Spinach, and Mixed Veggies

Total time: 35 minutes
Serving: 4
Nutrient per serving: Calories: 550, Fats: 121g, Carbohydrates: 237g, Proteins: 82g, Sodium: 20mg, Calcium: 10mg, Iron: 21mg
Ingredients:
- 1 cup of Cilantro-Cashew Dressing
- 2 tablespoons of fresh cilantro
- 2 15-oz. cans of red kidney beans
- 2 cups of frozen mixed vegetables
- 1 cup of finely chopped tomatoes
- ½ cup of finely chopped green onions
- 2 cups of fresh spinach leaves
- 3 cups of cooked brown rice

Directions:
1. 1/2 cup water and the beans should be combined in a medium pot. Cook over medium heat, stirring periodically until the vegetables are cooked through.
2. Cook frozen veggies in a little quantity of boiling water for 5 minutes, or until they are just soft, in a small pan while you prepare the other ingredients.

3. Using a slotted spoon, distribute spinach among soup and salad dishes. Combine beans, veggies, and rice in a large pot.

4. Dressing: Splash with Cilantro-Cashew Dressing after adding the tomatoes and green onions. Fresh cilantro may be sprinkled on top if desired. Warm the dish before serving.

110. No-Fry Fried Rice

Total time: 45 minutes
Serving: 2
Nutrient per serving: Calories: 621, Fats: 123g, Carbohydrates: 71g, Proteins: 41g, Sodium: 5mg, Calcium: 1mg, Iron: 5mg
Ingredients:
- 1 8-ounce can have chopped pineapple, or fresh if available
- 2 cups of baby spinach
- 1 small head broccoli
- 2 cups of uncooked brown jasmine rice
- 1 cup of frozen or fresh corn
- 2 carrots
- 1 red chili
- ½ cup of chopped cilantro
- 3 green onions
- 4 mushrooms

Directions:
1. Give your rice a thorough wash before cooking it according to the box instructions or in a crockpot to your liking.
2. Stir one tablespoon of water into a nonstick deep fryer or wok over medium-high heat until the water simmer. Cook until the carrot, cabbage, and green onions are transparent, approximately 5 minutes, then remove from the heat and set aside.
3. Combine the mushroom, maize, papaya, lettuce, Chile, and cilantro in a large mixing bowl. Reduce the heat to medium and combine the ingredients. Pour in 1–2 tablespoons of water at a time, as required, to prevent the veggies from adhering to the pan while cooking.
4. To make the sauce, combine the ginger, garlic, tamari, and coco sugar in a medium

saucepan until fragrant. Stir constantly for one minute or when the sugar is completely dissolved. 1/2 cup of water should be added.

5. In a small bowl, whisk together the flour and water until smooth. To finish thickening the sauce, add the starch mixture and whisk thoroughly. Cook for another 2 minutes, stirring constantly.

6. Once the rice is done, combine it with the cooked vegetables in a large skillet, pour your wonderful sauce over the top, and stir everything together! Serve as soon as possible.

111. Vegan Mashed Potatoes and Gravy

Total time: 65 minutes
Serving: 5
Nutrient per serving: Calories: 541, Fats: 312g, Carbohydrates: 87.2g, Proteins: 2.8g, Sodium: 41mg, Calcium: 19mg, Iron: 31.1mg
Ingredients:
- 4 cups low-sodium vegetable broth
- ½ teaspoon of dried sage
- ⅛ teaspoon of freshly ground white or black pepper, plus ¼ teaspoon freshly ground black pepper
- Pinch of Sea salt
- ¼ cup of cashews
- 2 pounds of russet potatoes
- 1 clove of garlic
- 2 tablespoons of fresh lime juice
- 2 cups of cooked brown rice
- 8 ounces of button mushrooms
- ½ teaspoon of dried marjoram
- ½ teaspoon of dried thyme

Directions:
1. Pour 1 cup of water over the walnuts in a small mixing bowl and set aside. Set aside for 30 minutes to let the flavors blend.
2. Place the potato in a medium skillet and cover with cold water to bring them up to a boil. Boil the potatoes for approximately 20 minutes on high heat, then turn the heat down to medium and continue cooking until the potato is extremely soft

when poked with the point of a sharp knife. Drain the water completely and put it aside to cool.

3. In the meanwhile, mix the rice, mushroom, and vegetable broth in a saucepan over medium heat. Boil for approximately 10 minutes over medium-high heat, lower the heat to medium-low, and continue to cook until the mushroom is soft, about 10 minutes more. Remove the remove from heat and set it aside to cool slightly. Transfer the solution to a food processor or blender and blend until completely smooth, taking care not to overprocess it. (Alternatively, you may mixture was left in the pan and combine it with an immersion blender until smooth.)

4. Transfer the mix to the pan if it becomes necessary. Combine the mint, oregano, herbs, garlic, lime juice, 1/8 teaspoon pepper, and season with salt in a large mixing bowl. Cook for 10 minutes over medium heat, occasionally stirring, to combine the flavors. Cover the pan with a lid to make the gravy heated and put it aside.

5. Put the cashews and soaked water into a sterile blender and mix until smooth. Blend in until smooth, adding a sprinkle of pepper and the remaining 14 teaspoon pepper as needed. Using a potato masher or a handheld electric mixer, mash the cashew cream into the potatoes until smooth and creamy. Season with salt and pepper to taste.

6. Serve the mashed potatoes over a bed of gravy on a serving plate.

112. Veggie And Apple Slaw

Total time: 25 minutes
Serving: 8
Nutrient per serving: Calories: 312, Fats: 278g, Carbohydrates: 77g, Proteins: 54.2g, Sodium: 73.1mg, Calcium: 11mg, Iron: 65mg
Ingredients:
- 2 tablespoons of pure maple syrup

- 3 red apples
- 2 carrots
- 2 cups of shredded green cabbage
- 2 cups of shredded red cabbage
- 1 teaspoon of Dijon-style mustard
- Pinch of sea salt
- 1 cup of thinly sliced celery
- ¼ cup of white wine vinegar

Directions:
1. In an extra-large mixing bowl, toss together the red cabbage, green cabbage, and celery.
2. In a small bowl, mix the mustard, maple syrup, vinegar, and salt until well combined.
3. Apples and carrots should be spiralized or shredded, either using the fine blade of a spiralizer or the fine side of a box grater and then added to the cabbage mixture. Toss to coat with a dressing after drizzling it on.

113. Potato Salad with Avocado and Dill

Total time: 90 minutes
Serving: 6
Nutrient per serving: Calories: 411, Fats: 51g, Carbohydrates: 64.3g, Proteins: 41.4g, Sodium: 64mg, Calcium: 19mg, Iron: 0mg
Ingredients:
- 3 stalks celery
- ½ white onion
- 2 pounds small red potatoes
- 1 large avocado
- ⅓ cup of fresh dill, packed and then chopped
- ½ bunch of green onions (green part), sliced
- 2 teaspoons of fresh lemon juice
- 1 tablespoon of Dijon mustard
- 1½ teaspoons of maple syrup
- Freshly ground black pepper
- ¼ teaspoon of smoked paprika
- ½ teaspoon (or less) of Herbamare or sea salt

Directions:

1. Remove any unhealthy patches or eyes from the potatoes by washing and cutting them out. Continue to steam for approximately 10 minutes, or until the vegetables are fork-tender through the middle. Run the pan under cold water as soon as possible to avoid additional cooking.
2. Freeze the potato cubes for approximately an hour before serving for optimum results. (This helps to keep them from falling apart while you're slicing them.)
3. Potatoes should be quartered and peeled if desired. Place all of the ingredients in a large mixing bowl.
4. In a small bowl, slice and smash the avocado until smooth. To make the dressing, combine the lime juice, paprika, mustard, salt, and maple syrup in a separate bowl and whisk until well combined. Season with freshly ground pepper to taste.
5. Toss the potatoes with the green onion, dill, avocado, onion, and celery dressing. Gently toss until everything is evenly covered. Taste the dish and make any necessary spice adjustments.
6. Serve immediately, or chill and serve the next day, whichever is most convenient as the avocado darkens and breaks down quickly.

114. Italian-Style Zucchini and Chickpea Sauté

Total time: 25 minutes
Serving: 6
Nutrient per serving: Calories: 199, Fats: 45.6g, Carbohydrates: 64.1g, Proteins: 6.5g, Sodium: 58mg, Calcium: 18.1mg, Iron: 1.1mg
Ingredients:
- ½ teaspoon of dried thyme
- A pinch of Sea salt
- Pinch of freshly ground black pepper
- 8 to 10 fresh basil leaves
- 1 onion, diced
- 1 large red bell pepper
- 1 cup of oil-free marinara sauce
- 1 tablespoon of white wine vinegar
- 6 cloves garlic
- 1 teaspoon of dried oregano
- 3 medium zucchinis
- 1 15-oz. can of chickpeas

Directions:
1. Using an extra-large skillet, heat the ingredients over medium to high heat. Cook for ten min, mixing often and adding more water, 1–2 Tablespoon. At a time, if necessary, to keep the mixture from sticking to the bottom of the pan.
2. Cook for another 10 minutes, or till the zucchini is soft if using fresh zucchini. Combine the marinara sauce, chickpeas, and vinegar in a large mixing bowl. Sprinkle with salt and freshly ground black pepper. Continue to heat until the desired temperature is reached. Serve immediately with a sprinkle of basil on top.

115. Spicy French Fries

Total time: 1 hour
Serving: 32
Nutrient per serving: Calories: 612, Fats: 37.1g, Carbohydrates: 7g, Proteins: 82g, Sodium: 64.1g, Calcium: 1mg, Iron: 5.8mg
Ingredients:
- 2 tablespoons of fresh lemon juice
- Ketchup and Dijon mustard
- 1 tablespoon of onion powder
- 1½ teaspoons of garlic powder
- Pinch of Sea salt
- 1½ pounds of russet potatoes
- 1½ teaspoons of sweet paprika
- 1 teaspoon of ground turmeric
- 1 teaspoon of ground coriander
- ¼ teaspoon of cayenne pepper

Directions:
1. Preheat the oven to 450 degrees Fahrenheit. Prepare a baking sheet by lining it with parchment paper.
2. Place a steamer basket in a big saucepan with about two inches of water and bring to a boil. Put the potatoes in a steamer,

cover with a lid, and steam for 10 minutes on a high heat setting. The potatoes would be approximately 75 percent done when you get them home.

3. To prepare the seasonings in the meanwhile, combine them in a medium-sized mixing bowl and mix well. Add the turmeric, paprika, coriander, cayenne pepper, lemon juice, and salt to taste and mix well.

4. Move the potato to the mixing bowl with the spices and gently toss to combine the potatoes equally. Place the mashed potatoes on a baking pan, allowing plenty of space between each wedge. Bake for 30 minutes.

5. Preheat the oven to 200°F and bake for 20-25 minutes.

6. If preferred, warm up the fries and serve them hot, with sauce and Dijon mustard on the side.

116. Celeriac, Hazelnut & Truffle Soup

Total time: 45 minutes
Serving: 6
Nutrient per serving: Calories: 155, Fats: 14.4g, Carbohydrates: 0.7g, Proteins: 0.2g, Sodium: 5.8mg, Calcium: 12.1mg, Iron: 29mg
Ingredients:
- 1 fat clove of garlic
- 1 celeriac
- 1 potato, chopped
- 50g blanched hazelnuts
- 1 tablespoon of truffle oil
- 1 tablespoon of olive oil
- 1 small bunch of thyme
- 1 veg stock
- 100ml of soya cream
- 2 bay leaves
- 1 onion

Directions:
1. Cook for another 1 minute after adding the garlic, add the potato and celeriac and mix well. Season with a generous sprinkle of salt and freshly ground white pepper after giving everything a thorough swirl. Put in

the stock and bring to a boil, then reduce the heat and simmer for about 30 minutes, or until the veggies are fully soft.

2. Remove the herbs from the pan and whisk in the cream until fully smooth. Remove the pan from the heat and blend until completely smooth. Start with less truffle oil and gradually add more, tasting as you go. Because the intensity of the truffle oil will vary, it's better, to begin with, less and add a bit at a time, rather than using all of it at once.

3. Prepare the soup till it is hot and bubbly before ladling it into bowls and garnishing with the hazelnuts, a pinch of black pepper, and an additional spray of truffle oil

117. Squash & Spinach Fusilli with Pecans

Total time: 50 minutes
Serving: 2
Nutrient per serving: Calories: 530, Fats: 140g, Carbohydrates: 71g, Proteins: 2g, Sodium: 8mg, Calcium: 10.5mg, Iron: 29.1mg
Ingredients:
- 1 tablespoon of chopped sage leaves
- 2 teaspoon of rapeseed oil
- 115g of whole meal fusilli
- 125g bag of baby spinach
- 160g of butternut squash
- 3 cloves of garlic
- 1 large courgetti
- 6 pecan halves

Directions:
1. Preheat the oven to 200 degrees Celsius/180 degrees Celsius fan/gas 6. Stir together the butternut squash, garlic, and sage in the oil and spread out in a roasting pan. Bake for 20 minutes, then add the courgettes and roast for another 15 minutes. Stir everything together, then include the pecans and simmer for another 5 minutes, or until the pecans are browned, and the veggies are soft and beginning to caramelize.

2. In the meanwhile, cook pasta according to the package directions (approx. 12 minutes). Drain the pasta, then spoon it into a serving dish and mix it with the spinach, allowing the spinach to wilt in the warmth from the pasta. Serve immediately. Mix in the roasted vegetables and walnuts, break up the nuts a bit as you go, then toss well again just before serving

118. Artichoke & Aubergine Rice

Total time: 50 minutes
Serving: 6
Nutrient per serving: Calories: 340, Fats: 31.4g, Carbohydrates: 86.1g, Proteins: 61g, Sodium: 0mg, Calcium: 4.0mg, Iron: 7.1mg
Ingredients:
- 1 small pack of finely chopped parsley
- 2 x 175g packs of chargrilled artichokes
- 2 lemons 1 juiced, 1 cut into wedges to serve
- 60ml of olive oil
- 2 aubergines
- 400g of paella rice
- 1 ½l of Kallo vegetable stock
- 1 large onion
- 2 garlic cloves
- 2 teaspoons of smoked paprika
- 2 teaspoons of turmeric

Directions:
1. In a large nonstick hot pan or paella pan, heat 2 tablespoons of the oil over medium heat. Sauté the aubergines until they are well browned across all surfaces (add another teaspoon of oil if the eggplant starts to catch too much), then take them from the pan and put them aside to cool.
2. Continue to cook the onions for 2-3 minutes, or until it is tender, in the remaining tablespoon of oil in the pan. Boil for a few minutes more after adding the parsley and garlic stems, then add the seasonings and rice and mix until all are well covered. Boil, uncovered, over a moderate flame for 20 minutes, stirring periodically to keep it from sticking, after

heating for 2 minutes and adding half the stock. Cook for a further 20 minutes, or when the rice is cooked through, after which you may add the aubergine and artichokes.
3. Cut the parsley leaves and combine them with the lime juice and salt and pepper to taste. Take the entire pan to the tables and divide it among the bowls, serving it with lime slices on the side.

119. Guacamole & Mango Salad with Black Beans

Total time: 15 minutes
Serving: 2
Nutrient per serving: Calories: 130, Fats: 82.1g, Carbohydrates: 60.8g, Proteins: 20g, Sodium: 61mg, Calcium: 41.1mg, Iron: 30g
Ingredients:
- 1 small avocado
- 100g of cherry tomatoes
- ½ small pack of coriander
- 400g can of black beans
- 1 lime for juice
- 1 small mango
- 1 red chilli
- 1 red onion, chopped

Directions:
1. In a large mixing bowl, combine the lemon juice and zest, mango, avocado, tomatoes, chili, and onion; toss in the coriander and beans until well combined.

120. Veggie Olive Wraps with Mustard Vinaigrette

Total time: 10 minutes
Serving: 1
Nutrient per serving: Calories: 350, Fats: 43g, Carbohydrates: 65.1g, Proteins: 79g, Sodium: 0.8mg, Calcium: 40mg, Iron: 29 mg
Ingredients:
- handful of basil leaves
- 5 green olives
- 1 tablespoon of cider vinegar
- 4 tortillas
- 1 carrot
- 80g wedge red cabbage

- ½ teaspoon of English mustard powder
- 2 teaspoon of extra virgin rapeseed oil
- 2 spring onions
- 1 courgetti, shredded or grated

Directions:

1. Toss together all of the ingredients (except the tortilla) until thoroughly combined.
2. Place the tortillas on a piece of aluminum foil and arrange the filling down one edge of the wrapping — it may almost seem there is too much material, but as you begin to roll it tightly, it will compress itself. As you roll the tortillas from the filled side inside, be sure to fold in the edges as you go. Fold the ends of the foil in to keep the contents of the wrap contained.

121. Black Beans & Avocado on Toast

Total time: 30 minutes
Serving: 4
Nutrient per serving: Calories: 470, Fats: 50g, Carbohydrates: 7g, Proteins: 20g, Sodium: 8mg, Calcium: 0.3mg, Iron: 29.2mg

Ingredients:

- 2 garlic cloves
- 4 slices of bread
- 1 avocado
- 270g of cherry
- tomatoes, quartered
- 1 red or white onion, finely chopped
- 2 x 400g cans of black beans, drained
- small bunch of coriander, chopped
- ½ lime, juiced
- 4 tablespoon of olive oil
- 1 teaspoon of ground cumin
- 2 teaspoon of chipotle paste
- 1 teaspoon of chili flakes

Directions:

1. Set aside the tomatoes, 1/4 onion, lime juice, and 1 tablespoon oil that have been mixed. Sautee the leftover onions in 2 tablespoons oil till it begins to soften, about 5 minutes. Add the garlic and cook for 1 minute. Next, add the cinnamon and chipotle and cook until fragrant, stirring

constantly. Add the soybeans and a bit of water, mix, and simmer on low heat until the beans are cooked through.

2. Cook for 1 minute after stirring in the majority of the tomato mixture. Season with salt and pepper and stir in the majority of the coriander. Warm the bread and sprinkle with the remainder 1 tablespoon olive oil to finish it off. Place a piece of bread on each dish and top with a mound of beans. Sprinkle the leftover tomatoes mixture and parsley leaves on top of the avocado slices, then serve immediately.

122. Spinach, Sweet Potato & Lentil Dhal

Total time: 45 minutes
Serving: 4
Nutrient per serving: Calories: 430, Fats: 140g, Carbohydrates: 76g, Proteins: 42g, Sodium: 49.1mg, Calcium: 20mg, Iron: 50mg

Ingredients:

- 1 red chili, finely chopped
- 1½ teaspoon of ground turmeric
- 1½ teaspoon of ground cumin
- 4 spring onions
- ½ small pack of Thai basil
- 1 tablespoon of sesame oil
- 1 red onion
- 600ml of vegetable stock
- 80g bag of spinach
- 1 garlic clove, crushed
- thumb-sized piece ginger
- 2 sweet potatoes
- 250g of red split lentils

Directions:

1. 1 tablespoon sesame oil is heated in a broad pan with a narrow cover until shimmering.
2. Toss in 1 coarsely diced red onion and simmer for 10 minutes on low heat, turning periodically until the onion is tender.
3. Continue to simmer for 1 minute after adding 1 smashed garlic clove, 1 coarsely

diced thumb-sized piece of ginger, and 1 coarsely diced red chili. After 1 minute, add 112 teaspoon ground turmeric and 112 teaspoon ground cumin and continue to boil for 1 minute longer.

4. Stir in 2 sweet potatoes that have been sliced into even pieces while increasing the heat to medium and mixing everything until the sweet potatoes are covered in the spice's mixture.

5. Add 250g reddish split lentils, 600ml veggie stock, and a pinch of salt and pepper to taste.

6. After bringing the liquid to a boil, turn down the heat to low and cover the pot. Cook for 20 minutes, or when the lentils are cooked, and the potatoes are barely holding together.

7. Test and adjust the seasonings, then carefully fold in the 80g spinach until everything is well combined. Once the spinach has wilted, garnish with 4 diagonally cut spring onions and 12 tiny package torn basil leaves before serving.

8. Instead, let it cool fully before dividing it into sealed containers and storing it in the refrigerator for a nutritious lunchbox.

123. Kidney Bean Curry

Total time: 35 minutes
Serving: 2
Nutrient per serving: Calories: 780, Fats: 54.1g, Carbohydrates: 30g, Proteins: 29g, Sodium: 5mg, Calcium: 10mg, Iron: 51mg
Ingredients:
- 1 small pack coriander, stalks finely chopped, leaves roughly shredded
- 400g can of kidney beans, in water
- cooked basmati rice, to serve
- 1 tablespoon of vegetable oil
- 1 onion, finely chopped
- 2 teaspoons of garam masala
- 400g can have chopped tomatoes
- 2 garlic cloves
- thumb-sized piece of ginger
- 1 teaspoon of ground cumin

- 1 teaspoon of ground paprika

Directions:
1. In a large skillet, heat the oil over medium heat until shimmering. Toss in the onions and a sprinkle of salt and heat, turning periodically until the onion is tender and just beginning to brown. Cook for another 2 minutes, or until the garlic, ginger, and coriander stems are aromatic, before adding the tomatoes.

2. Heat for another 1 minute after adding the spices, at which time everything should be smelling delicious. Bring the kidney beans and chopped tomatoes to a boil in their water, then remove from the heat.

3. Simmer for 15 minutes, or until the curry has hardened and become very fragrant. Season with salt and pepper to suit, then serve over basmati rice and coriander leaves.

124. Roasted Cauli-Broc Bowl with Tahini Hummus

Total time: 40 minutes
Serving: 2
Nutrient per serving: Calories: 230, Fats: 30.9g, Carbohydrates: 60g, Proteins: 7.9g, Sodium: 6.9mg, Calcium: 0.9mg, Iron: 2mg
Ingredients:
- large handful baby spinach
- 3 tablespoons of hummus
- 1 lemon
- 10 walnuts
- 2 tablespoons of tahini
- 400g pack of cauliflower & broccoli florets
- 2 tablespoon of olive oil
- 250g of ready-to-eat quinoa
- 2 cooked and sliced beetroots

Directions:
1. Preheat the oven to 200°C/180°C fan/gas 6 the night before. Place the broccoli and cauliflower in a large roasting pan with the oil as well as a sprinkling of flaky sea salt and roast for 30 minutes or until the vegetables are tender. Roast for 25-30 minutes, or until the vegetables are

browned and cooked. Allow cooling fully before using.

2. Start by placing half of the oats in each of the four bowls. Place the lemon slices on top, next by the asparagus, spinach, broccoli, and walnuts, and then the rest of the ingredients. Mix the hummus, tahini, lemon juice, and 1 tablespoon water in a small saucepan until smooth. Before you begin to eat, coat your hands with the dressing. Toss with the lemon slices before serving.

125. Vegan Shepherd's Pie

Total time: 1 hour 20 minutes
Serving: 8
Nutrient per serving: Calories: 355, Fats: 51g, Carbohydrates: 0.5g, Proteins: 30g, Sodium: 41mg, Calcium: 23.7mg, Iron: 7.9mg
Ingredients:

- 1 vegetable stock cube
- 3 cloves of garlic,
- 2 tablespoon of tomato purée
- 20ml of olive oil
- A small pack of leaf parsley, chopped
- 50ml of vegetable oil
- 30g of dried porcini mushrooms
- 400g can of chickpeas
- 300g of frozen peas
- 300g of frozen spinach
- Some tomato ketchups, to serve
- 2kg of floury potatoes
- 2 large leeks
- 2 small onions, chopped
- 4 medium carrots
- ½ small pack of thyme
- ½ small pack of sage
- 4 celery sticks, chopped
- 2 teaspoons of smoked paprika
- 1 small butternut squash
- ½ small pack of marjoram or oregano

Directions:

1. Place the peeled and cut potatoes in a medium skillet with enough water to cover them. Bring to a boil, then reduce the heat and boil for 40 minutes, or till the skins begin to split. Pour the water out and set it aside to cool a bit.

2. Meantime, boil the veggie oil in a heavy-bottomed frying pan or flame-resistant casserole dish over medium heat until shimmering and hot. Cook over low heat for 5 minutes, occasionally stirring, until the carrots, leeks, mushrooms, onions, and stock cube have softened somewhat. Cook on a lower heat. Stir more often, scraping the pieces from the bottom of the pan if it begins to stick. Vegetables should be tender but not mushy when cooked.

3. Combine the paprika, tomato purée, garlic, squash, and herbs in a large mixing bowl. Cook for 3 minutes after stirring and increasing the heat a little. Add the celery and simmer for another few minutes after stirring.

4. Place the chickpeas in a large mixing bowl with the water from the can and the leftover mushroom stock. Stir in the spinach and peas until everything is well combined. Cook for 5 minutes, stirring periodically, then season with salt and pepper, turn off the heat and put aside. There should be plenty of water left in the pan, and the vegetables should be vibrant and somewhat firm.

5. Remove the skins from the potatoes and set them aside. 200g of the potatoes should be mashed with a spoon and mixed with the vegetables. Break the remaining potatoes into pieces and combine with the olive oil, parsley, and salt & pepper to taste.

6. Divide the contents amongst the pie plates and arrange the potatoes on top of the mixture. Preheat the oven to 190°C/170°F fan/gas 5 and cook the pie for 40-45 minutes, or until their tops are brown and the mixture is hot throughout. If you are preparing individual pies, check them after 20 minutes of baking. Shepherd's pies are

served better with tomato ketchup, as are all excellent shepherd's pies.

126. Easy Healthy Falafels

Total time: 35 minutes
Serving: 6
Nutrient per serving: Calories: 130, Fats: 42g, Carbohydrates: 30g, Proteins: 72g, Sodium: 5.8mg, Calcium: 10.1mg, Iron: 6.2mg
Ingredients:

- 1 small chili, roughly chopped
- 1 teaspoon of ground cumin
- 80g of flour
- 100ml of vegetable oil
- 250g dried chickpeas
- ½ teaspoon of bicarbonate of soda
- Handful of chopped coriander
- Handful of chopped parsley
- 3 cloves of garlic
- 1 onion
- 1 teaspoon of cayenne pepper
- 1 teaspoon of sumac
- 1 leek chopped
- 1 celery stick chopped

Directions:

1. Soak the chickpeas in ice water for 8 hours or overnight, depending on your preference.
2. Rinse the chickpeas and process them in a mixing bowl with the bicarb until they are coarsely minced. Remove about 3/4 of the batter and put it aside for later.
3. In a food processor, combine the remaining ingredients (garlic, veggies, spices, and herbs) and purée until a paste is formed. Mix the mixture into the rough chickpea purée, mix the gram flour and season with salt and pepper to taste.
4. Preheat the oven to 110 degrees Celsius/90 degrees Celsius fan/gas 1/4. Melt part of the oil in an extra-large, nonstick frying pan over medium heat before adding the rest. After mixing the ingredients, form the patties with your hands. There should be enough to make about 16. Fry for 2 minutes on each side,

or until the chicken is crisp. Keeping the mixture warm in the oven will allow you to finish frying the rest in batches, adding just little oil in a frying pan with each round. Serve with the houmous, tabbouleh, pickled red onion and radish on flatbreads, if desired, with the tabbouleh on the side.

127. Lentil Ragu with Courgetti

Total time: 55 minutes
Serving: 6
Nutrient per serving: Calories: 280, Fats: 82g, Carbohydrates: 42.1g, Proteins: 72.2g, Sodium: 28mg, Calcium: 12mg, Iron: 61mg
Ingredients:

- 2 tablespoons of balsamic vinegar
- 1-2 large courgettes
- 2 tablespoon of rapeseed oil
- 3 celery sticks
- 1l of reduced-salt vegetable bouillon
- 1 teaspoon of dried oregano
- 2 carrots
- 4 cloves of garlic
- 500g pack of dried red lentils
- 500g pack of passata
- 2 onions
- 140g button mushrooms

Directions:

1. In a big sauté pan, heat the 2 tablespoons of oil until shimmering. Fry the celery, carrots, garlic, and onions for 4-5 minutes over high heat, until the vegetables are tender and beginning to brown. Fry for another 2 minutes after adding the mushrooms.
2. Combine the passata, lentils, bouillon, oregano, and balsamic vinegar in a large mixing bowl. Stir occasionally for 30 minutes or when the lentils are soft and pulpy, depending on how large your pan is. Check and stir the mixture periodically to ensure that it does not cling to the bottom of the bowl; if it does, put in a drop of water.
3. Cook the courgetti in another frying pan with the remaining oil until it is soft and

heated throughout before transferring it to a serving dish.

128. Lentil Lasagna

Total time: 1 hour 15 minutes
Serving: 6
Nutrient per serving: Calories: 480, Fats: 21g, Carbohydrates: 62.1g, Proteins: 50g, Sodium: 1.1mg, Calcium: 10mg, Iron: 29mg
Ingredients:
- 1 tablespoon of corn flour
- 400g can have chopped tomato
- 1 teaspoon of mushroom ketchup
- pinch of freshly grated nutmeg
- 9 dried egg-free lasagna sheets
- 1 tablespoon of olive oil
- 1 onion
- 2 cauliflower heads
- 2 tablespoon of unsweetened soya milk
- 1 carrot
- 1 celery stick
- 1 teaspoon of chopped oregano
- 1 teaspoon of vegetable stock powder
- 1 garlic clove
- 2 x 400g cans of lentils

Directions:
1. In a large skillet, heat the oil over medium heat. Add the onion, celery, and carrot, and slowly cook for 10-15 minutes, or until the vegetables are tender. Simmer for a few minutes after adding the garlic, before adding the corn flour and lentils.
2. Combine the tomatoes with a can of liquid, the mushroom ketchup, the oregano, the stock powder, and some spice in a large mixing bowl. Cook for 15 minutes, stirring periodically until the vegetables are tender.
3. In the meanwhile, simmer the cauliflower for 10 minutes, or until it is soft, in a pan of water. Drain the soy milk and purée it with it in a handheld food processor or blender until smooth. Season with salt and pepper and sprinkle with nutmeg.
4. Preheat the oven to 180 degrees Celsius/160 degrees Celsius fan/gas 4.

Distribute a quarter of the legume mix over the bottom of a clay baking dish, approximately 20 x 30cm in size. Top with a thin layer of lasagna, snapping the sheets together to form a tight fit. Using half of the legume mixture, place a part of the cauliflower puree on top, then add a layer of spaghetti on top of that. Finish with the final third of the lentils and lasagna, accompanied by the remaining puree and serve immediately after.

5. Cover loosely with an aluminum baking sheet and bake for 35-30 mins, discarding the paper for the last 10 minutes of cooking time to finish cooking.

129. Sweet Potato & Cauliflower Lentil Bowl

Total time: 1 hour
Serving: 3
Nutrient per serving: Calories: 226, Fats: 10g, Carbohydrates: 75g, Proteins: 20g, Sodium: 18mg, Calcium: 12mg, Iron: 50mg
Ingredients:
- 2 cloves of garlic
- 200g of lentils
- ¼ red cabbage
- ½ small pack of coriander
- 1 large, sweet potato
- 1 cauliflower
- 1½ lime juice
- 2 carrots
- 1 tablespoon of garam masala
- 3 tablespoon of groundnut oil
- thumb-sized piece ginger
- 1 teaspoon of Dijon mustard

Directions:
1. Preheat the oven to 200 degrees Celsius/180 degrees Celsius fan/gas 6. Mix the cauliflower and sweet potato with the cumin seeds, half the oil, and a pinch of salt and pepper until well combined. Distribute out on a big roasting pan or baking sheet. Roast for 30-35 minutes, or until the garlic is soft and cooked.

2. In the meanwhile, add the legumes to a pot with 400ml ice water and bring to a boil. Bring to a boil, then reduce the heat and simmer for 20-25 minutes, or until the legumes are done but still have a bite to them. Drain.

3. The garlic cloves should be removed from the pan and squashed together with the tip of your knife. Place the garlic in a bowl and mix with the residual oil, ginger, mustard, a sprinkle of sugar, then one-third of the lime juice. Toss well to combine. Whisk in the heated lentils, then season to taste with salt and pepper after a few minutes. Grate the carrots coarsely, shred the cabbage, and finely chop the coriander before assembling the dish. Season with salt and pepper to taste after squeezing in the remaining lime juice.

4. Divide the lentil mixture into four serving dishes (or four containers if saving and chilling). Using half of the carrot salad and half of the potato and cauliflower mixture, top each dish with a quarter of the dressing.

130. Smoky Spiced Veggie Rice

Total time: 1 hour 15 minutes
Serving: 6
Nutrient per serving: Calories: 550, Fats: 14g, Carbohydrates: 42.1g, Proteins: 43g, Sodium: 28mg, Calcium: 10mg, Iron: 9mg
Ingredients:
- 2 tablespoon caster sugar
- 2 spring onions
- 25g cashews
- 4 tablespoon of olive oil
- 400ml of vegetable or vegan stock
- 1 tablespoon of red vinegar
- 1 corn cob
- 250g of rainbow baby carrots
- 400g can of cherry tomatoes
- 300g long-grain rice
- 2 red onions
- 2 celery sticks
- 200g of heirloom cherry tomatoes

Directions:
1. Cook the nuts in a large skillet or Dutch oven over medium heat, often stirring, until golden brown. Remove from the fire and set aside to cool before chopping roughly. In the same pan, heat 1 tablespoon oil over a high temperature until shimmering, then cook the corn for 20 seconds on each side to sear. Remove the chicken from the pan, put it aside, and add the vegetables and cook for 5 minutes. Remove the pan from the heat and put it aside.

2. Continue to cook the onion and celery for another 10 minutes in the same pan over medium-high heat until tender and slightly browned. Remove from the pan and set aside. Season with Cajun spice before adding the smoked paprika, chipotle paste, and tomato purée. Continue to cook for another 5 minutes before adding the other ingredients. Continue to cook for 1 minute, or when the spices are aromatic, before adding the tomatoes and continuing to fry for just another 2 minutes.

3. Mix in the black beans, tomato paste, rice, stock, vinegar, and sugar until everything is well-combined, perhaps 5 minutes more or so. Stir halfway through and cook for 35-40 minutes on a moderate flame, occasionally stirring, until the food is cooked, and the liquid has been absorbed, stirring halfway through.

4. The corn should be cut from the cob and mixed into the rice and carrots to taste. Season with salt and pepper, then garnish with red onions and cashews.

131. Cauliflower Lentil Bowl

Total time: 55 minutes
Serving: 4
Nutrient per serving: Calories: 330, Fats: 70g, Carbohydrates: 50g, Proteins: 100g, Sodium: 19.1mg, Calcium: 20mg, Iron: 23mg
Ingredients:
- 2 garlic cloves

- 200g lentils
- ¼ red cabbage
- ½ small pack of coriander
- 1 large, sweet potato
- 1 cauliflower, stalk diced
- 1½ teaspoon of lime juice
- 2 carrots
- 1 tablespoon of garam masala
- 3 tablespoon of groundnut oil
- thumb-sized piece ginger
- 1 teaspoon of Dijon mustard

Directions:

1. Preheat the oven to 200 degrees Celsius/180 degrees Celsius fan/gas 6. Mix the cauliflower and sweet potato with the seasoning, half the oil, and a pinch of salt and pepper until well combined. Distribute out on a big roasting pan or baking sheet. Roast for 30-35 minutes, or until the garlic is soft and cooked. In the meanwhile, place the beans in a pot with 5ml cold water and bring to a boil. Bring to a boil, then reduce the heat and simmer for 20-25 minutes, or until the legumes are roasted but still have a bite to them. Drain.

2. The garlic cloves should be removed first from the tray and squashed together with the tip of your knife. Place the garlic in a mixing bowl with the residual oil, mustard, ginger, a sprinkle of sugar, and one-third of the lemon juice. Toss well to combine. Whisk in the heated lentils, then season to taste with salt and pepper after a few minutes. Grate the carrots coarsely, shred the cabbage, and finely chop the coriander before assembling the dish. Season with salt and pepper to taste after squeezing in the remaining lime juice.

3. Divide the lentil mixture into four serving dishes (or four containers if saving and chilling). Using a quarter of the carrot slaw and a quarter of the sweet potato and cauliflower mixture, top each dish with a quarter of the dressing.

132. Sesame Parsnip & Wild Rice Tabbouleh

Total time: 55 minutes
Serving: 3
Nutrient per serving: Calories: 320, Fats: 29.9g, Carbohydrates: 41.9g, Proteins: 50g, Sodium: 19mg, Calcium: 30mg, Iron: 49mg
Ingredients:

- 1 small pack coriander
- 2 tablespoon of pomegranate seeds
- 500g of parsnips
- 2 ½ tablespoon of cold pressed rapeseed oil
- 3 tablespoons of tahini
- 1 small pack mint
- 1 teaspoon of ground turmeric
- 2 teaspoon of ground coriander
- 2 red onions
- 2 tablespoon of white wine vinegar
- 2 tablespoon of sesame seeds
- 130g of wild rice

Directions:

1. Preheat the oven to 200 degrees Celsius/180 degrees Celsius fan/gas 6. Toss the parsnips with 112 tablespoons of the oil, turmeric, coriander, and a pinch of salt and pepper, then pour over the sesame seeds so that each piece is thoroughly covered with the seeds. Bake in the oven at 60 ° c or until the vegetables are soft.

2. In the meanwhile, prepare the wild rice according to the package directions. In a second pan, heat and cook 1 tablespoon oil until shimmering, then add the chopped onion and 3 tablespoon waters. Cook for 10-15 minutes, stirring periodically, or until the vegetables are fully soft and tender. Increase the heat to high, add 1 tablespoon of the vinegar, and continue cooking, or until the liquid is bright pink.

3. Whisk the tahini, remaining vinegar with just enough warm water to create a creamy dressing by constantly whisking. Season with salt and pepper to taste.

72

4. Rinse the wild rice and combine it with the onions and 34 chopped parsleys in a large mixing bowl. To assemble, divide the mixture among three dishes and top with the sunflower parsnips, pomegranate seeds, and the remaining herbs. Serve with a dollop of tahini dressing on top of each serving.

133. Acai Bowl

Total time: 5 minutes
Serving: 1
Nutrient per serving: Calories: 180, Fats: 19g, Carbohydrates: 60.1g, Proteins: 65g, Sodium: 43mg, Calcium: 80mg, Iron: 35mg
Ingredients:
- ½ a very ripe banana
- handful of ice cubes
- 1 teaspoon of coconut flakes
- 5 pineapple chunks
- ½ cup of passionfruit
- 1 tablespoon toasted oats
- 2 teaspoons of açai powder
- handful of frozen berries

Directions:
1. Blend the powder, frozen berries, banana, and ice cubes in a high-powered blender with 100ml water until completely smooth. Blend until smooth, then transfer to a serving dish and top with your favorite toppings.

134. Vegan Kebabs with Avocado Dressing

Total time: 40 minutes
Serving: 4
Nutrient per serving: Calories: 330, Fats: 39g, Carbohydrates: 4.0g, Proteins: 62g, Sodium: 20mg, Calcium: 46mg, Iron: 41mg
Ingredients:
- 3 rosemary sprigs
- 4 Portobello mushrooms
- large bag rocket
- watercress
- spinach salad
- 2 tablespoons of toasted mixed seeds
- 3½ tablespoon of olive oil
- 2 garlic cloves

- 1 teaspoon of lemon juice
- ½ teaspoon of wholegrain mustard
- 1 teaspoon of chili flakes
- 3 rosemary sprigs
- 2 large red onions
- 1 avocado
- 4 peaches
- 2 large courgettes

Directions:
1. Combine 3 tablespoon oil, the smashed garlic, the chili flakes, and the rosemary in a mixing bowl. Each skewer should have alternating bits of mushroom, peach, courgette, and red onion on it - you should be able to get 2 parts of everything on each skewer. Season the kebabs with salt and freshly ground black pepper after brushing them with the flavored olive oil. Set them aside. The kebabs may be prepared beforehand and stored refrigerated until needed.
2. Preheat the barbeque or grill to its maximum possible temperature. Then, blend the avocado, half of the lemon juice, and 50ml water in a blender until smooth and salt to taste with salt and pepper. Toss the combined rocket salads and toasted seeds with the leftover lemon juice, remaining 12 tablespoon olive oil, and mustard in a large mixing bowl until well combined.
3. Grill or barbecue the skewers for about 4-5 minutes on each side, or until they are cooked through and attractively browned. To serve, arrange the meat on a dish and top with the avocado sauce and lettuce on the side.

135. Cauliflower Steaks with Roasted Red Pepper & Olive Salsa

Total time: 20 minutes
Serving: 2
Nutrient per serving: Calories: 280, Fats: 25g, Carbohydrates: 43g, Proteins: 1.2g, Sodium: 3.8mg, Calcium: 10mg, Iron: 3.4mg
Ingredients:

- black olives, pitted
- ½ tablespoon red wine vinegar
- 2 tablespoon toasted flaked almonds
- 1 cauliflower
- ½ teaspoon smoked paprika
- small handful parsley
- 1 teaspoon capers
- 2 tablespoon olive oil
- 1 roasted red pepper

Directions:

1. Prepare a baking pan by lining it with baking paper and preheating the stove to 220C/200C fan/gas 7. Cauliflower should be separated into 2 1-inch steaks — utilize the central section since it is bigger and reserve the remainder for another time. Season the steaks with salt and pepper after rubbing the paprika and 12 tablespoon oils into them. Place on a baking sheet and bake for 15-20 minutes, or until the chicken is cooked through.

2. In the meanwhile, prepare the salsa. Cut the pepper, olives, parsley, and capers and place them in a bowl with the leftover oil and vinegar. Toss to combine. Season with salt and pepper to taste. When the steaks are done, spoon the salsa over them and sprinkle with flaked almonds before serving.

136. Fennel, roast lemon & tomato salad

Total time: 40 minutes
Serving: 6
Nutrient per serving: Calories: 310, Fats: 20g, Carbohydrates: 50.1g, Proteins: 11g, Sodium: 8mg, Calcium: 6mg, Iron: 9.1mg
Ingredients:

- pinch of sugar
- 1/2 small pack of parsley leaves
- 1/2 small pack of mint leaves
- 2 lemons
- 2 tablespoon of extra virgin olive oil
- 100g pomegranate seeds
- 1/2 small pack of tarragon leaves
- 500g mixed tomatoes
- 3 fennel bulbs

Directions:

1. Preheat the oven to 200 degrees Celsius/180 degrees Celsius supporter 6 and line a baking dish with baking parchment. 1/4 cup sugar and 1/2 tablespoon oil should be drizzled over the lemon slices before spreading them out on a baking sheet. Roast for 20-25 minutes, or until the vegetables are wilted and caramelized in spots. Always keep an eye on them, as you may need to remove some from the cooker already when the others are finished baking. These can be prepared in the morning and stored at room temperature.

2. The tomatoes and fennel should be chopped coarsely while the limes are cooking, but you should save the fronds for garnishing. Combine the residual olive oil, the juice from another lemon, and the pomegranate seeds in a large mixing bowl. Season with salt and pepper to taste, then combine everything thoroughly.

3. Before serving, roughly chop all herbs and combine them with the cooked lemon slices and fennel fronds in the salad bowl, stirring well.

Chapter: 4 Plant Based Diet Dinner Options

If you believe that eating healthfully is monotonous, think again. Hundreds of strong-flavored food ideas for each meal of the day may be derived from this source. The only tools you would need to cook one of these easy, healthy plant diet dishes are a wood spoon, a pan, and some vegetables. Ingredients that are fresh Despite the fact that traditional stir-fry dishes call for higher-sodium ingredients, this dish is low in sodium. These Plant based meals are tasty and low in salt due to the use of natural ingredients. Have the pan out and start cooking. Start by preparing these delectable supper entrees, then sit back and enjoy them.

137. Portobello Burritos

Preparation time: 50 minutes
Cooking time: 40 minutes
Servings: 4
Ingredients:

- 3 large portobello mushrooms
- 2 medium potatoes
- 4 tortilla wraps
- 1 medium avocado, pitted, peeled, diced
- ¾ cup salsa
- 1 tablespoon cilantro
- ½ teaspoon salt
- ⅓ cup water
- 1 tablespoon lime juice
- 1 tablespoon minced garlic
- ¼ cup teriyaki sauce

Directions:

1. Preheat the oven to 400°F. Use olive oil to grease a sheet pan lightly (or line with parchment paper) and set it aside. Combine the water, lime juice, teriyaki, and garlic in a small bowl.
2. Slice the portobello mushrooms into thin slices and add these to the bowl. Allow the mushrooms to marinate thoroughly for up to three hours.
3. Cut the potatoes into large matchsticks, like French fries. Sprinkle the fries with salt, and then transfer them to the sheet pan.

4. Place the fries in the oven and bake them until crisped and golden, around 30 minutes. Flip once halfway through for even cooking.
5. Heat a large frying pan and add the marinated mushroom slices with the remaining marinade to the pan. Cook until the liquid has absorbed, around 10 minutes. Remove from heat.
6. Fill the tortillas with a heaping scoop of mushrooms and a handful of potato sticks. Top with salsa, sliced avocados, and cilantro before serving.
7. Serve immediately, enjoy, or store the tortillas, avocado, and mushrooms separately for later!

Per serving: Calories: 239kcal; Fat: 9.2g; Carbs: 34g; Protein: 5.1g

138. Plant-Strong Power Bowl

Preparation time: 25 minutes
Cooking time: 0 minutes
Servings: 4
Ingredients:

- 2 cups white or brown rice, cooked
- 1 (14 ounces) can of black beans, drained and rinsed
- 1 (14 ounces) can of chickpeas, drained and rinsed
- 4 cups spinach, chopped
- 1 cucumber, chopped
- Microgreens, for garnish
- Lemon parsley dressing

Directions:

1. Divide the rice evenly among 4 food storage containers, and then add ¼ cup of black beans, ¼ cup of chickpeas, 1 cup of spinach, and ¼ of chopped cucumber.
2. Garnish each container with a small handful of microgreens. Serve.

Per serving: Calories: 514kcal; Fat: 22g; Carbs: 70g; Protein: 14g

139. Millet Fritters

Preparation time: 5 minutes
Cooking time: 20 minutes
Servings: 4
Ingredients:

- 2 tablespoons coconut oil
- ⅓ cup psyllium husk
- ½ cup chickpea flour
- 1 cup millet
- ⅛ teaspoon mustard powder
- Pepper to taste
- ½ teaspoon onion powder
- ½ teaspoon paprika
- 1 teaspoon dried parsley
- ⅛ teaspoon coriander
- Salt to taste

Directions:

1. To start this recipe, cook your millet according to the directions on the package. Once this is cooked through, place the millet into a mixing bowl.
2. Next, add the flour, psyllium husk, and all the seasonings into your bowl and mix everything well.
3. Once a "dough" is formed, use your hands to create patties from the ingredients and set them on a plate to the side.
4. When you bake the fritters, take a medium skillet, and put it over medium heat. Add coconut oil and your first batch of fritters to the pan as it warms up.
5. You should grill the fritters for nearly five minutes on either side or up until the fritter is a nice, golden color and crunchy on the outer surface.
6. Finally, remove the dish from the stove and enjoy your creation!

Per serving: Calories: 410kcal; Fat: 15g; Carbs: 50g; Protein: 10g

140. Satay Tempeh with Cauliflower Rice

Preparation time: 60 minutes
Cooking time: 15 minutes
Servings: 4
Ingredients:

- ¼ cup water
- 4 tablespoons peanut butter
- 3 tablespoons low sodium soy sauce
- 2 tablespoons coconut sugar
- 1 garlic clove, minced
- ½ inch ginger, minced
- 2 teaspoons rice vinegar
- 1 teaspoon red pepper flakes
- 4 tablespoons olive oil
- 2 8-ounce packages of tempeh, drained
- 2 cups cauliflower rice
- 1 cup purple cabbage, diced
- 1 tablespoon sesame oil
- 1 teaspoon agave nectar

Directions:

1. Combine the sauce fixings in a large bowl, and then whisk until the mixture is smooth and any lumps have dissolved.
2. Cut the tempeh into ½-inch cubes and put them into the sauce, stirring to ensure the cubes get coated thoroughly.
3. Put the bowl in your fridge to marinate the tempeh for up to 3 hours. Before the tempeh is done marinating, preheat the oven to 400°F.
4. Spread the tempeh in one layer on a baking sheet lined with parchment paper or lightly greased with olive oil. Bake the marinated cubes until browned and crisp — about 15 minutes.
5. Heat the cauliflower rice in a saucepan with 2 tablespoons of olive oil over medium heat until it is warm. Rinse the large bowl with water, mixing the cabbage, sesame oil, and agave.
6. Serve a scoop of the cauliflower rice topped with the marinated cabbage and cooked tempeh on a plate, and enjoy, or store for later.

Per serving: Calories: 531kcal; Fat: 33g; Carbs: 31.7g; Protein: 27.6g

141. Freekeh Bowl with Dried Figs

Preparation time: 15 minutes
Cooking time: 35 minutes

Servings: 2
Ingredients:

- ½ cup freekeh, soaked for 30 minutes, drained
- 1 ⅓ cups almond milk
- ¼ teaspoon sea salt
- ¼ teaspoon ground cloves
- ¼ teaspoon ground cinnamon
- 4 tablespoons agave syrup
- 2 ounces dried figs, chopped

Directions:

1. Place the freekeh, milk, sea salt, ground cloves, and cinnamon in a saucepan.
2. Bring to a boil over medium-high heat.
3. Immediately turn the heat to a simmer for 30 to 35 minutes, occasionally stirring to promote even cooking.
4. Stir in the agave syrup and figs. Ladle the porridge into individual bowls and serve. Bon appétit!

Per serving: Calories: 458kcal; Fat: 6.8g; Carbs: 90g; Protein: 12.4g

142. Lentil Vegetable Loaf

Preparation time: 15 minutes
Cooking time: 55 minutes
Servings: 4
Ingredients:

- 2 cups cooked lentils, drained well
- 1 tablespoon olive oil
- 1 small onion, diced
- 1 carrot, finely diced
- 1 stalk celery, diced
- 1 x 8 ounces package of white or button mushrooms, cleaned and diced
- 3 tablespoons tomato paste
- 2 tablespoons soy sauce
- 1 tablespoon balsamic vinegar
- 1 cup old-fashioned oats, uncooked
- ½ cup almond meal
- 1 ½ teaspoon dried oregano
- ⅓ cup ketchup
- 1 teaspoon balsamic vinegar
- 1 teaspoon Dijon mustard

Directions:

1. Warm your oven to 400°F and grease a 5 x 7-inch loaf tin, then pop it to one side. Add olive oil to a skillet and pop over medium heat.
2. Add the onion and cook for 5 minutes until soft.
3. Grab your food processor and add the lentils, tomato paste, soy sauce, vinegar, oats, almond, and oregano. Whizz well until combined, then transfer to a medium bowl.
4. Pop the veggies into the food processor and pulse until combined. Transfer to the bowl. Stir everything together.
5. Move the mixture into the loaf pan, press down, and pop it into the oven. Cook for 35 minutes, add the topping, and then bake for another 15 minutes. Remove from the oven and allow about 10 minutes to cool.

Per serving: Calories: 226kcal; Fat: 6g; Carbs: 25g; Protein: 12g

143. Chard Wraps with Millet

Preparation time: 25 minutes
Cooking time: 0 minute
Servings: 4
Ingredients:

- 1 carrot, cut into ribbons
- ½ cup millet, cooked
- ½ large cucumber, cut into ribbons
- ½ cup chickpeas, cooked
- 1 cup sliced cabbage
- ⅓ cup hummus
- Mint leaves, as needed for topping
- Hemp seeds, as needed for topping
- 1 bunch Swiss rainbow chard

Directions:

1. Spread hummus on one side of the chard, place some of the millet, vegetables, and chickpeas on it, sprinkle with some mint leaves and hemp seeds, and wrap it like a burrito. Serve straight away.

Per serving: Calories: 152kcal; Fat: 4.5g; Carbs: 25g; Protein: 3.5g

144. Stuffed Indian Eggplant

Preparation time: 90 minutes
Cooking time: 1 hour and 10 minutes
Servings: 5
Ingredients:

- ½ cup dry black beans
- 6 medium eggplants, peeled
- 3 large Roma tomatoes, diced
- 1 large purple onion, chopped
- 1 large yellow bell pepper, chopped
- 2 cups raw spinach
- 2 tablespoons olive oil
- 2 cloves garlic, minced
- 1 tablespoon tomato paste
- 1 teaspoon coconut sugar
- 1 teaspoon cumin
- 1 teaspoon turmeric
- Salt and pepper, to taste
- 2 Tablespoons thyme, chopped

Directions:

1. Preheat the oven to 400°F. Line a parchment paper on a large baking sheet and set it aside. Cut the peeled eggplants across the top from one side to the other, careful not to slice all the way through.
2. Sprinkle the inside of the cut eggplants with salt and wrap them in a paper towel to drain the excess water. It could take up to 30 minutes.
3. Bake the eggplants in the oven for 15 minutes. Then, remove the baking sheet from the oven and set it aside.
4. Heat 1 tablespoon olive oil in a large skillet. Add the chopped onions and sauté until soft, around 5 minutes.
5. Stir frequently, adding the bell peppers and garlic. Cook the fixings until the onions are translucent and the peppers are tender, for about 15 minutes.
6. Season the spinach with sugar, cumin, turmeric, salt, and pepper. Stir everything well to coat the ingredients evenly; then mix in the tomatoes, black beans, spinach, and tomato paste.
7. Heat everything for about 5 minutes, remove the skillet from the heat and set it aside.
8. Stuff the eggplants with heaping scoops of the vegetable mixture. Sprinkle more salt and pepper to taste on top.
9. Drizzle the remaining 1 Tablespoons of olive oil across the eggplants, return them to the oven, and bake until they shrivel and flatten — for 20–30 minutes.
10. Serve the eggplants and garnish with the optional fresh thyme if desired. Enjoy it right away, or store it to enjoy later!

Per serving: Calories: 145kcal; Fat: 6g; Carbs: 18.3g; Protein: 4.4g

145. Sweet Potato Quesadillas

Preparation time: 15 minutes
Cooking time: 1 hour and 9 minutes
Servings: 3
Ingredients:

- 1 cup dry black beans
- ½ cup dry rice of choice
- 1 large sweet potato, peeled and diced
- ½ cup salsa
- 3-6 tortilla wraps
- 1 tablespoon olive oil
- ½ teaspoon garlic powder
- ½ teaspoon onion powder
- ½ teaspoon paprika

Directions:

1. Preheat the oven to 350°F. Line a baking pan with parchment paper. Drizzle olive oil on the sweet potato cubes. Transfer the cubes to the baking pan. Bake the potatoes in the oven until tender, for around 1 hour.
2. Allow about 5 minutes for the potatoes to cool, and then add them to a large mixing bowl with the salsa and cooked rice. Use a fork to mash the fixings into a thoroughly combined mixture.
3. Heat a saucepan over medium-high heat and add the potato/rice mixture, cooked black beans, and spices to the pan. Cook

everything for about 5 minutes or until it is heated through.

4. Take another frying pan and put it over medium-low heat. Place a tortilla in the pan and fill half with a heaping scoop of the potato, bean, and rice mixture.
5. Fold the tortilla halfway to cover the filling and cook until both sides are browned — about 4 minutes per side. Serve the tortillas with some additional salsa on the side.

Per serving: Calories: 329kcal; Fat: 7.5g; Carbs: 54.8g; Protein: 10.6g

146. Vegan Curried Rice

Preparation time: 5 minutes
Cooking time: 25 minutes
Servings: 4
Ingredients:

- 1 cup white rice
- 1 tablespoon minced garlic
- 1 tablespoon ground curry powder
- ⅓ teaspoon ground black pepper
- 1 tablespoon red chili powder
- 1 tablespoon ground cumin
- 2 tablespoons olive oil
- 1 tablespoon soy sauce
- 1 cup vegetable broth

Directions:

1. Put oil in a saucepan over low heat, and when hot, add garlic and cook for 3 minutes.
2. Then stir in all spices, cook for 1 minute until fragrant, pour in the broth, and switch heat to a high level.
3. Stir in soy sauce, bring the mixture to boil, add rice, stir until mixed, switch heat to the low level, and simmer for 20 minutes until rice is tender and all the liquid has been absorbed. Serve straight away.

Per serving: Calories: 262kcal; Fat: 8g; Carbs: 43g; Protein: 5g

147. Cauliflower and Potato Curry

"**Preparation time:** 10 minutes"
"**Cooking time:** 27 minutes"
"**Servings:** 4"
"**Ingredients:**"

- "1 medium yellow onion, peeled and diced"
- "Water, as needed"
- "2 cloves garlic, peeled and minced"
- "1 tablespoon grated ginger"
- "½ jalapeño pepper, deseeded and minced"
- "1 medium head cauliflower, cut into florets"
- "2 medium tomatoes, diced"
- "1-pound (454 g) Yukon Gold potatoes, cut into ½-inch dices"
- "1 teaspoon ground coriander"
- "1 teaspoon ground cumin"
- "1 teaspoon crushed red pepper flakes"
- "½ teaspoon turmeric"
- "¼ teaspoon ground cloves"
- "2 bay leaves"
- "1 cup green peas"
- "¼ cup chopped cilantro or mint, for garnish"

Directions:

1. Sauté the onion in a big container at low to moderate flame for seven to eight mins, mixing rarely. "Add water, 1 to 3 Tablespoons at a time, to keep it from sticking to the pan."
2. "Stir in the garlic, ginger, and jalapeño pepper, and sauté for 3 minutes."
3. Include the cauliflower, tomatoes, potatoes, coriander, cumin, crushed red pepper flakes, turmeric, cloves, and bay leaves, and mix to associate — protect and cook for twelve to fifteen mins, or till the vegetables are tender.
4. "Mix in the peas and cook for an additional 5 minutes."
5. "Remove the bay leaves and sprinkle the chopped cilantro on top for garnish. Serve immediately."

Per serving: Calories: 175kcal; Fat: 0.9g; Carbs: 34.9g; Protein: 6.7g

148. Grilled Eggplant Steaks

"**Preparation time:** 15 minutes"
"**Cooking time:** 10 minutes"
"**Servings:** 4"
"**Ingredients:**"

- "4 Roma tomatoes, diced"
- "8 ounces cashew cream"
- "2 eggplants"
- "1 tablespoon olive oil"
- "1 cup parsley, chopped"
- "1 cucumber, diced"
- "Salt and pepper to taste"

"**Directions:**"

1. Slice the eggplants into three thick steaks, drizzle with oil, and season with salt and pepper. "Grill in a pan for 4 minutes per side. Top with the remaining ingredients. Serve and enjoy!"

Per serving: Calories: 86kcal; Fat: 7g; Carbs: 12g; Protein: 8g

149. Broccoli and Rice Stir Fry

"**Preparation time:** 5 minutes"
"**Cooking time:** 10 minutes"
"**Servings:** 8"
"**Ingredients:**"

- "16 ounces frozen broccoli florets, thawed"
- "3 green onions, diced"
- "½ teaspoon salt"
- "¼ teaspoon ground black pepper"
- "2 tablespoons soy sauce"
- "1 tablespoon olive oil"
- "1 ½ cup white rice, cooked"

"**Directions:**"

1. "Take a skillet pan, place it over medium heat, add broccoli, and cook for 5 minutes until tender-crisp."
2. Include the scallion as well as the remaining components, swirl till well combined, and cook for two mins until hot. Offer as soon as possible.

Per serving: Calories: 187kcal; Fat: 3.4g; Carbs: 33g; Protein: 6.3g

150. Grilled Veggie Kabobs

"**Preparation time:** 15 minutes"
"**Cooking time:** 12 to 15 minutes"
"**Servings:** 6"
"**Ingredients:**"
"Marinade:"

- "½ cup balsamic vinegar"
- "1½ tablespoons minced thyme"
- "1½ tablespoons minced rosemary"
- "3 cloves garlic, peeled and minced"
- "Sea salt, to taste (optional)"
- "Freshly ground black pepper, to taste"

"Veggies:"

- "2 cups cherry tomatoes"
- "1 red bell pepper should be seeded and cut into 1-inch pieces"
- "1 green bell pepper, without seeds and cut into 1-inch pieces"
- "1 medium yellow squash, cut into 1-inch rounds"
- "1 medium zucchini, cut into 1-inch rounds"
- "1 medium red onion, skinned and cut into large chunks"

"Special Equipment:"

- "12 bamboo skewers, make sure to soak them in water for 30 minutes"

"**Directions:**"

1. "Preheat the grill to medium heat."
2. In making the marinade: In a small container, stir together the balsamic vinegar, thyme, rosemary, garlic, salt (if desired), and pepper.
3. Thread the veggies onto skewers, alternating between different-colored veggies.
4. Grill the veggies for 12 to 15 minutes until softened and lightly charred; brush the veggies with the marinade, flipping the skewers every 4 to 5 mins.
5. "Remove from the grill and serve hot."

"**Per serving:** Calories: 98kcal; Fat: 0.7g; Carbs: 19.2g; Protein: 3.8g"

151. Grilled Cauliflower Steaks

"**Preparation time:** 10 minutes"
"**Cooking time:** 57 minutes"
"**Servings:** 4"
"**Ingredients:**"

- "2 medium heads of cauliflower"
- "2 medium shallots, peeled and minced"
- "Water, as needed"
- "1 clove of garlic, peeled and minced"
- "½ teaspoon ground fennel"
- "½ teaspoon minced sage"
- "½ teaspoon crushed red pepper flakes"
- "½ cup green lentils, rinsed"
- "2 cups low-sodium vegetable broth"
- "Salt, to taste (optional)"
- "Freshly ground black pepper, to taste"
- "Chopped parsley for garnish"

"**Directions:**"

1. Cut each of the cauliflower heads in half through the stem on a flat work surface, then trim each half, so you get a 1-inch-thick steak.
2. Arrange each piece on a baking sheet and set it aside. "You can reserve the extra cauliflower florets for other uses."
3. Sauté the shallots in a medium saucepan over medium heat for 10 minutes, stirring occasionally. "Add water, 1 to 3 Tablespoons at a time, to keep the shallots from sticking."
4. "Stir in the garlic, fennel, sage, red pepper flakes, and lentils, and cook for 3 minutes."
5. "Pour into the vegetable broth and bring to a boil over high heat."
6. Reduce the heat to medium, cover, and cook for 45 to 50 minutes, or until the lentils are very soft, adding more water as needed.
7. Using an immersion blender, purée the mixture until smooth. "Sprinkle with salt (if desired) and pepper. Keep warm and set aside."
8. "Preheat the grill to medium heat."
9. "Grill the cauliflower steaks for about 7 minutes per side until evenly browned."
10. Transfer the cauliflower steaks to a plate and spoon the purée over them. Serve garnished with parsley.

Per serving: Calories: 105kcal; Fat: 1.1g; Carbs: 18.3g; Protein: 5.4g

152. Vegetable Hash with White Beans

"**Preparation time:** 15 minutes"
"**Cooking time:** 23 minutes"
"**Servings:** 4"
"**Ingredients:**"

- "1 leek (white part only), finely chopped"
- "1 red bell pepper, deseeded and diced"
- "Water, as needed"
- "2 teaspoons minced rosemary"
- "3 cloves garlic, peeled and minced"
- "1 medium sweet potato, peeled and diced"
- "1 large turnip, peeled and diced"
- "2 cups of cooked white beans or 1 (15 ounces/425 grams) can drain and rinse"
- "Zest and juice of 1 orange"
- "1 cup chopped kale"
- "Salt, to taste (optional)"
- "Freshly ground black pepper, to taste"

Directions:

1. Put the leek and red pepper in a large saucepan over medium heat and sauté for 8 minutes, stirring occasionally. "Add water, 1 to 3 Tablespoons at a time, to keep them from sticking to the bottom of the pan."
2. "Stir in the rosemary and garlic, and sauté for 1 minute more."
3. Add the sweet potato, turnip, beans, orange juice, and zest, and stir well — heat until the vegetables are softened.
4. Add the kale and sprinkle with salt (if desired) and pepper. "Cook for about 5 minutes or more until the kale is wilted."
5. Serve on a plate.

Per serving: Calories: 245kcal; Fat: 0.6g; Carbs: 48.0g; Protein: 11.9g

153. Broccoli Casserole with Beans and Walnuts

"**Preparation time:** 10 minutes"
"**Cooking time:** 35–40 minutes"
"**Servings:** 4"
"**Ingredients:**"
- "¾ cup vegetable broth"
- "2 broccoli heads, crowns, and stalks finely chopped"
- "1 teaspoon salt (optional)"
- "2 cups cooked pinto or navy beans"
- "1 to 2 Tablespoons brown rice flour or arrowroot flour"

154. Best Buddha Bowl

Total time: 1 hour
Serving: 4
Nutrient per serving: Calories: 519, Fats: 52g, Carbohydrates: 51g, Proteins: 3g, Sodium: 43mg, Calcium: 30mg, Iron: 2mg
Ingredients:
- 2 cups of brown rice, cooked
- Microgreens
- Sea salt
- 8 kale leaves
- freshly cracked black pepper
- 1 large, sweet potato
- Extra-virgin olive oil
- 2 tablespoons of sesame seeds or hemp seeds
- Turmeric Tahini Sauce
- 1 watermelon radish
- 2 medium carrots
- 1 cup of cooked lentils or cooked chickpeas
- ¾ cup of fermented veggie or sauerkraut
- 1 cup of shredded red cabbage
- 1 teaspoon of lemon juice

Directions:
1. Preheat oven to 400 ° degrees Fahrenheit and line a huge pan with parchment paper to prevent sticking.
2. Prepare a baking sheet by tossing the potatoes with canola oil, sodium, and pepper and spreading them out evenly.

Twenty minutes, or until the top is golden brown, should suffice.
3. Use a mandoline to thinly slice the radish into rounds and a carrot peeler to peel the carrots into bows before combining them.
4. A squeeze of lemon should be squeezed over the daikon slices, vegetables, and shredded cabbage. Make a mental note to put it aside.
5. Put the cabbage leaves in a bowl and mix and throw with a pinch of sugar and just a few squeezes of lemon to combine the ingredients. Massage the leaves with your hands until they are soft and wilted and the amount of liquid in the bowl has decreased by about half.
6. Fill each serving bowl with rice, split peas, kale, veggies, cucumbers, cabbage, sweet potatoes, and sauerkraut. Top with sesame seeds and micro greens if you'd like to include them. Season with salt and serve with the Tamanu Tahini Sauce as a dipping condiment.

155. Kimchi Brown Rice Bliss Bowls

Total time: 40 minutes
Serving: 2
Nutrient per serving: Calories: 140, Fats: 41g, Carbohydrates: 90g, Proteins: 12g, Sodium: 7.1mg, Calcium: 10mg, Iron: 5.5mg
Ingredients:
- ½ avocado
- 8 ounces of Marinated Tempeh
- ½ recipe of Peanut Sauce
- Lime slices
- Microgreens (optional)
- 1 cup of cooked brown rice
- Heaping ¼ cup of kimchi
- ½ teaspoon of sesame seeds
- 2 Thai chiles
- 1 Persian cucumber
- ½ cup of thinly sliced red cabbage

Directions:
1. Assemble the bowls by layering the rice, cabbage, cucumber, kimchi, avocado, and tempeh on top of the ingredients.

2. Using a liberal quantity of peanut sauce, drizzle it over the topping and garnish with sesame and Thai chilies if using. Serve with lime wedges and the leftover peanuts sauce to complete the meal. Depending on your preference, garnish with microgreens.

156. Adzuki Bean Bowls

Total time: 50 minutes
Serving: 4
Nutrient per serving: Calories: 370, Fats: 24g, Carbohydrates: 52g, Proteins: 1.2g, Sodium: 26mg, Calcium: 14mg, Iron: 3mg
Ingredients:
- 1 cup of sugar snap peas
- 2 tablespoons of sesame seeds
- 1 cup of cooked brown rice
- 2 avocados
- 1 small fresh red chili
- 1/2 large Napa of cabbage head
- 3 small carrots
- 2 tablespoons chopped fresh cilantro leaves
- 1 1/2 cups of cooked adzuki beans

Directions:
1. Prepare the salad dressing. In a small mixing bowl, mix the rice, miso, vinegar, tamari, olive oil, and sesame seeds until well combined and smooth.
2. Using a large mixing bowl, combine the carrots, cabbage, sesame oil, and snap peas with ¼ cup of the sauce. Serve immediately.
3. Just before serving, mix the cilantro into the cabbage salad until it is evenly distributed. Make four separate serving dishes and divide the cabbage, salad, rice, beans, and avocados evenly among them. More dressing may be drizzled on top if desired, and more coriander and sesame seeds can be sprinkled on top for extra flavor if wanted.

157. Roasted Veggie Grain Bowl

Total time: 45 minutes
Serving: 4
Nutrient per serving: Calories: 320, Fats: 24g, Carbohydrates: 50g, Proteins: 24g, Sodium: 20mg, Calcium: 12mg, Iron: 30mg
Ingredients:
- ¼ cup of fresh lemon juice
- ½ teaspoon of sea salt
- ½ cup of water
- ½ teaspoon of maple syrup or honey
- ½ cup of pepitas
- 2 small cloves of garlic
- freshly ground black pepper
- ½ cup of extra-virgin olive oil
- 1 packed cup of chopped kale
- 1 packed cup of cilantro
- 1 cup of raw quinoa
- 1¾ cups of water

Directions:
1. Using parchment paper, line two baking pans with parchment paper and cook the chicken to 425°F.
2. To begin, prepare the quinoa. In a medium-sized saucepan, combine the washed quinoa and water. It should be brought to a boil before being covered and simmered for around 15 minutes. Remove the pan from the oven and let it aside for another 10 minutes, covered. Using a fork, fluff the mixture. This recipe will yield 2 to 3 cups.
3. After that, prepare the sauce. Blend the garlic, spinach, pepitas cilantro, lemon juice, pepper, sea salt, water, olive oil, and syrup or honey until smooth in a blender until well combined and blended.
4. The vegetables should then be roasted. A big baking sheet can hold the parsnips, Cauliflower, and cabbage all at the same time. Place the sauteed greens on the other baking sheet and bake for another 15 minutes. Pour olive oil and seasonings over the veggies, tossing to coat thoroughly, then spread out on the baking

trays in an equal layer to bake. Bake the parsnips/brussels sprouts/cauliflower for 20 to 25 minutes, or until they are lightly browned around the edges until they are golden brown. 10-12 minutes, or until the broccolini is soft, roast the broccolini. When the broccolini stems are cold to the touch, cut them up.

5. Assemble the plates with a spoonful of quinoa, the grilled veggies, approximately 14 cups chickpeas, a scoop of sauerkraut, and a sprinkle of pepitas on top, and serve immediately. Drizzle the sauce over the top. Season with extra salt and pepper to taste, if needed, and then serve the dish. I divided the ingredients into a medium bowl and kept the leftovers for tomorrow's meal - stay tuned for further details!

6. Refrigerate any leftover sauce, quinoa, and chickpeas that haven't been used up.

158. Cauliflower Rice Kimchi Bowls

Total time: 1 hour
Serving: 4
Nutrient per serving: Calories: 550, Fats: 22g, Carbohydrates: 40g, Proteins: 12g, Sodium: 9.3mg, Calcium: 10mg, Iron: 2mg
Ingredients:

- 6 leaves curly kale
- 14 ounces of baked tofu
- 1 avocado
- Sea salt
- Lime slices
- 1 small head of cauliflower
- ½ cup of chopped scallions
- Sprinkle of sesame seeds
- Extra-virgin olive oil
- ½ clove of garlic
- 7 ounces shiitake mushrooms
- ½ cup of kimchi
- ¼ cup of microgreens
- ½ teaspoon of rice vinegar
- ½ teaspoon of tamari

Directions:

1. Prepare the coconut sauce by whisking together all the coconut milk, lime juice or rice wine vinegar, ginger, miso paste and pepper in a small mixing bowl until smooth. Make a mental note to put it away.

2. A splash of olive oil is heated in a wide nonstick pan over low heat until hot. Cook, stirring regularly, for 3 minutes, just long enough to cook out the raw taste of the cauliflower. Add the mid-engine cauliflower, onions, ginger, and a few teaspoons of salt. Remove the remove from heat and mix in 1/12 of the mango sauce until well combined. Divide the cauliflower florets into four serving dishes.

3. Remove any residual cauliflower parts from the pan with a paper towel. With a couple of drops of olive oil, bring the pan back up to medium heat. Cook, turning periodically, until the mushrooms are soft, approximately 5 minutes, adding a few teaspoons of salt as needed. Remove the pan from the heat and mix in the rice wine vinegar and tamari until well combined. Place the mushrooms in the cauliflower dishes and mix well.

4. Remove the kale from the pan and cook it over medium-high heat, uncovered, for 1 minute, or until it is mildly wilted. Remove the skillet from the heat and set it aside.

5. Finalize the bowls by spreading additional mango sauce over the cauliflower portions in each dish. To assemble the bowls, combine the tofu, avocado, kale, and kimchi, along with the hydroponics and tahini, if desired. Serve with any leftover sauce and lime wedges on the side to complete the dish.

159. Macro Veggie Bowl

Total time: 40 minutes
Serving: 4
Nutrient per serving: Calories: 430, Fats: 23g, Carbohydrates: 20g, Proteins: 21g, Sodium: 12mg, Calcium: 8mg, Iron: 10mg

Ingredients:

- 1 small head of broccoli florets
- 1 cup of microgreens
- Pinch of Sea salt
- Pinch of freshly cracked black pepper
- 1 watermelon radish
- squeeze of lemon juice
- ¾ cup of sauerkraut
- 2 tablespoons of sesame seeds
- 1 uncooked cup of sprouted mung beans
- 3 medium steamed carrots
- 8 kale leaves
- 2 cups of brown rice

Directions:

1. Make the sauce in a separate bowl. Prepare the dressing by combining the tahini, olive oil, lemon juice, water (if using), garlic, turmeric, and a large pinch of salt and pepper in a small mixing bowl. Make a mental note to put it away.
2. Toss the radish slices with a splash of lemon once they have been thinly sliced. Make a mental note to put it away.
3. Boil the mung beans in salted boiling water according to the package guidelines or until they are cooked for about 20 minutes. Drain.
4. Cook the carrots, covered, in a crockpot over a saucepan of boiling water for 7 to 10 minutes, or until they are just barely soft. Remove the item and place it away. After that, steam the broccoli for 4 to 5 minutes, or until it is soft but still brilliant green. Finally, steam the kale for 15 to 30 seconds, or until it is barely soft.
5. Preparing the brown rice and mung beans is the first step. Then you may add the vegetables like carrots and broccoli. Then you can add the sauerkraut and

microgreen if you like. Add salt and pepper, then serve with the Curcumin Tahini Sauce as a dipping condiment.

160. Best Veggie Burger

Total time: 40 minutes
Serving: 8
Nutrient per serving: Calories: 110, Fats: 13g, Carbohydrates: 51.1g, Proteins: 21g, Sodium: 1.8mg, Calcium: 0mg, Iron: 51mg

Ingredients:

- 1 tablespoon of mirin,
- 2 cloves of garlic
- ½ teaspoon of smoked paprika
- 2 teaspoons of sriracha
- Hamburger buns
- Pinch of Sea salt
- Pinch freshly ground black pepper
- 2 tablespoons of extra-virgin olive oil
- 2 shallots
- Vegan Worcestershire sauce
- Nonstick cooking spray
- 16 ounces of mushrooms
- 2 tablespoons of tamari
- 2 cups of cooked short-grain brown rice
- 1 cup of panko breadcrumbs, divided
- 2 tablespoons of balsamic vinegar
- 1 tablespoon of mirin
- ½ cup of chopped walnuts
- ¼ cup of ground flaxseed

Directions:

1. In a medium pan, heat the oil over medium heat until shimmering. Stir the shallot and cook for 1 minute or until it is tender. Add the garlic and a liberal teaspoon of salt to the pan and cook, occasionally stirring, until the mushrooms are soft and brown, 6 to 9 minutes. Reduce the heat if necessary.
2. Combine the soy, vinegar, and mirin in a large mixing bowl. Stir in the onion, smoked paprika, and jalapenos and cook until fragrant, about 2 minutes. Take the remove from heat and set it aside to cool a little.

3. Mix the sauteed mushrooms, nuts, flaxseed, basmati rice, and 12 cups of panko to make a crumble-like crumble in a stick blender. Pulse until the ingredients are barely blended. Pinching the mixture should result in its remaining together, but it should have some texture.

4. Transfer the mixture to a medium bowl and fold in the leftover panko until well combined.

5. Form the mixture into 8 patties and lay them on a big platter in the refrigerator for 1 hour to firm up.

6. If you're cooking the patties, prepare a grill to medium-high heat before you begin cooking them. Brush the burgers with canola oil and coat the skillet with cooking spray before grilling them on the grill. Put the steaks on the grill and softly push down with a spatula to ensure they are not sticking. Cook for 10 mins on the first side, then turn and grill for another 6 - 8 minutes on the bottom layer, or until the meat is well-charred and completely done.

7. Cooking the burgers on the stove is an alternative method. Using a cast-iron skillet, cook the ingredients over medium heat. Fry the burgers for 5 to 6 minutes on each side, or until they are well-charred and cooked through, in an oiled pan coated with cooking spray or olive oil.

8. When finished, remove from the pan and spray with Worcestershire sauce before serving with selected toppings.

161. Portobello Mushroom Burger

Total time: 18 minutes
Serving: 4
Nutrient per serving: Calories: 480, Fats: 65g, Carbohydrates: 18g, Proteins: 26g, Sodium: 4.1mg, Calcium: 2mg, Iron: omg
Ingredients:
- Balsamic vinegar
- Tamari
- Pinch of Sea salt
- Pinch of freshly ground black pepper
- 4 large portobello mushrooms
- Extra-virgin olive oil

Directions:
1. The mushrooms should be cleaned with a moist cloth or paper towel after they have been prepared by removing the stems. Using a wide-rimmed platter, arrange the mushrooms and sprinkle with salt, olive oil, tamari, balsamic vinegar, and pepper to taste. Make use of your hands to gently cover all sides of the mushrooms with the sauce.

2. Preheat a grill or barbecue pan on the stove until hot but not smoking. Place the mushrooms on the grill pan with the gills facing up. Cook the mushrooms for 5 - 6 minutes on each side, or until they are soft.

3. Put the mushrooms on top of the buns and top with the selected toppings to complete the meal.

162. Crispy Baked Falafel

Total time: 40 minutes
Serving: 4
Nutrient per serving: Calories: 170, Fats: 17g, Carbohydrates: 41.1g, Proteins: 65.1g, Sodium: 5.2mg, Calcium: 1mg, Iron: 7.8mg
Ingredients:
- 1 cup of fresh parsley leaves and stems
- 1 tablespoon of extra-virgin olive oil
- 1 cup of uncooked chickpeas dry
- ½ cup of chopped shallot
- ¼ teaspoon of baking powder
- 1 cup of chopped
- ½ cup of chopped shallot
- 3 cloves of garlic
- ¾ teaspoon of sea salt
- ¼ teaspoon of cayenne pepper
- 1 teaspoon of ground cumin
- 1 teaspoon of ground coriander

Directions:
1. Preheat oven to 400 ° degrees Fahrenheit and prepare a wide pan with parchment paper to prevent sticking.

2. Place the chickpeas, shallot, garlic, lemon zest, cinnamon, coriander, salt, cayenne pepper, baking powder, coriander, parsley, and olive oil in a large food processor and pulse until smooth. Pulse until everything is fully blended, but do not purée. Scrape the edges of the bowl with a spatula as often as necessary to ensure even cooking.

3. Using a 2-tablespoon scoop and your hands, shape the mixture into 12 to 15 thick patties, depending on your preference for them too tight. If they aren't sticking together after a few more cycles in the food processor, add a few more.

4. Put the patties on a baking sheet and bake for 20 minutes. To make them juicy and crispy since we're not frying them, gently drizzle them with olive oil and bake them for 14 minutes at 350°F. Turn the pan over and bake for another 10 to 12 minutes, or until the exterior is golden brown and crunchy. When baking the pita, cover it tightly in aluminum foil and place it in the oven to reheat.

5. Stack pitas with a smear of hummus, diced vegetables, falafel, spices, pickled red onions, and liberal splatters of tahini sauce on the side, if desired

163. Vegan Bacon

Total time: 45 minutes
Serving: 2
Nutrient per serving: Calories: 380, Fats: 30g, Carbohydrates: 62.1, Proteins: 13g, Sodium: 1mg, Calcium: 4.1mg, Iron: 2.1 mg
Ingredients:
- Heaping ½ teaspoon of smoked paprika
- Pinch of Freshly ground black pepper
- 8 ounces tempeh
- ¼ cup of tamari
- 1 tablespoon of extra-virgin olive oil
- ½ teaspoon of cumin

Directions:
1. Making tempeh bacon is simple: Preheat your oven to 425 degrees Fahrenheit, then line your pan with parchment paper. Put the cooked tofu in an 8x8 baking dish or a baking dish of equivalent size. In a small mixing bowl, mix all the miso, rice wine vinegar, syrup, olives, cumin, paprika, and a few grinds of pepper until well combined and smooth. Place the tempeh in a large mixing bowl and cover with the marinade. Cast aside for fifteen min. Bake for 8 - 10 mins, or until the tempeh strips are crisp and burnt around the edges, on a baking sheet lined with parchment paper. Remove from the oven and set aside for 10 minutes to cool on the pan. If desired, create "bacon bits" by crumbling the crisp tempeh into little pieces with your hands.

2. Preparing the mushroom bacon: Preheat the oven to 300°F and prepare a baking tray before starting. To clean the mushrooms, use a moist towel to wipe them down (if you wash them in water, they will not become crisp in the oven). Remove the stems and slices from the mushrooms and set them on a baking sheet with the olive oil and tamari, tossing to coat well. Spread the mushrooms in an equal layer on the baking sheet and bake for 30 to 40 minutes, stirring halfway through, or until the stems are wilted and crispy.

3. Preheat the oven to 350°F and prepare a baking tray before beginning to make the coconut bacon. Gently mix the cocoa flakes, tamari, syrup, and chili powder into the pan to cover them all with the sauce. Sprinkle evenly on the baking sheet and bake for 6 to 10 minutes, or until the topping is rich golden brown and somewhat crunchy. Keep an eye on everything since oven temperatures might fluctuate, and the chocolate flakes can burn rapidly.

164. Stuffed Acorn Squash

Total time: 40 minutes
Serving: 4
Nutrient per serving: Calories: 210, Fats: 31g, Carbohydrates: 42g, Proteins: 2g, Sodium: 5.8mg, Calcium: 3mg, Iron: 2.2mg

Ingredients:

- ⅓ cup of coarsely chopped walnuts
- 1 tablespoon of tamari
- Parsley and a few pomegranates arils
- Pinch of Sea salt
- Pinch of freshly ground black pepper
- 2 acorn squashes
- 1 package of tempeh
- ¼ cup of chopped sage
- ⅓ cup of dried cranberries
- 1 tablespoon of extra-virgin olive oil
- ½ yellow onion
- 1 tablespoon of apple cider vinegar
- ½ tablespoon of chopped rosemary
- 8 ounces of cremini mushrooms
- 3 cloves of garlic

Directions:

1. Preheat the oven to 425 degrees Fahrenheit and prepare a baking tray to prevent sticking. Scoop out the seed from the squash and throw them away. Put the squash halves on a baking sheet and sprinkle them with canola oil and a pinch of salt and pepper. Bake for 30 minutes. Roast for 40 minutes, cut side up, or until the vegetables are soft.

2. Preparation Time: Cut the tempeh into 12-inch pieces and put in a steamer basket placed over a saucepan covered with 1 inch of water while the squash roasts. Preparation Time: Bring water to a simmer in a large saucepan, cover it, and let it steam for ten min. Remove the tempeh from the water, drain any extra moisture, and crumble it with your hands.

3. In a large pan, heat the oil over medium heat until shimmering. Cook for 5 minutes, occasionally stirring, until the onion is translucent. Season with 12 teaspoon salts

as well as several pinches of black pepper. Cook the mushrooms, constantly stirring, for approximately 8 minutes, or until they are tender. Cook for another 2 to 3 minutes, constantly stirring, until the crumbled tofu, garlic, walnuts, soy, apple cider vinegar, thyme, and sage are well combined. If the pan becomes too dry, add 14 cups of water at a time. Season with salt and pepper to taste after stirring in the cranberries. Scoop the contents into the baked acorn pumpkin halves and top with the herbs and pomegranates to complete the presentation.

165. Twice Baked Sweet Potatoes

Total time: 1 hour 5 mins
Serving: 8
Nutrient per serving: Calories: 170, Fats: 24g, Carbohydrates: 71g, Proteins: 72g, Sodium: 5.8mg, Calcium: 10mg, Iron: 29 mg

Ingredients:

- ½ teaspoon of Dijon mustard
- 1 tablespoon of fresh lemon juice
- ⅓ cup of chopped scallion
- ½ cup of chopped parsley
- Pinch Sea salt
- Pinch of freshly ground black pepper
- 4 medium sweet potatoes
- 4 cups of small broccoli florets
- 1 cup of cheddar cheese
- ¼ cup of hemp seeds
- 1 teaspoon of extra-virgin olive oil
- 1 small garlic clove

Directions:

1. Preheat oven to 400 ° degrees Fahrenheit and prepare a baking tray to prevent sticking. Sweet potatoes should be pierced in many places with a fork before being placed on a baking pan to bake. Roasted for fifteen minutes, or until the vegetables are soft. To prepare the filling, cut the potatoes in halves and scoop off a tablespoon of mash from each side to create a place for it (12 cups total). This will be used in the Potato Cashew Cream.

2. To make the Potato Cashew Cream, follow these steps: Mix the milk, sweet potato mush, walnuts, lemon zest, garlic, rosemary, salt, and pepper in a rising blender and mix until smooth. Make a mental note to put it away.

3. Steam the broccoli for 5 minutes, or until it is crisp but still brilliant green, in a steamer set over boiling water.

4. In a medium-sized mixing bowl, whisk the olive oil, chopped garlic, mustard, lemon juice, and scallions until well combined. Toss in the steamed vegetables and a couple of teaspoons of salt and black pepper until everything is well-coated.

5. Then top with a scoop of cashew cream, some cheddar (if using), the cauliflower mixture, scallions and hemp seeds before baking for 30 minutes at 350°F (180°C). Remove from the oven and bake for an additional 10 minutes, or until the shredded cheddar cheese. Garnish with cilantro and culinary herbs and dish with the leftover cashew sauce for pouring on top if you want. Tip: If the cashews butter is too sticky to drizzle, thin it up with a little milk until it's a drizzle-worthy thickness).

166. Stuffed Poblano Peppers

Total time: 40 minutes
Serving: 8
Nutrient per serving: Calories: 150, Fats: 31g, Carbohydrates: 72g, Proteins: 28g, Sodium: 5.2mg, Calcium: 2mg, Iron: 9.5mg
Ingredients:
- 1/2 teaspoon of coriander
- ½ teaspoon of oregano
- Pinch of Sea salt
- Pinch of freshly ground black pepper
- Monterey Jack cheese
- 4 medium poblano peppers
- Extra-virgin olive oil
- 2 tablespoons of lime juice
- ¼ cup of tomatillo salsa
- 1/3 cup of diced red onion
- 1 heaping cup of cauliflower florets
- 1 cup of cooked white or brown rice
- 3 cups of fresh spinach
- 1/2 cup of diced bell pepper
- 1 garlic clove
- 1 cup of cooked black beans
- 1/2 teaspoon of cumin

Directions:
1. Preheat the oven to 400 ° degrees Fahrenheit and line a pan with parchment paper or pepper.

2. Deseed and ribs from the peppers by slicing them in half and removing the seeds. Place the vegetables on a baking pan, sprinkle with olive oil, and season with salt and pepper before roasting for 15 minutes. Cut side up.

3. 1 tablespoon of olive oil is heated in a large pan over medium heat until shimmering. Combine the onion, carrot, bell pepper, cinnamon, paprika, basil, garlic, 1 teaspoon, as well as several grinds of smoked paprika in a large mixing bowl until everything is well-combined. Cook for 5 to 8 minutes, or until the onion is tender and the broccoli is gently browned, depending on how big your cauliflower is.

4. Remove the pan from the heat and toss in the butter beans, rice, greens, lime juice, and tomatillo salsa until everything is well combined. Season with salt and pepper to taste.

5. Bake the peppers for 15 minutes after filling them with the filling.

6. Avocados slices, coriander, Verde salsa, salsa Verde cashew cream, and lime slices should be served on the side to complement the dish.

167. Spaghetti Squash w/ Chickpeas & Kale

Total time: 1 hour
Serving: 3
Nutrient per serving: Calories: 350, Fats: 29g, Carbohydrates: 21g, Proteins: 46g, Sodium: 2mg, Calcium: 10mg, Iron: 13mg
Ingredients:

- ½ tablespoon of minced fresh rosemary
- Pinch of chili flakes
- ½ cup of chickpeas
- Pinch of Sea salt
- Pinch of freshly ground black pepper
- Freshly grated Parmesan cheese
- 1 spaghetti squash
- 1 to 2 tablespoons of extra-virgin olive oil
- 1 shallot
- 1 whole garlic clove
- 2 cups of chopped kale leaves
- 1 tablespoon of lemon juice

Directions:

1. Preheat oven to 400 ° degrees Fahrenheit.
2. Cooking your squash according to the instructions in this article is recommended.
3. Add sufficient olive oil to gently cover the bottom of a large skillet, then add the onions, the entire garlic clove the rosemary, the chili flakes, and a sprinkle each of salt and pepper. Cook until the shallots are translucent, about 5 minutes.
4. Once the shallot has begun to soften, add the garbanzo and simmer for a few minutes, or until they are faintly golden brown. Serve immediately. When using roasted chickpeas, please put them in towards the end of the dish rather than at the beginning. Discard the garlic clove and toss in the greens and lemon juice until well combined.
5. Then, after the kale has begun to wilt, add the squash strips and just a little grated cheese and more salt and black pepper to taste. Toss well to combine. Toss in order to integrate. Remove from the pan and sprinkle with roasted pine nuts and more grated cheese, if desired.

168. Sesame Soba Noodles

Total time: 20 minutes
Serving: 4
Nutrient per serving: Calories: 200, Fats: 51g, Carbohydrates: 22.5g, Proteins: 81g, Sodium: 5.3mg, Calcium: 10mg, Iron: 4mg
Ingredients:

- 2 cups of blanched snap peas
- 1/4 cup of fresh mint leaves
- Sesame seeds
- 6 ounces of soba noodles
- Sesame oil
- ¼ cup of edamame
- 1 watermelon radish
- 2 avocados
- Squeezes of lemon

Directions:

1. Make the dressing by following these steps: In a small mixing bowl, whisk together the tamari, vinegar, sesame oil, ginger, honey, and garlic until well combined. Make a mental note to put it away.
2. Bring a saucepan of unsalted water to a boil, add the soba noodles, and cook according to the package instructions. Drain and thoroughly rinse with cold water. This aids in the removal of starches that contribute to clumping. Stir in the dressing until the noodles are well coated, then split into 2 to 4 serving dishes. Fresh lemon juice should be squeezed over the avocado slices before adding them to the bowls with the green beans, soybeans, radish, mint, and sesame seeds. Optional: Sprinkle with more miso or sesame oil if preferred.

169. Maki Sushi Recipe

Total time: 1 hour 20 minutes
Serving: 2
Nutrient per serving: Calories: 480, Fats: 24g, Carbohydrates: 55.2g, Proteins: 11.2g, Sodium: 62mg, Calcium: 20mg, Iron: 1.6mg
Ingredients:

- 1 teaspoon of extra-virgin olive oil
- 2 tablespoons of rice vinegar3 long thin strips of cucumber
- Tamari
- Pickled ginger
- 3 nori sheets
- 1 cup of thinly sliced red cabbage
- ½ avocado
- Sesame seeds
- 1 tablespoon of cane sugar
- 1 teaspoon of sea salt
- 1 cup of short grain brown rice
- 2 cups of fresh water

Directions:

1. The following steps are required to make the roasted shitake mushrooms: Preheat oven to 400°F and line two large baking sheets with parchment paper. Using your hands, coat the mushrooms mushroom with the canola oil and tamari until they are well coated. On a large baking sheet, spread the mixture in a uniform layer. Roasted for 25 minutes, or until the edges are browned and crisped. Fry the onions for the condiment on the second layer of parchment paper.
2. To make the carrots ginger dipping sauce, follow these steps: Mix all of the ingredients in a blender until they are smooth and creamy: roasted carrots, water, canola oil, rice wine vinegar, garlic, and salt. Cast aside the shitake mushrooms till you're ready to use them and chill till you're ready to use them.
3. Prepare the sushi rice as follows: In a pan over medium heat, bring the grains, milk, and olive oil to a boil while stirring constantly. Cover the pan with a lid and decrease the heat to low for 45 minutes. Take the rice from the heat and let it rest for another 10 minutes, covered. With a fork, fluff the rice and mix in the rice wine vinegar, honey, and salt until well combined. Cover with plastic wrap until prepared to use.
4. Make the maki rolls according to package directions. Because your fingers will get greasy while you work, have a little bowl of milk and a kitchen roll close by your work area. Placing one nori sheet on a bamboo mat with the shiny side facing up, push a scoop of rice into the bottom 25 of the sheet with your fingers. Your toppings should be stuck at the base of the rice (see picture). Don't overfill the container since it will make rolling more difficult. To fold and roll the nori, place it on the bamboo mat. Once the roll has been formed, use the reed mat to then and shape it. Put the rolls to the side with the sliced side facing up. Repeat the same with the remaining rolls.
5. To cut the sushi, use a chef's knife that is razor-sharp. Use a moist cloth to wipe the blade clean in between each cut.
6. Sesame seeds may be sprinkled on top. Prepare the sauce and tamari as requested, along with any pickled ginger you choose to include in the dish.

170. Radish Salad

Total time: 10 minutes
Serving: 6
Nutrient per serving: Calories: 200, Fats: 18g, Carbohydrates: 51, Proteins: 35g, Sodium: 2.9mg, Calcium: 11.0mg, Iron: 1.9mg
Ingredients:

- 1/4 cup of pine nuts
- 1 tbs of lemon juice
- Pinch of Sea salt
- Pinch of freshly ground black pepper
- 1 1/2 cups of cooked navy beans
- ¼ cup of Lemon Vinaigrette
- 1/4 cup of fresh mint leaves

- 2 tablespoons of shaved pecorino
- 9 roasted radishes
- 2-3 thinly sliced of red radishes
- 1 tablespoon of capers
- 1/4 cup of Radish Green Pesto

Directions:

1. Mix the legumes with 2 tablespoon of the Lemon zest in a medium-sized mixing dish
2. Arrange the salad on a tray, alternating the beans with roasted red peppers, sliced raw radishes, pecans, capers, and a dollop of pesto. Serve immediately.
3. To finish, drizzle with the remaining dressing and garnish with fresh basil and pecorino if desired. Season with additional salt and black pepper to taste and additional compresses of lemon, if preferred.

171. Kale Salad with Carrot Ginger Dressing

Total time: 40 minutes
Serving: 4
Nutrient per serving: Calories: 550, Fats: 37g, Carbohydrates: 20g, Proteins: 46g, Sodium: 15mg, Calcium: 0mg, Iron: 2.3mg
Ingredients:

- 1 small carrot
- 1 small red beet
- 1 teaspoon of sesame seeds
- Pinch of Sea salt
- Pinch of Freshly ground black pepper
- 1 batch of Roasted Chickpeas
- 1 bunch of curly kale
- 2 tablespoons of dried cranberries
- ¼ cup of pepitas, toasted
- 1 teaspoon of lemon juice
- ½ teaspoon of extra-virgin olive oil
- ½ watermelon radish
- 1 avocado

Directions:

1. Preparing the dressing and roasting the chickpeas is as follows: Preheat oven to 400 ° degrees Fahrenheit and prepare a large pan with parchment paper to prevent sticking. A sprinkle of olive oil, as well as salt and pepper, should be drizzled on top of the chickpeas before serving. To roast with the chickpeas, put the carrot slices for the sauce in their area of the baking sheet and roast them at the same time. Roast for 20 - 25 minutes, or when the beans are brown and crusty, and the carrot are tender, depending on how big your roasting pan is. Remove the roasted chickpeas from the pan. Transfer the carrot to a mixer and add water, olives, rice wine vinegar, garlic, and salt. Blend until the carrots are smooth and creamy. Mix the dressing until it is smooth and set it aside in the refrigerator until you are ready to use it.
2. Put the cabbage leaves in a large mixing bowl and toss with the lemon, 12 teaspoon canola oil, and just a few sprinkles of salt to taste. Massage the leaves with your hands until they are limp and wilted, and the amount of liquid in the dish has decreased by roughly half.
3. Toss in the carrots, beets, watermelon radish, 1⁄2 of the diced avocado, figs, pepitas, a few more generous pinches of salt, and a few grindings of pepper until everything is well distributed. Dress the salad with a large amount of carrot spice dressing. Finish with the leftover avocado, additional dressing, the roasted chickpeas, and a sprinkling of sesame seeds on the lettuce. Season with salt and pepper to taste, then serve.

172. Healthy Taco Salad

Total time: 25 minutes
Serving: 3
Nutrient per serving: Calories: 382, Fats: 19g, Carbohydrates: 48.9g, Proteins: 1.2g, Sodium: 9.8mg, Calcium: 10.1mg, Iron: 29mg
Ingredients:

- ½ cup of cooked black beans, drained and rinsed
- 2 red radishes
- Pinch of Sea salt
- Lime wedges

- 2 corn tortillas
- Extra-virgin olive oil
- Jalapeno slices
- Cilantro Lime Dressing
- 1 medium head romaine lettuce
- 1 cup of shredded red cabbage
- ½ cup of sliced cherry tomatoes
- 1 avocado

Directions:

1. Preheat oven to 400 ° degrees Fahrenheit and prepare a baking tray to prevent sticking. Mix the tortillas strips with a little drizzle of olive oil and a couple of pinches of salt until they are well coated. Spread the mixture onto a baking sheet and cook for 10–14 minutes, or until crispy and golden.

2. Create the Shiitake Taco "Meat" by following these steps: Heat the oil in a medium pan over medium heat until shimmering. Cook, stirring periodically for 3 to 4 minutes, or until the mushrooms start to darken and soften, depending on how big they are. Toss in the nuts and softly roast for 2 minutes, or until fragrant. Add in the vinegar and chili powder and mix well. Stir in the balsamic vinegar until well combined. After removing the skillet from the heat, season with salt to taste.

3. Gather all of your ingredients for the salad and toss them together with large globs of coriander lime avocado dressing. Top with spaghetti noodles, radishes, tomatoes, and jalapeno, if using, and serve immediately. Spray with canola oil and season with salt and pepper to taste. Garnish with lime slices and additional vinaigrette on the side to complete the presentation.

173. Butternut Squash Soup

Total time: 45 minutes
Serving: 6
Nutrient per serving: Calories: 443, Fats: 29g, Carbohydrates: 23g, Proteins: 11.9g, Sodium: 12.9mg, Calcium: 34g, Iron: 23.9mg
Ingredients:

- 3 garlic cloves
- 1 tablespoon of chopped fresh sage
- 3 to 4 cups of vegetable broth
- Pinch of Freshly ground black pepper
- 2 tablespoons of extra-virgin olive oil
- 1 large yellow onion
- ½ tablespoon of minced fresh rosemary
- 1 teaspoon of grated fresh ginger
- ½ teaspoon of sea salt
- 1 butternut squash

Directions:

1. In a large saucepan, heat the oil over medium heat until shimmering. Continue to cook until the onion is tender, 5 to 8 minutes, while adding salt as well as several pinches of fresh pepper as needed. Cook, stirring periodically, for 8 - 10 mins, or until the squash starts to soften, depending on how large your squash is.

2. Combine the onion, sage, thyme, and ginger in a large mixing bowl. After 15 to 30 seconds of stirring and cooking, put three cups of the stock and bring to a boil. Boil for a couple of minutes, then cover and decrease bring to a simmer. Cook for 20 to 30 minutes, or until the pumpkin is fork tender.

3. Allow the soup to cool somewhat before pouring it into a mixer, working in stages if necessary, and blending until completely smooth. You may add approximately 1 cup extra broth and mix if your stew is too thick to your liking. Season with salt and pepper to taste, then garnish with herbs and crusty bread.

174. Vegan Broccoli Soup

Total time: 50 minutes
Serving: 4
Nutrient per serving: Calories: 199, Fats: 23g, Carbohydrates: 98g, Proteins: 21.8g, Sodium: 2.1mg, Calcium: 20mg, Iron: 5.1mg
Ingredients:

- 3/4 teaspoon of sea salt
- Pinches of freshly ground black pepper
- 2 tablespoons of extra-virgin olive oil

- 1 small yellow onion
- ¼ cup of fresh dill
- 1 tablespoon of fresh lemon juice
- ½ cup of chopped celery
- ⅓ cup of chopped carrots
- 1½ teaspoons of apple cider vinegar
- 1/2 teaspoon of Dijon mustard
- 1 lb. broccoli
- 1 small Yukon of gold potato
- 3 cups of cubed bread
- ½ cup of raw cashews
- 4 garlic cloves
- 4 cups of vegetable broth

Directions:

1. Preheat the oven at 350 degrees Fahrenheit and prepare two small baking pans with parchment paper to prevent sticking.
2. In a large saucepan or Dutch oven, heat the oil over medium heat until shimmering. Add the onions, celery, carrot, broccoli stalks, salt, and pepper to the pan and cook until the vegetables are tender about 10 minutes. Stir in the potato and garlic until the potato is cooked, then add the water and boil for 20 minutes, or until the potatoes are completely soft. Allow for a brief cooling period.
3. To make the soup's topping, cast aside half a cup of the cauliflower florets to roast and use as a garnish. Place the leftover florets in a crockpot and lay them over a saucepan filled with one inch of water to steam them through. To steam, the broccoli, bring water to a boil, cover, and let it steam for 5 minutes, or until it's soft.
4. In the meanwhile, arrange the broccoli florets and baguette cubes on the oven sheets that have been set aside. Toss with a splash of olive oil and a bit of salt and roast for 10 to 15 minutes, or until the bread is crisp and the broccoli is soft and caramelized around the edges, depending on your preference.

5. Put the soup to a blender and process until smooth, adding the cashews, cider vinegar, and sriracha as needed. If necessary, work in batches to save time. In a food processor, pulse in batches until the broccoli is well-incorporated but still chunky, about 30 seconds. Remove from the processor and set aside. The soup should have a thick consistency; if it is too heavy, add ½ cup water to dilute it to the consistency you prefer.
6. Season with salt and pepper, then ladle the soup into bowls and garnish with the roast broccoli and croutons.

175. Best Lentil Soup

Total time: 45 minutes
Serving: 3
Nutrient per serving: Calories: 400, Fats: 48g, Carbohydrates: 35g, Proteins: 23g, Sodium: 1.2mg, Calcium: 30mg, Iron: 6.7mg
Ingredients:

- 1 can of fire roasted tomatoes
- 1 cup of dried French green lentils
- ½ cup of diced cilantro
- 2 tablespoons of fresh lime juice
- 1 medium onion
- ½ teaspoon of sea salt
- Pinch of Freshly ground black pepper
- 4 garlic cloves
- 3 tablespoons of minced ginger
- 2½ cups of water
- 1 can of full-fat coconut milk
- 1 tablespoon of mild curry powder
- ¼ teaspoon of crushed red pepper flakes

Directions:

1. In a large saucepan, heat the oil over medium heat until shimmering. Using a pinch of salt, sauté the onion for 8 to 10 minutes, occasionally stirring, until tender and gently browned around the edges. Reduce the heat to low as necessary.
2. Stir constantly for approximately 2 minutes, or until the garlic and ginger are fragrant. Reduce the heat to low and add

the curry powder and red pepper flakes, cooking until fragrant.

3. Cook for 30 minutes on low heat until the tomatoes, lentils, and water are tender. Add the coconut milk, 12 teaspoon peppers, as well as several pinches of black pepper. Bring to the boil, lid, and lower to low heat, stirring only periodically, for 25 to 35 minutes, or when the lentils are cooked, and the liquid has evaporated. If the soup is too dense, add 1/2 cup extra water to thin it out to the consistency you prefer.

4. Combine the parsley and lime juice in a large mixing bowl. Season with salt and pepper, and then plate and serve.

176. Easy Coconut Curry

Total time: 50 minutes
Serving: 4
Nutrient per serving: Calories: 210, Fats: 65g, Carbohydrates: 21g, Proteins: 44g, Sodium: 1.8mg, Calcium: 28mg, Iron: 42.1mg
Ingredients:
- ¼ teaspoon of turmeric
- ¼ teaspoon of cardamom
- ½ cup of fresh or frozen peas
- Pinch of Freshly ground black pepper
- 1 tablespoon of coconut oil
- 1 cup of chopped yellow onion
- 1 tablespoon of fresh lime juice
- 4 cups of fresh spinach
- 2 garlic cloves
- ½ teaspoon of grated fresh ginger
- 1 can of full-fat coconut milk
- 1 tablespoon of fresh lemon juice
- ½ teaspoon of cumin
- ¼ teaspoon of coriander
- 3 red Thai chiles
- 2 cups of cauliflower florets
- 1 teaspoon of sea salt
- 2 cups of cubed butternut squash

Directions:
1. In a big Dutch oven, heat the oil over medium heat until shimmering. Cook for approximately 10 minutes, occasionally

stirring, until the onion is tender and thoroughly browned, decreasing the heat to medium-low halfway through.

2. In a small mixing bowl, combine the onion, ginger, cinnamon, cilantro, turmeric, cayenne, and salt until well combined. Make a mental note to put it away.

3. Simmer for 5 minutes after adding the sweet potato and chilies to the saucepan, stirring constantly. Mix in the cauliflower until it is well coated, then add the coco milk and spice combination. Place a lid on the pot and cook for 20 minutes, or until the veggies are soft.

4. Stir in the lemon, lime juice, spinach, and peas until well combined. Taste and adjust spices, adding more lemon zest, salt, and pepper to taste if necessary, and serve immediately. If wanted, use fresh basil and naan bread and lime slices on the side, garnish the curry with fresh basil and serve.

177. Easy Vegetarian Chili

Total time: 45 minutes
Serving: 6
Nutrient per serving: Calories: 240, Fats: 35g, Carbohydrates: 29g, Proteins: 56.1g, Sodium: 11mg, Calcium: 34mg, Iron: 45mg
Ingredients:
- 1 cup of water or broth
- 3 chipotle peppers
- Pinch of Freshly ground black pepper
- 1 tablespoon of lime juice
- 1 tablespoons of extra-virgin olive oil
- 1 small yellow onion
- 1 cup of corn kernels
- ½ teaspoon of sea salt
- 2 garlic cloves
- 1 red bell pepper
- 1 can of red beans
- 1 can of pinto beans

Directions:
1. In a large saucepan, heat the oil over medium heat until shimmering. Stir in the onion and a couple of teaspoons of salt

and black pepper until everything is well-combined. Cook for 5 minutes, or when the onion is transparent, before adding the cloves and red pepper flakes. Cook, often stirring, until the vegetables are tender, 5 - 10 minutes, reducing the heat if necessary.

2. Combine the chipotles, beans, water, garlic, adobo sauce, maize, salt, and just a few pinches of pepper in a large saucepan. Bring the pot to a boil, then reduce the heat to low. Cover with a lid and decrease the heat to low; cook for 30 min, stirring periodically, until chili has thickened somewhat.

3. Season with salt and pepper to taste after stirring in the lime juice. Toss with preferred toppings before serving.

178. Tomato Basil Soup

Total time: 1 hour 30 minutes
Serving: 6
Nutrient per serving: Calories: 328, Fats: 46g, Carbohydrates: 53g, Proteins: 53g, Sodium: 39mg, Calcium: 0.6mg, Iron: 23mg
Ingredients:

- 2 cloves of garlic
- 3 cups of vegetable broth
- 1 loose-packed cup of basil leaves
- Pinch of Sea salt
- Pinch of freshly ground black pepper
- ¼ cup of extra-virgin olive oil
- 1 tablespoon of balsamic vinegar
- 1 teaspoon of thyme leaves
- 1 medium yellow onion
- ⅓ cup of chopped carrots

Directions:

1. Preheat the oven to 350 degrees Fahrenheit and prepare a wide pan with parchment paper to prevent sticking. Toss the tomatoes on a baking sheet with 2 tablespoon of the canola oil and add salt and pepper. Bake for 20 minutes, or until the tomatoes are soft. Preheat the oven to 350 degrees for 1 hour, or until the rims are just starting to fade, but the interiors are still juicy.

2. In a large saucepan, heat. Add 2 tablespoons of oil over medium heat until shimmering. Cook for 8 minutes, occasionally stirring, until the onions, carrots, pepper, and 12 teaspoon salts are tender. Cook for 20 minutes, occasionally stirring; after adding the tomatoes, bring vinegar and thyme leaves to a simmer.

3. Allow the soup to cool somewhat before transferring it to a mixer, working in stages if required. Blend until the mixture is smooth. Toss in the mint and pulse until everything is well combined.

4. Serve the soup with fresh basil leaves on top and crusty bread on the side.

179. Cream of Mushroom Soup

Total time: 40 minutes
Serving: 4
Nutrient per serving: Calories: 250, Fats: 31g, Carbohydrates: 59.9g, Proteins: 12g, Sodium: 23.1mg, Calcium: 15mg, Iron: 23mg
Ingredients:

- 2 large garlic cloves
- 1 tablespoon of balsamic vinegar
- Pinch of Sea salt
- Pinch freshly ground black pepper
- 2 tablespoons of extra-virgin olive oil
- 2 medium leeks
- 1 pound cauliflower
- 1 teaspoon of Dijon mustard
- 2 celery stalks
- 16 ounces of cremini mushrooms
- 2 tablespoons of fresh thyme leaves
- 4 cups of vegetable broth
- 2 tablespoons of tamari
- ¼ cup of dry white wine

Directions:

1. In a large saucepan, heat the oil over medium heat until shimmering. Cook for 5 minutes after adding the leeks, celery, and 14 teaspoon salts. Cook for another 8 to 10 minutes, or until the mushrooms are tender.

2. Simmer for 15 to 30 seconds, or until the soy, wine, onion, and thyme are

completely evaporated, after which removed from heat. Combine the broth and cauliflower in a large mixing bowl.

3. Cook the cauliflower, uncovered, for twenty minutes, or until it is very soft. Transfer the mixture to a blender and process until smooth, adding the Dijon and vinegar as needed. Season with salt and pepper to taste, then garnish with chosen garnishes.

180. Zucchini Verde Vegan Enchiladas

Total time: 35 minutes
Serving: 4
Nutrient per serving: Calories: 280, Fats: 23g, Carbohydrates: 42g, Proteins: 12g, Sodium: 2.9mg, Calcium: 1.4mg, Iron: 7.1mg
Ingredients:
- 1/2 teaspoon of freshly ground black pepper
- 1 cup of cooked black beans
- 1/2 jalapeno or serrano pepper
- 8 Lime slices
- 1 tablespoon of extra-virgin olive oil
- 1 small yellow onion
- 1/2 avocado
- 1/2 cup of chopped fresh cilantro
- 1 poblano pepper
- 1/2 teaspoon of sea salt
- 8 corn tortillas
- 1/4 cup of diced red onion
- 1 small zucchini
- 1/2 teaspoon of ground coriander
- 6 ounces of firm tofu
- 1 1/2 cups of tomatillo salsa
- 1/2 teaspoon of ground cumin
- 2 cloves of garlic

Directions:
1. Preheat oven to 400 ° degrees Fahrenheit.
2. To make the cashews lime sour cream, follow these steps: Put the cashews, water, ginger, lemon zest, and salt in an elevated blender and mix until completely smooth and creamy. Refrigerate until prepared to use.

3. Prepare the enchilada filling by heating the olive oil in a large pan over medium heat until hot. Cook for approximately 5 minutes, occasionally stirring, until the onions are tender. Add the poblano pepper and a touch of salt. Cook until the courgette, coriander, and cumin are gently browned, approximately 5 minutes longer. Remove from the heat and set aside.

4. Combine the cloves, salt, and peppercorns in a large mixing bowl. Transfer the mixture to a big mixing bowl when it has been removed from the heat. Combine the kidney beans and tofu in a large mixing bowl.

5. After lightly brushing a 9 x 13-inch baking sheet with olive oil, distribute an even 1 12 cup of tomato salsa across the bottom and sides of the pan. About 12 cups of the enchiladas filling should be used to fill each tortilla. To assemble the tortillas, roll them up and lay them in the oven dish seam-side down. Poured 1 cup chili over the enchiladas, dividing them along the center and leaving a little amount of space around the borders. I do this in order for the tortillas' edges to get a bit crispy while they cook. Bake for 15 minutes with the lid on. Remove the lid and bake for another 10 minutes.

6. Set aside to cool somewhat, and then sprinkle with 1/2 of the cashews lime sour cream if you want to go all out. Add the chopped red onion, radish, avocado, cilantro, and jalapenos, if desired, to the top of the salad. As a finishing touch, garnish with lime wedges and the leftover cashew cream.

181. Sushi Salad

Total time: 15 minutes
Serving: 4
Nutrient per serving: Calories: 180, Fats: 32g, Carbohydrates: 42.2g, Proteins: 15g, Sodium: 0.3mg, Calcium: 1.5mg, Iron: 4mg
Ingredients:

- 1 pinch of sea salt
- 1 pinch of black pepper
- 2 cups of frozen shelled edamame beans
- 4 cups of cooked brown rice
- 1 tablespoon of sesame seeds
- 4 nori seaweed sheets
- 4 Persian cucumbers
- 3 avocados
- 2 handfuls of baby spinach leaves
- 1 splash of extra-virgin olive oil

Directions:

1. Bring a small saucepan of saltwater to a boil, then add the edamame and cook until tender. Cook for 1-2 min, or until they're delicate yet still crispy, depending on how crunchy you want your vegetables. Drain the water and rinse it under cold water.
2. When you prepare the dressing, whisk it together until it has the texture of the cream. Whisk in the miso paste, olive oil, miso, sugar, and 1-2 teaspoons of water or when it is thoroughly blended. Add in the sesame and mix well.
3. Toss together the grains, soybeans, cucumbers, avocados, and baby spinach in a large mixing bowl until everything is well distributed. Place salad on a serving platter and drizzle with the soybean sauce and a little olive oil. Sprinkle with salt and pepper and garnish with the sesame and nori strips before serving.

182. Gingery Noodle Salad

Total time: 20 minutes
Serving: 4
Nutrient per serving: Calories: 130, Fats: 42g, Carbohydrates: 12.2g, Proteins: 0.5g, Sodium: 28mg, Calcium: 6.2mg, Iron: 29mg
Ingredients:

- 2 tablespoons of fresh lemon juice
- 2 tablespoons of dark sesame oi
- 1 pound of snow peas
- 8 ounces of whole wheat angel hair pasta, broken in half
- 2 tablespoons of sesame seeds
- 1 2-inch piece of fresh ginger
- 2 tablespoons of good-quality vegetable oil
- Pinch of Pepper
- 6 scallions
- 1/4 cup of soy sauce

Directions:

1. Bring a big saucepan of bringing to a boil, and season it with salt to taste. Pour sesame seeds into a medium skillet and toast for 3 to 5 minutes, stirring the pan regularly, until they are brown and aromatic, about 3 to 5 minutes. Transfer to a large mixing bowl.
2. To shred the ginger, use the tiniest teeth on a grater to grate it into a large mixing bowl. Salt and pepper to taste, then stir in the green onion white people, soy sauce, lemon zest, and oils until well combined. Season with salt and pepper to taste.
3. Stacked in a single layer, thinly slice the snow peas crosswise into three or four thin strips and set aside. It's OK if some peas burst out or break; keep them all together in a single container. Remove all of the leftover pods from the pan.
4. When the water comes to a boil, add the noodles, and toss to coat. Keep stirring until the squash is soft but not mushy, about 5 minutes. Regularly check after 5 minutes. When the pasta is finished cooking, mix in the snow peas, and immediately drain, brushing off as enough excess liquid as possible (but do not rinse) before removing from the heat. Toss gently to coat the vegetables with the dressing in a large mixing bowl. Allow it to settle for up to 1 hour before serving at room temperature. Decorate with the scallion leaves and sesame seeds and serve warm or at room temperature.

183. Twice-Baked Potatoes with Creamy Chive Pesto

Total time: 1 hour 20 minutes
Serving: 2
Nutrient per serving: Calories: 415, Fats: 64g, Carbohydrates: 48g, Proteins: 22g, Sodium: 3.6mg, Calcium: 21mg, Iron: 34mg
Ingredients:

- 2 cups of packed arugula
- 2 tablespoons of fresh lemon juice, divided, plus more
- 1/2 cup of roasted cashews
- 2 medium russet potatoes
- 5 tablespoons of olive oil, divided
- 5 tablespoons of finely chopped scallions
- 1/4 cup of finely chopped chives, divided
- Pinch of Kosher salt
- Pinch of freshly ground pepper
- 2 garlic cloves

Directions:

1. Preheat oven to 425 degrees Fahrenheit. Poke the potato over with a spoon to ensure even cooking. Rub the outsides of the chicken breasts with 1 tablespoon oil, season with a touch of salt and black pepper, and lay on a baking sheet with a rim. Bake for 50 to 60 minutes, rotating once halfway through or when the skins are crispy, and a knife can be inserted into the middle with just a little amount of resistance beyond the peel. Remove from the oven and set it aside until cooled enough to handle. In the meanwhile, raise the temperature of the oven to 450°F.
2. Slice the potato in half lengthwise, then in half again widthwise. To make a medium-sized mixing bowl, scoop off the majority of the meat, leaving approximately a 14-inch border around the inner peels. (Keep the potato skins on the cookie sheet to prevent them from sticking.) Salt and pepper to taste. To a large mixing bowl, combine the cloves, 1 cup greens, 3 tablespoons sliced onions and chives, 2 tablespoons olive oil, and 1 tablespoon lemon juice; toss well to combine. Mix until smooth and well-combined, similar to boiled potatoes, with a handful of chopped greens thrown in for good measure. Use salt, peppercorns, and lemon juice to season the dish to your liking, being sure to use as much salt so that almost all of the accompanying tastes are brought to life.
3. Place the blended potato mix back into the mashed potatoes and bake for approximately 20 minutes until the mixture is brown on top of the potatoes.
4. In the meanwhile, prepare the creamy pesto. Salt and black pepper and process until smooth in a food processor. Add the rest 1 cup of arugula, 2 tablespoon scallions, 2 tablespoon onions, 2 tablespoon oil, and 1 teaspoon lemon juice and process until smooth. Process the mixture in a food processor, wiping down the sides as necessary until it is uniform, the spices are very finely minced, and the nuts are finely chopped. While the engine is running, slowly pour in 2 to 3 teaspoons of hot water until the batter is smooth and the texture of loose sour cream is achieved. Salt and pepper, salt, and lemon juice to taste, and adjust seasoning as needed.
5. Allow the potatoes to cool slightly once they have done cooking so that you do not burn your tongue. Serve with a dollop of pesto on the side.

184. Stuffed Zucchini with Freekeh Pilaf and Currants

Total time: 1 hour 15 minutes
Serving: 6
Nutrient per serving: Calories: 220, Fats: 18g, Carbohydrates: 44g, Proteins: 98g, Sodium: 4mg, Calcium: 36mg, Iron: 2.8mg
Ingredients:

- 1 teaspoon of ground cumin
- crushed red pepper flakes
- 1/2 cup of chopped parsley leaves
- 4 medium zucchinis

- Kosher salt
- Pinch of freshly ground black pepper
- 3 tablespoons of toasted pine nuts
- 2-3 teaspoons of ed wine vinegar (to taste)
- 1/2 cup of dry freekeh, rinsed
- 2 tablespoons of olive oil
- 1 teaspoon of ground coriander
- 3 tablespoons of currants
- 1 small red onion
- 3 cloves garlic

Directions:

1. Preheat oven to 375 degrees Fahrenheit. Using a cantaloupe baller or a tiny spoon, gently scrape out the seeds from the zucchini halves that have been cut in half lengthwise. Place the zucchini on a baking pan, cut side up, and drizzle with some olive oil. Bake for 30 minutes. Season the squash with salt and black pepper. Cook for 10 min, or until the squash is fork soft but still retain their form and are still keeping their shape after being fork-tender. Remove the zucchini from the pan.

2. In a medium-sized pot or saucepan, bring 1/2 cup water to a boil. After adding the freekeh, reduce the heat to low and cover the pan. Cook, occasionally stirring, for 20-30 min, or when the freekeh is soft. Remove the freekeh from the pot and put it aside to drain any excess water.

3. In a large pan, heat the 2-tablespoon oil over medium heat until shimmering. Cook, turning regularly, for 5-10 mins, or when the onions are very soft and just beginning to brown, depending on how large the onion is. Cook for another minute, stirring regularly, after which remove the garlic. Pan and add freekeh, cumin, cilantro, and 1 teaspoon coarse salt to a pan and mix everything until everything is well-combined and the freekeh is warm. Season with salt and freshly ground black pepper to taste after adding the currants and pine nuts. Test the mixture and make any

necessary adjustments to the salt and vinegar. Add in the parsley and mix well.

4. Once you're ready to complete cooking the meal, fill every zucchini boat with more of the freekeh mix to make a rounded top but not so much that it spills over the edges of the zucchini boat. Set aside. Return the zucchini to the oven to bake for another fifteen min, or when the zucchini is entirely forked soft, and the edges are just beginning to brown. Serve the zucchini topped with additional chopped parsley and drizzled with your favorite lemony tahini dressing or drizzled with a drizzle of lemon zest before cutting into wedges.

185. Boiled Potato on Rye Bread, aka Potato Salad on Toast

Total time: 45 minutes
Serving: 4
Nutrient per serving: Calories: 450, Fats: 28g, Carbohydrates: 56g, Proteins: 2g, Sodium: 7.3mg, Calcium: 20mg, Iron: 6.4mg
Ingredients:

- 1 teaspoon of chopped chives
- 1 dash red wine vinegar
- 1 dash of freshly cracked pepper
- 1/2 cup of Veganize
- 1 1/2 teaspoons of finely chopped capers
- 1 teaspoon of finely chopped flat leaf parsley
- 1 dash of hot sauce
- 1 teaspoon of whole grain Dijon mustard
- 1 teaspoon of finely chopped dill

Directions:

1. Bring a saucepan of salted water to a boil, then add the potatoes. Meanwhile, prepare the remoulade as follows: In a medium-sized mixing bowl, combine the Veganize, Dijon, chopped herb, diced olives, hot sauce, and freshly cracked pepper. Stir until everything is well-combined. Season with salt and pepper to taste.

2. Whenever the potato is fork-tender, drain them and put them away to cool until they

are safe to handle again. Cut the rounds into 14-inch-thick slices. Taste and salt and black pepper to your liking.

3. Avoid even considering attempting to consume this sandwich in the traditional manner! Use a knife and fork to cut your food so that all of the toppings don't come off.

186. Spiced Peanut Sweet Potato Salad

Total time: 50 minutes
Serving: 4
Nutrient per serving: Calories: 330, Fats: 81g, Carbohydrates: 42g, Proteins: 24g, Sodium: 5.6g, Calcium: 39mg, Iron: 2.7mg
Ingredients:
- 2 teaspoons of ground cumin
- 1 handful of peanuts
- 1 handful of chopped radicchios for serving
- 2 large, sweet potatoes
- 2 tablespoons of olive oil
- 1 tablespoon of black sesame seeds
- Salt and pepper
- 2 teaspoons of ground ginger
- 2 teaspoons of ground cinnamon
- 1 handful of parsley
- 45 grams of dates

Directions:
1. Preheat oven to 240 degrees Celsius (464 degrees Fahrenheit, fan 220 degrees Celsius).
2. Place the potatoes in a big baking dish and sprinkle with olive oil. Add the spices and a pinch of salt and pepper and toss to combine, making sure everything is thoroughly coated with the olive oil. Allow 45-50 minutes of baking time to ensure that they are soft.
3. While the potatoes are cooking, prepare the dressing by whisking together all of the Ingredients with a pinch of salt until smooth.
4. Place the parsley, dates, and sesame seeds in a large mixing bowl and toss to combine. Once the potatoes have been cooked, please place them in a large mixing dish

with the sauce and toss to combine everything. If you're using roasted peanuts, sprinkle them on top before serving.

187. Spicy Miso Eggplant & Broccoli Salad

Total time: 45 minutes
Serving: 2
Nutrient per serving: Calories: 150, Fats: 38g, Carbohydrates: 21g, Proteins: 76g, Sodium: 31mg, Calcium: 9.8mg, Iron: 4.9mg
Ingredients:
- 1 pinch of Chile flakes
- 1 handful of coriander
- 1 handful of sesame seeds
- Salt and pepper to taste
- 2 medium aubergines
- 1 large head of broccoli

Directions:
1. Preheat oven to 240 degrees Celsius (464 degrees Fahrenheit, fan 220 degrees Celsius).
2. The dressing may be made in a blender by blending the miso, lime juice, white wine vinegar, sesame oil, ginger, salt, and pepper until smooth. For those who don't have access to a mixer, melt the miso in a teaspoon of hot water before stirring in the rest of the dressing components.
3. Cook the aubergine for 30-35 minutes in a big baking dish after mixing it with the dressing. At this stage, remove the baking pan from the heat and turn the oven's temperature down to the grill position. Combine the broccoli florets and eggplant in a large mixing bowl, return the baking dish to the oven for another 10 minutes, or until the cauliflower is gently browned on topping aubergine is tender and golden.
4. Removing the chicken from the oven and placing it in a serving dish, sprinkle with the chili flakes, parsley, and sesame seeds, and then serve it immediately.

188. Indian Peanutty Noodles

Total time: 35 minutes
Serving: 2

Nutrient per serving: Calories: 200, Fats: 40g, Carbohydrates: 21g, Proteins: 63g, Sodium: 11.2mg, Calcium: 54mg, Iron: 29mg

Ingredients:
- 1 cup of broccoli florets
- 2 tablespoons of peanut chutney
- 1 to 2 tablespoons of light soy sauce
- 8 ounces of udon or soba noodles
- 2 tablespoons of vegetable oil
- 1 cup of red bell pepper
- 3/4 cup of thinly sliced scallions

Directions:
1. Roasted the nuts in a 350°D e oven (or toaster oven, as I use) for 8 to 12 minutes, or until they are a dark brown color that is a touch darker than golden brown, stirring halfway through. Maintain vigilance over them! Then, after 3 minutes, flip the pan to bring the peanuts at the rear to the front. (Turn off the oven and remove the peanuts to a cooling rack to cool.
2. In a blender or food processor, pulse or mix all chutney components (cumin powder, red pepper powder, salt, and sugar) until they are a coarse powder, adding the peanuts last. Store in a knot bag or a jar with a tight-fitting lid.
3. Noodles with peanut sauce from India. Prepare the vermicelli according to the directions on the package and put them aside to cool. Save half a cup of the water in which the noodles were cooked aside.
4. In a skillet, boil the vegetable oil until shimmering. Cook for 5 minutes after adding the broccoli. You are welcome to include broccoli stalks as well. Add in the red bell pepper and cook for another 3 to 4 minutes. (We want both of these veggies to lose their fresh taste while yet maintaining a bite to them.) To make substitutions, use veggies of your choosing that hold some bite and form, rather than being mushy or soft. Carrot, red onions, snapping peas, squash, water chestnut, baby corn, mushrooms, and French beans are excellent alternatives for the vegetables listed above. Cook for a minute after adding 1/2 of the scallions to the pan.
5. Toss in the peanut chutney and combine well, then add the soy sauce and cook until the sauce is evenly coated over the veggies.
6. In a separate bowl, combine the boiling noodles and soy sauce mixture until the noodles are equally covered with the sauce mixture. If you prefer your noodle to be a little drier, add some of the starch noodle water.
7. Remove from heat and garnish with the remainder of the scallions. Serve immediately with a side of fresh bell pepper chili-garlic butter to taste.

189. Turmeric-Roasted Cauliflower with Pistachio Gremolata

Total time: 25 minutes
Serving: 4
Nutrient per serving: Calories: 280, Fats: 43g, Carbohydrates: 34.7g, Proteins: 22.2g, Sodium: 7.29mg, Calcium: 93.0mg, Iron: 40mg

Ingredients:
- 6 to 8 dates
- 1 large lemon
- 1/4 cup of pomegranate arils
- 1/2 teaspoon of Aleppo pepper
- 1 large head of cauliflower
- 2 tablespoons of finely grated fresh turmeric
- 1/3 cup of shelled pistachios
- 1/2 cup of finely chopped
- 3 tablespoons of olive oil
- Pinch of Kosher salt

Directions:
1. Preheat the oven to 425 degrees Fahrenheit.
2. Prepare a sheet pan by tossing the broccoli with ginger and olive oil, seasoning with salt, and arranging the cauliflower in a single, uniform layer. After 15 minutes of roasting, take the pot from the heat and set it aside. In a large mixing bowl, combine all ingredients and disperse in a

single, equal layer. Continue roasting for another 10 minutes or until the broccoli is well browned and soft, and the date and little amounts of powdered turmeric are beginning to caramelize, depending on how large your cauliflower is. Remove the pan from the oven and squeeze half a lemon over the whole dish (be sure to zest it first—you'll need it for the gremolata in Step 3!); season with more lemon juice and salt to taste.

3. Meanwhile, to prepare the pistachio gremolata, follow these steps: Pistachios should be toasted in a small pan over medium heat for 3 to 4 minutes, or until they're aromatic, for 3 to 4 minutes. Once they have cooled enough to handle, remove them from the fire and cut them into fine but irregular pieces using a knife. Season with salt and pepper to taste after mixing the walnuts, citrus zest, cilantro, grape arils, and Aleppo peppers in a small mixing dish.

4. Arrange the cabbage and date on a large serving dish and sprinkle with the pistachio gremolata to finish. Hot or at ambient temperature are both acceptable serving temperatures.

190. Crispy Roasted Shallot and Lentil Sheet-Pan Mujadara

Total time: 1 hour
Serving: 4
Nutrient per serving: Calories: 354, Fats: 28g, Carbohydrates: 64g, Proteins: 9.8g, Sodium: 25.8mg, Calcium: 12.0mg, Iron: 9mg
Ingredients:

- 1 1/2 cups of long grain white rice
- 1/4 cup of finely chopped fresh flat-leaf parsley leaves or cilantro leaves
- 8 medium-sized shallots
- 2 tablespoons of extra-virgin olive oil
- 3/4 cup of brown lentils

- 4 cups of boiling water
- 1 tablespoon of ground cumin
- 2 teaspoons of dried thyme
- 2 1/2 teaspoons of kosher salt, plus extra as needed
- 1 teaspoon of freshly ground black pepper

Directions:

1. Preheat oven to 375° F. Move an oven rack to the center point and lay a rimmed baking sheet on top of it.

2. In a large mixing bowl, mix the onions with the canola oil, cinnamon, rosemary, 1 teaspoon sugar, and pepper until well combined. Spread the onions onto the preheated cookie sheet in an equal layer and cook for approximately 25 minutes, or until golden brown.

3. Pull the oven temperature out halfway and toss the beans into the onion mixture on the cookie sheet, using oven gloves to prevent burning yourself. Prepare your tinfoil (you may need 2 sheets) by carefully adding hot water to the sheet pan and crimping it around the sides to seal. Turn down the preheated oven to 350 degrees Fahrenheit and cook for 10 minutes longer.

4. Extend the rack roughly halfway again, open the foil, and toss in the rice and the remaining 12 tablespoons salt until well combined. Continue to simmer until the rice is cooked, approximately 25 minutes longer, after re-covering the sheet pan and crimping the foil over the sides to lock it in place again.

5. Take the pan out of the oven and set it aside. Season to taste the salt level if necessary to your liking. Serve hot or at room temperature, garnished with parsley or cilantro with a dressing made of yogurt, Jabal al pepper, and more olive oil.

191. White Bean Soup with Garlic and Parsley

Total time: 1 hour 5 minutes
Serving: 4
Nutrient per serving: Calories: 540, Fats: 32g, Carbohydrates: 12.9g, Proteins: 23g, Sodium: 56mg, Calcium: 9.5mg, Iron: 21mg
Ingredients:
- 6 cups cooked beans
- Pinch of Salt
- 2 tablespoons of chopped fresh parsley
- toasted slices of crusty bread
- 1/2 cup of extra virgin olive oil
- 1 teaspoon of garlic
- Pinch of Black pepper
- 1 cup of homemade broth or water

Directions:
1. Combine the oil and minced garlic in a soup pot and bring to a simmer over medium heat. Sauté the garlic, constantly stirring, until it becomes a very light-yellow color, about 10 minutes.
2. Toss in the dried cooked or tinned beans, a sprinkle of salt, and several grinds of pepper until everything is well combined. Cover and cook for 4 - 5 minutes on a low heat setting.
3. Remove approximately 1/2 cup of the beans from the saucepan and purée them through with a food mill before returning them to the pot with the rest of the stock. Alternatively, you may puree the soup in a blender, loosening it with a little of the liquid. Taste and adjust seasonings with salt and pepper if necessary. Continue to cook for another 6 - 8 minutes. Remove the pan from the heat and stir in the chopped parsley.
4. Pour the soup into separate soup bowls and top with the grilled bread pieces.

192. Vegan Cauliflower Alfredo Bake

Total time: 45 minutes
Serving: 6
Nutrient per serving: Calories: 220, Fats: 54g, Carbohydrates: 10g, Proteins: 39g, Sodium: 8.1mg, Calcium: 47mg, Iron: 1.5mg
Ingredients:
- 3/4 cup of unsweetened almond, soy, or rice milk
- 1/3 cup of nutritional yeast
- 1 cup of fresh green peas
- 1/2 cup of vegan breadcrumbs
- 12 ounces of penne pasta
- 1 medium head of cauliflower
- 1 tablespoon of fresh lemon juice
- 3/4 teaspoon of salt
- 1 tablespoon of olive oil
- 2 to 3 small cloves of garlic

Directions:
1. Preheat the oven to 375 degrees Fahrenheit. Prepare a saucepan of salted water by bringing it to a boil. Remove from fire and toss in the penne until it's cooked through but still a bit al dente, around 5 to 7 minutes, depending on how much time you have on your hands. Reserve a few teaspoons of the pasta cooking water after draining it. Setting the pasta aside after tossing it with boiling water helps prevent it from sticking.
2. Prepare a second pot of water by bringing it to a boil. Cook the cauliflower for 5 to 6 mins, or until it is soft, depending on how big it is. Drain. Part of the florets should be placed in the blender, with the other half being set aside.
3. In a small saucepan, heat the olive oil over medium-low heat until shimmering. 3 minutes, stirring regularly, or until the garlic is aromatic and heated through but not burned. Remove from heat and set aside. Half of the chopped broccoli is blended with the onion, non-dairy milk, nutritious yeast, lime juice, salt, and pepper to form a smooth sauce. The gravy should be extremely smooth, so, if necessary, add more milk or a drop of olive oil to get a silky texture. Serve immediately.

4. Prepare a 9-by-13-inch baking dish by lightly oiling it. Combine the pasta, the leftover cauliflower, the peas, and the rest of the sauce in a large mixing bowl. Toss the ingredients together and season with a little salt or salt if preferred. All of the ingredients should be placed in a baking dish. Breadcrumbs should be sprinkled on top. Cook for 20 to 30 minutes, or until the breadcrumbs are browned, and the spaghetti is bubbling until the crumbs are toasted. Serve.

193. Rutabaga Laksa

Total time: 1 hour 15 minutes
Serving: 4
Nutrient per serving: Calories: 320, Fats: 54g, Carbohydrates: 23.4g, Proteins: 21g, Sodium: 8mg, Calcium: 4.0mg, Iron: 3.1mg
Ingredients:
- 1/4 cups of vegan vegetable stock
- 7 ounces of rice vermicelli noodles
- 2 limes
- 6 cloves garlic
- 1 inch ginger
- 1 1/2 teaspoons of granulated sugar
- 2 pounds of rutabaga (3/4 of a large one), peeled
- 4 teaspoons of red chili powder, such as Kashmiri
- 2 1/2 teaspoons of ground cumin
- 14 ounces (1 can) of full-fat coconut milk
- 1 1/2 teaspoons of kosher salt
- 2 lemongrass stalks
- 3/4 cup of packed cilantro
- 6 shallots
- 1 splash of canola oil

Directions:
1. Set the oven to 425°F and prepare 2 huge baking sheets by lining them with aluminum foil.
2. The laksa paste may be made by blending the garlic, ginger root, chili powder, coriander, lemon, and cilantro leaves in a blender with about 2/3 cup of stock to form a smooth paste. 2 shallots, peeled and coarsely chopped, should be added to the blender with the rest of the ingredients and blended until smooth.
3. To make the paste, heat tablespoon of oils in a depth saucepan over a low flame until hot, then scoop the dough into the pot. After 15 minutes, often stirring to ensure that it does not catch, gently pour the coconut cream until it is completely incorporated. Pour in the remaining stock along with the salt and sugar and cook for 20 minutes, or until the sauce is rich and flavorful. Remove the pan from the heat and season with salt and pepper to taste.
4. Prepare rutabaga by cutting it in half and slicing it into 1/2-inch-thick slices, then arranging them on one of the prepared baking pans while the soup is heating. Continue to peel and half the current shallots lengthways, then divide them into "petals" by detaching the individual segments and arranging them on the second lined sheet of parchment paper. Lightly pour oil over each veggie and mix with your hands to evenly cover them with the oil. Season with a little salt if desired. 20 minutes at 400 degrees, followed by 30 minutes at 400 degrees, or until the shallots are cooked through, and the rutabaga is caramelized. Cook the pasta in boiling water according to package directions (typically 2–3 minutes), then strain and run under cold water to stop the cooking process.
5. Reheat the soup over medium heat until it is ready to serve. Distribute the noodles into four soup bowls and pour the heated soup over the top. Place the heated rutabaga and caramelized shallots on top of the quinoa, and garnish with fresh cilantro. Serve with a slice of lime squeezed over each dish and more lime wedges on the side.

194. Instant Pot No-Soak Black Bean Soup

Total time: 50 minutes

Serving: 6

Nutrient per serving: Calories: 410, Fats: 29g, Carbohydrates: 32g, Proteins: 11g, Sodium: 8.6mg, Calcium: 30.1mg, Iron: 4.9mg

Ingredients:

- 2 cups of canned pureed tomato
- 2 cups of broth (chicken or vegetable)
- 1 tablespoon of dark brown sugar
- pinch of salt
- 2 tablespoons of olive oil
- 1 large, pickled onion
- 1/2 cup of red wine vinegar
- 1/4 cup of hot (but not boiling) water
- 4 cloves of garlic
- 1 teaspoon of Hungarian hot paprika
- 2 teaspoons of kosher salt
- 1/2 teaspoon of freshly cracked pepper
- 3 tablespoons of tomato paste
- 3 tablespoons of red wine vinegar
- 3 cups of water
- 1 pound of dried black beans

Directions:

1. Set the sauté function on your multi-cooker. Add the garlic and onions once the olive oil is sizzling and cook until the onion is translucent. Sauté until the onions are transparent and aromatic, and the edges are just beginning to brown, about 5 minutes.
2. Transfer the veggies to the outside edges of the saucepan and place the paprika in the middle of the pot. Allow the mixture to simmer for 30 seconds in the oil before stirring to combine it with everything. Stir in the tomato paste until everything is well combined. Pour in the red wine vinegar and use it to deglaze the saucepan, if necessary, Combine the pureed tomato, vegetable broth, water, and beans in a large mixing bowl. Stir. Pressure cooks on high for 10 mins in the multi-cooker using the pressure cooker setting.

3. During this time, prepare the fast pickled onions. In a medium-sized mixing bowl, whisk the wine vinegar, boiling water, sugar, and salt until well combined. Stir until the sugars and salt are completely dissolved. Stir in the onion and set the pot aside till the soup is finished. Drain the water and use it as a garnish.
4. Allowing the pressure to naturally release for at least a few minutes after the pressure-cooking process is complete is recommended before using the quick release option. Once the pressure has been released, remove the lid and season with salt and pepper. Using your taste buds, adjust the spice as needed.
5. Spoon the beans and broth into soup bowls and top with pickled onions and any other additional toppings that you choose.

195. Vegan Chicken Phở

Total time: 1 hour

Serving: 4

Nutrient per serving: Calories: 710, Fats: 21g, Carbohydrates: 30g, Proteins: 53g, Sodium: 1.8mg, Calcium: 3.5mg, Iron: 0mg

Ingredients:

- 2 medium celery stalks
- 1 large carrot
- 2/3 cup of hot water
- 1 teaspoon of organic sugar,
- 1 whole clove
- 1 teaspoon of coriander seeds
- 2 teaspoons of fine sea salt
- 2 1/2 tablespoons of nutritional yeast powder
- Chubby 1-inch section ginger
- 1 medium-large yellow onion
- 7 cups of cold water
- 1 pound of napa cabbage leaves
- 1 cup of coarsely chopped cilantro sprigs
- 7 cups of cold water
- 1 small Fuji apple

Directions:

1. Set the sauté function on your multi-cooker. Add the garlic and onions once the

olive oil is sizzling and cook until the onion is translucent. Sauté until the onions are transparent and aromatic, and the edges are just beginning to brown, about 5 minutes.

2. Transfer the veggies to the outside edges of the saucepan and place the paprika in the middle of the pot. Allow the mixture to simmer for 30 seconds in the oil before stirring to combine it with everything. Stir in the tomato paste until everything is well combined. Pour in the red wine vinegar and use it to deglaze the saucepan, if necessary (aka, scrape up any browned bits clinging to the bottom). Combine the pureed tomato, vegetable broth, water, and beans in a large mixing bowl. Stir. Pressure cooks on high for 10 mins in the multi-cooker using the pressure cooker setting.

3. During this time, prepare the fast pickled onions. Whisk the wine vinegar in a medium-sized mixing bowl, boiling water, sugar, and salt until well combined. Stir until the sugars and salt are completely dissolved. Stir in the onion and set the pot aside till the soup is finished. Drain the water and use it as a garnish.

4. Allowing the pressure to naturally release for at least a few minutes after the pressure-cooking process is complete is recommended before using the quick release option. Once the pressure has been released, remove the lid and season with salt and pepper. Using your taste buds, adjust the spice as needed.

5. Spoon the beans and broth into soup bowls and top with pickled onions and any other additional toppings that you choose.

196. Bartha

Total time: 1 hour 20 min
Serving: 4
Nutrient per serving: Calories: 420, Fats: 21g, Carbohydrates: 29.1g, Proteins: 2g, Sodium: 31.7mg, Calcium: 42mg, Iron: 31mg

Ingredients:
- 2 teaspoons of curry powder
- 2 teaspoons of cumin
- 1/2 teaspoon of salt
- 1 pinch of Black pepper
- 1 large eggplant
- 2 tablespoons of vegetable oil
- 1/2 teaspoon of chili powder
- 1 cup of frozen peas
- 1 medium onion
- 3 cloves garlic
- 2 teaspoons of cumin
- 1/2 teaspoon of turmeric
- 3 cloves of garlic
- 2 medium tomatoes

Directions:
1. Cook the entire eggplant (with the stem and leaves removed) over high heat on your stove, often rotating, until the interior is mushy, and the exterior is charred, approximately 20 minutes total time. Alternatively, you may puncture the eggplant with a knife and bake it at 350° F for approximately an hour, or until it is soft and mushy.

2. Take the eggplant from the heat or the oven, let it cool, and then cut it up; the purple will be mush and will entirely crumble into a pulpy mass — this is exactly what you want. Assist it in completing this task and then remove it from consideration.

3. In a large skillet, heat the oil over medium heat until shimmering. Sautee the onions and garlic for 5 to 7 minutes, or until they are almost transparent. Combine the tomato so all of the ingredients (except the salt) in a large mixing bowl. Reduce the heat to a low setting and simmer for 5 minutes.

4. Cook until the eggplant and peas are completely cooked through, stirring often. Just use the back of a spoon to mash the entire thing together if you like a smoother mix (in which case, raise your hand), or

continue living and then let live if you prefer your mix on the bulkier side. Season with salt and pepper to suit, and any extra spices that you choose. Season with freshly ground black pepper.

197. One-Pot Skinny Pasta Primavera

Total time: 35 minutes
Serving: 6
Nutrient per serving: Calories: 120, Fats: 32g, Carbohydrates: 16g, Proteins: 27g, Sodium: 13.5mg, Calcium: 5mg, Iron: 19mg
Ingredients:

- 1/2 cup of vegetable broth
- 1/8 teaspoon of red pepper flakes
- 1 teaspoon of kosher salt
- 6 fresh thyme sprigs
- 1/2 cup of grated parmesan cheese
- 1/3 cup of dill leaves
- 8 ounces of spaghetti noodles
- 1 leek
- 3/4 cup of English peas
- 1/2 lemon
- 1/2 pound of asparagus
- 1/4 pound of broccoli florets
- 1 tablespoon of olive oil
- 10-12 of kale sprouts
- 1 cup of brown mushrooms
- 4 cloves of garlic
- 1 tablespoon of olive oil
- 10-12 kale sprouts
- 1 cup of brown mushrooms
- 4 cloves of garlic

Directions:

1. Break up the spaghetti noodles and place them in a huge stockpot or Dutch oven with the leek, spears, broccoli, mushrooms, and garlic. Season with cayenne pepper, kosher salt, thyme leaves, and olive oil. Cook on low heat for 30 minutes.
2. Stir periodically so that the spaghetti does not stay together while cooking for 8 minutes at a low simmer but with a good amount of boiling.

3. Then add the kale sprouts and peas, cooking for another 2-3 mins or until the pasta is done and the water has reduced to resemble sauce consistency.
4. Combine the lime juice, parmesan cheese, and dill in a large mixing bowl. As the sauce cools, it will thicken even more. Sprinkle with additional kosher salt to taste if necessary.
5. Sprinkle extra dill leaves, parmesan cheese, and lemon zest on top of the dish before serving.

198. Spicy Tuna Poke Bowls

Total time: 15 minutes
Serving: 4
Nutrient per serving: Calories: 245, Fats: 34g, Carbohydrates: 15g, Proteins: 61g, Sodium: 2.8mg, Calcium: 40mg, Iron: 21mg
Ingredients:

- 2 tablespoons of black sesame seeds
- 1 sheet of organic roasted nori
- 2 cans of albacore tuna in olive oil
- 2 cups of organic brown rice cooked
- 1 jalapeno
- 1/4 cup of organic scallions diced
- 1 cup of organic leafy greens
- 1 avocado
- 1/2 cup of organic edamame shelled
- 1/2 cup of organic Persian cucumbers diced
- 1/2 cup of pickled carrots

Directions:

1. Mix the components for the eel's sauce in a medium saucepan over medium heat until well combined. Reduce the heat to low and cook, stirring regularly, until the syrup is thick. Pour the contents into a glass dish and put it aside.
2. In the meanwhile, mix the components for the hot mayo in a big glass mixing bowl. Mix everything with a whisk. Toss in the canned tuna, breaking it up with such a fork, then toss it all together with the hot mayo to combine completely.

3. To construct the bowls, distribute the rice among four serving bowls in an equal layer. Finish with a sprinkling of leafy greens. In a large mixing bowl, combine the spicy tuna, avocados, carrots, soybeans, cucumbers, and jalapeño rings. Garnish with onions, sesame seeds, and seaweed, if desired. Sprinkle with eel sauce and serve. Prepare the dish and serve it to your guests.

199. Spiralized Zucchini, Quinoa and Turkey Sausage Stuffed Peppers

Total time: 1 hour
Serving: 2
Nutrient per serving: Calories: 410, Fats: 21g, Carbohydrates: 35g, Proteins: 2g, Sodium: 1.5mg, Calcium: 15mg, Iron: 22.9 mg
Ingredients:
- 1/2 cup of grated Parmesan cheese plus more for garnish
- 1/4 cup of chopped fresh basil
- 6 bell peppers of assorted color
- Kosher salt
- Pinch of freshly ground black pepper
- 1 cup of crushed tomatoes or tomato sauce
- 4 cups of cooked quinoa
- 2 medium zucchini spiralized
- 2 tablespoons of olive oil divided
- 1/8 teaspoon of crushed red pepper flakes
- 1 cup of chopped yellow onion
- 1 pound of ground turkey
- 4 cloves garlic minced
- 1/2 teaspoon of dried fennel seed crushed

Directions:
1. Preheat oven to 375 degrees Fahrenheit.
2. Remove the bell peppers' stems and core them, being sure to remove all of the seeds before rinsing. Using kosher salt, lightly coat the insides of the peppers and set them in a microwave-safe dish with 14 cups of water to cook. Microwave on high for 5 - 6 minutes, or until they begin to soften until they are warm to the touch. Remove the item and place it away.

3. Prepare the zucchini by spiralizing or dicing it. In a large pan, heat 1 tablespoon of the canola oil over medium heat until shimmering. Season with a pinch of kosher salt and toss in the zucchini, if desired. Toss the squash and heat until it just starts to soften, approximately 2 minutes, before transferring it to a bowl and allowing it to cool completely.
4. To make the ground turkey, heat the remaining olive oil in a large skillet until hot before adding the squeezed garlic, star anise, crushed red pepper flakes, and seasoning with basic salt and black pepper in the same skillet. Cook for approximately 5 minutes, or until the vegetables are nearly cooked through, stirring often. Sauté until the onion is softened, about 5 minutes after adding the onion. Sauté for another minute once you've added the smashed tomatoes to the pan. Remove the remove from heat and mix in the grains and zucchini until well combined. Season with salt and pepper to taste after tossing with the Grated parmesan and fresh basil.
5. Fill the peppers in a 3 quarts baking dish with the meat and quinoa mixture. Bake for 30 minutes at 350 degrees. Bake for 20 minutes, or until the peppers are soft and the cheese has browned on top if using extra Parmesan cheese on top is preferred. Serve when still heated.

200. Vegan Black Bean Burgers

Total time: 30 minutes
Serving: 4
Nutrient per serving: Calories: 340, Fats: 18g, Carbohydrates: 43g, Proteins: 52g, Sodium: 38mg, Calcium: 30mg, Iron: 37mg
Ingredients:
- 1 Teaspoon of Salt
- 1/2 Teaspoon of Paprika
- 1-2 Tbs of Water
- Neutral Vegetable Oil
- 1/4 Cup of Red Onion chopped
- 1 Clove of Garlic

- 1 15 oz Can of Black Beans rinsed and dried
- 2 Tbs of Olive Oil
- 1/4 Cup of Rolled or Quick Oats
- 1/4 Cup of Breadcrumbs
- 1/4 Teaspoon of Cumin
- Pinch of Black Pepper
- 1/4 Cup of Walnuts
- 2 Tbs of Ground Flaxseed

Directions:

1. Combine the shallots and garlic clove in a stick blender and mix until smooth. Process until all of the ingredients are finely chopped.
2. Afterward, include the oats, crumbs, walnuts, flax, salt, and spices into the mixture. Process the ingredients until it resembles a chunky meal.
3. After that, put in the black beans, olive oil, and 1 tablespoon of water. The mixture should be chunky and bendable at this point (there should still be some bits of kidney beans in the mix - you don't want it to be completely smooth - but not completely smooth).
4. If the mixture is too crumbly, put in 1 tablespoon of water at a time until it comes together.
5. Allow for a 10–15-minute resting period for the dough. DO NOT miss this step at any cost!!
6. After that, cut the mixture into four equal halves.
7. Heat a sauté pan over medium heat, adding a dab of neutral vegetable oil if desired.
8. During the time that the skillet is heating, form the batter into burger patties. (You may use the photographs on this page as a guide.)
9. Cook each burger for approximately 4-5 minutes on each side in a hot pan with a little oil.
10. With lettuce, tomato, and red onion on top, assemble your burgers on your preferred bread. (Or any fillings you choose!)
11. Enjoy!

201. Vegetable Lasagna with Butternut Squash and Shiitake Mushroom

Total time: 1 hour 5 minutes
Serving: 2
Nutrient per serving: Calories: 235, Fats: 34g, Carbohydrates: 44g, Proteins: 51g, Sodium: 38mg, Calcium: 20.1mg, Iron: 21mg
Ingredients:

- 1/4 cup of all-purpose flour
- 1/2 cup of grated Parmesan cheese
- kosher salt
- Pinch of pepper
- 2 tablespoons of olive oil
- 2 pounds of butternut squash
- 3 cups of mozzarella cheese, shredded
- 1 cup of ricotta cheese
- 1/2 cup of water, fresh
- 4 amaretti cookies
- 1 cup of fresh basil leaves
- 13 ounces of DeLallo no-boil lasagna noodles
- 8 ounces of shiitake mushrooms sliced
- 1/4 cup of butter
- 3 1/2 cups of whole milk
- 1/2 teaspoon of ground nutmeg

Directions:

1. Bake at 400 degrees Fahrenheit (180 degrees Celsius).
2. In a large pan, heat 1 tablespoon oil over medium-high heat until shimmering. The squash should be seasoned with salt and black pepper at this point, and then add the water to the skillet. Pour in the stock and bring to a simmer over medium-high heat for 15-20 minutes or when the pumpkin is fork-tender. You may also use the Instant Pot to prepare it. Put the pumpkin in a blender. Blend until smooth. Blend in the almond meal or biscotti cookies until they are completely smooth.
3. Remove the skillet from the heat and pour the remaining tablespoon of oil on

110

medium heat. Cook for 8-10 minutes, stirring periodically until the mushrooms are tender and the 1/4 teaspoon kosher salt has been dissolved. Remove the pan from the heat, wipe off the pan, and put it aside.

4. Using medium heat, melt the butter in the pan, pour the flour and stir until smooth, about 1 minute's total. Over medium-high heat, mix in the milk and come to a mild boil, then decrease the heat to medium and continue to cook until the sauce is slightly thickened approximately 5 minutes. Add the nutmeg, 1/4 teaspoon kosher salt, and freshly ground black pepper to taste. Allow for minor cooling. Place one-half of the sauce in a blender and mix until smooth. Add the basil. Because the combination will be hot, lay a cloth or cloth over the top of the blender to prevent the mixture from exploding. Blend until smooth, then add the basil sauce back to the pan with the rest of the sauce and swirl to combine. Taste and salt and black pepper to your liking.

5. Lightly grease a glass baking dish that measures 13 x 9 x 2 inches. Pour 3/4 cups of the sauce into the base of the baking dish that has been prepared. Using a layer of spaghetti noodles, cover the pan with the sauce. Spread one-third of the pumpkin puree over the noodles, followed by one-third of the mushrooms. Using 1/2 cup mozzarella and 1/3 cup feta cheese, top the pizza with a generous amount of cheese. Pour 1/2 cup of the liquid over the noodles and toss to combine. Continue stacking for a total of three more times, finishing with a layer of provolone and parmesan cheese.

6. Cover the baking sheet with aluminum foil that has been coated with nonstick spray and bake for 40 minutes at 350°F. Cover with foil and bake for another 15 minutes, or when the topping is golden brown. Remove the lasagna from the oven and allow it to cool for 15-20 minutes before adding.

202. Vegetarian Thai Pineapple Forbidden Fried Rice

Total time: 1 hour 20 minutes
Serving: 4
Nutrient per serving: Calories: 435, Fats: 14g, Carbohydrates: 0.9g, Proteins: 2g, Sodium: 8mg, Calcium: 11.4mg, Iron: 9.1mg
Ingredients:
- 2 tablespoons of gluten free soy sauce
- 1/3 cup of coarsely chopped honey roasted
- 1 ½ tablespoons of toasted sesame oil
- 1 ½ cups of fresh cubed pineapple
- 1/2 cup of frozen shelled edamame
- 1 tablespoon of chili paste
- 3 cloves garlic
- 1/2 tablespoon of freshly grated ginger
- 3 cups of shredded red cabbage
- 1/2 cup of shredded carrots
- 1 bunch of green onions
- 1 red bell pepper

Directions:
1. The prohibited rice should be prepared as follows: Combine the rice with coconut oil and cook over medium heat in a medium-sized saucepan. To increase the taste and texture of the rice, toast it for two min with the oil. After two min, add the water and salt and mix well to combine. Bring water to a boil, then reduce heat to a low setting, cover, and simmer for 45-55 minutes or until vegetables are tender. After removing the dish from the heat, please leave it cool in the pan for 10 minutes before fluffing with a fork. The rice should have a small crunch to it while remaining soft.

2. Meanwhile, whereas the rice is boiling, you may prepare the vegetables and cook the eggs. In a mixing dish, mix the eggs and water and softly whisk together with a fork. Using nonstick cooking spray, coat the bottom of a big pan or wok and set it

over medium-low heat. Eggs should be scrambled in the pan with some salt and pepper until cooked but still somewhat moist, then removed from the pan and set aside. Place the eggs in a separate dish and put them aside.

3. Once the rice is finished cooking, you may begin preparing the vegetables. Clean the same big skillet or wok you used for the previous step with a towel, then add 1 tablespoon olive oil or sesame seeds and heat over medium heat until hot. Sauté the pineapple, garlic, mustard, green onion, and red bell pepper for 4-6 minutes, or until the fruit begins to caramelize and the pineapple edges become slightly golden brown.

4. After that, put in the remaining vegetables, which include red cabbage, carrots, and edamame. Continue to cook for another 3-5 minutes, stirring often. Place all of the vegetables on a big plate or in a large dish.

5. We may start frying the rice right now. In the same pan, heat the remaining 12 tablespoons of oil over medium heat until shimmering. Cook, often stirring, for 2-4 minutes once you've added your prepared rice.

6. Return all of the cooked vegetables, as well as the scrambled eggs, to the pan. Simmer for a few more minutes after adding the sweet chili sauce, soy sauce, and honey-roasted cashews, stirring constantly. Season with salt and pepper to taste and season with salt as needed. Another teaspoon of miso or some smashed red pepper for a little kick may be necessary to complete the flavor profile. It is all up to you.

7. Garnish with more nuts, cilantro, and a little amount of green onion, if desired.

203. Grilled Vegetable Sandwich

Total time: 1 hour 10 minutes
Serving: 3

Nutrient per serving: Calories: 332, Fats: 98g, Carbohydrates: 21g, Proteins: 42g, Sodium: 2.8mg, Calcium: 19.2mg, Iron: 4.3mg

Ingredients:
- 1/2 cup of arugula leaves
- Balsamic glaze
- 1 cup of ricotta cheese
- 1 tablespoon of each of fresh basil chives and parsley, chopped
- 2 teaspoons of dried oregano
- 1 loaf of ciabatta bread or other soft bread
- 1 clove of garlic minced
- 1 tablespoon of extra virgin olive oil
- ½ cup of red onion
- ½ of red bell pepper seed
- Pinch of kosher salt
- Pinch of freshly ground black pepper
- 1 portobello mushroom
- 1 medium zucchini sliced
- 1 medium yellow squash

Directions:
1. Blend the mozzarella cheese, fresh basil, garlic clove, 1 tablespoon olive oil, kosher salt, and freshly ground pepper in a small mixing bowl until smooth. Make a mental note to put it away.
2. Grill grates should be gently covered with grapeseed or soybean oil after being oiled with paper towels. Heat the grill on high for 10-15 minutes, depending on the size of the steaks.
3. Season the veggies with dried oregano, kosher salt, and freshly ground pepper after drizzling them with olive oil.
4. Drizzle some more canola oil on the sliced side of the bread to finish it off.
5. Place the veggies on the barbecue and allow them to cook for 5 minutes without moving them. When the vegetables begin to wilt, and grill marks appear, gently turn them with a spatula to ensure even cooking. Continue cooking for another five min. Both sides of the bread should be toasted. Place the vegetables and ciabatta on a serving plate.

6. To assemble the sandwiches, distribute the herbed mascarpone mixture on both cut surfaces of the bread pieces. Cover the bottom slices of bread with layers of roasted veggies and arugula, then sprinkle with balsamic sauce to finish the sandwich.

7. Hot or even at room temp are both acceptable serving temperatures.

Chapter: 5 Plant Based Dessert Options

By include them on the menu, we are able to feel fuller after a dinner and adjust for low blood sugar levels that may occur after a meal. Sugar intake may also be motivated by a desire to improve one's mood, which may be a contributing factor. Sweet meals encourage the production of a hormone described as the "happy hormone." "hormone" that exists in our bodies. Your own actions and behaviors are critical in this process as well. The vast majority of people. Desserts are enjoyed by many people. Drinking dairy sweets may be both healthful and delightful while also being tasty excellent way to get your daily vitamin and mineral intake, as well as your protein and calories (kilojoules). Desserts are acceptable on a Plant based diet in the same manner that they are on a standard diet. Here are a few dessert recipes that you may like. You might want to think about the following:

204. Easy Vegan Paleo Chocolate Cupcakes

Total time: 40 minutes
Serving: 4
Nutrient per serving: Calories: 211, Fats: 12g, Carbohydrates: 34g, Proteins: 22.1g, Sodium: 1.8mg, Calcium: 50mg, Iron: 71mg
Ingredients:

- 1 teaspoon of baking soda
- 1/2 teaspoon of salt
- 1/2 cup of Hu Gems
- 3/4 cup of coconut sugar
- 1 1/4 cup of cassava flour
- 1/2 cup of cocoa powder
- 1 1/4 cup of almond milk
- 1 tablespoon of apple cider vinegar

Directions:

1. Preheat oven to 350 degrees Fahrenheit.
2. Melt the chocolate in a small saucepan with almond butter. Stir until the mixture is smooth.
3. Combine the cocoa sugar and cider vinegar in a separate bowl.
4. Mix in the remainder of the cupcake materials until well combined.
5. Fill each cupcake liner three-quarters of the way with the mixture and place in a cupcake pan lined with paper liners.

6. Preheat the oven to 350°F and bake for 25 minutes.
7. Allow for thorough cooling before icing.
8. To make the frosting, combine all ingredients in a mixing bowl and beat until thick and creamy using an electric mixer. To thicken, place in the refrigerator.
9. Cupcakes should be frosted after they have cooled. Reheat leftovers in the refrigerator for up to a week or freeze cakes for long shelf life.

205. Banana Split Deluxe

Total time: 10 minutes
Serving: 2
Nutrient per serving: Calories: 230, Fats: 14g, Carbohydrates: 7g, Proteins: 41g, Sodium: 2.6mg, Calcium: 56mg, Iron: 23mg
Ingredients:

- 1 cup of fresh berries
- 1 cup of shaved raw chocolate
- 1 cup of almond flakes
- 1 banana
- 2 cups of Date and coconut mixture

Directions:

1. Place the banana on a platter after slicing it in half along its length. Using the scoop, place many ices cream scoops on top, then garnish with fruit, shaved cocoa, and almond flakes.
2. Serve and take pleasure in it!

206. Date & Coconut Ice Cream

Total time: 2 hours
Serving: 1
Nutrient per serving: Calories: 480, Fats: 51g, Carbohydrates: 21g, Proteins: 37g, Sodium: 4.1mg, Calcium: 32mg, Iron: 25mg
Ingredients:

- 2-3 tablespoon of organic honey
- 1 teaspoon of vanilla powder
- 2/3 cup of dried dates
- ½ cup of toasted coconut flakes
- 1 cup of cashews

- 1 can of full-fat coconut milk

Directions:
1. Place the walnuts in a large mixing bowl and cover with lots of water. Allow the cashews to soak overnight or for at least 4-6 hrs. before using them to make the ice cream.
2. Rinse and drain the cashews, then place them in a blender with the other ingredients. Blend in the coconut cream, honey, and vanilla until the mixture is smooth. The mixture should have a creamy texture and be very smooth. Taste and adjust the sweetness if necessary.
3. Fill the ice cream maker with the mixture and process the ice cream. Before the ice cream is finished, fold in the crushed date and toasted coconut until well combined. Serve the ice cream right away, transfer it to a freezer-safe container and store it in the freezer for a couple of hours. Allow for around 15 minutes of thawing time before serving the ice cream.

207. Healthy Cookie Dough Blizzard Recipe

Total time: 30 minutes
Serving: 3
Nutrient per serving: Calories: 130, Fats: 14g, Carbohydrates: 77g, Proteins: 12g, Sodium: 1.8mg, Calcium: 30mg, Iron: 2mg

Ingredients:
- 1/2 cup of unsweetened almond milk
- 1 tablespoon of natural cashew butte
- 2 bananas
- 1 scoop of natural vegan vanilla protein powder

Directions:
1. Bananas should be peeled and sliced into quarters before freezing.
2. Make the cookie dough in accordance with the directions provided here - Vegan Cookie Dough is a delicious treat.
3. Make a total of 20 cookie dough balls.
4. Put the ball in the refrigerator to chill.

5. Once banana chunks have been frozen, you may proceed to produce the 'ice cream.
6. Blend or process the banana milkshake, almond butter, protein shakes, and cashew butter in a food processor or blender until smooth. Blend until the mixture is smooth.
7. Pour ice cream into two glasses and serve immediately.
8. Add two chocolate chip cookies balls to every glass and mix to combine. Serve and enjoy.

208. Vegan Apple Cider Donuts

Total time: 45 minutes
Serving: 4
Nutrient per serving: Calories: 320, Fats: 34g, Carbohydrates: 20g, Proteins: 33.1g, Sodium: 29.1mg, Calcium: 21mg, Iron: 4.9mg

Ingredients:
- 1/4 cup of vegan butter
- 1 teaspoon of vanilla extract
- 2 cups of flour
- 1/2 cup of organic cane sugar
- 1 teaspoon of apple cider vinegar
- 1/3 cup of apple sauce
- 2 teaspoon of baking powder
- 2 teaspoon of baking soda
- 1/4 teaspoon of ground nutmeg
- 1 1/4 cups of apple cider
- 1/4 teaspoon of salt
- 2 teaspoons of cinnamon

Directions:
1. Bake at 400 degrees Fahrenheit and coat a doughnut pan with nonstick cooking spray before starting.
2. In a large mixing bowl, combine the dry ingredients.
3. In a separate dish, whisk together all of the wet ingredients.
4. Put the cooking liquid into the dry ingredients and stir just until everything is mixed. Don't overmix the ingredients. The presence of a few tiny chunks in the batter is OK. It doesn't need to be perfectly smooth.

5. Fill the donut molds 3/4 of the way with the dough using a sewing bag (or a big Ziploc bag with the tip cut off.

6. Bake for 9-11 minutes, and until a toothpick inserted into the center comes out clean.

7. Mix the honey and cinnamon in a plastic baggie and use it to coat the doughnuts as a coating. Coat each donut with cooking spray, then put each doughnut in the sack and shake around till it's completely coated with cooking spray. Repeat the process with the remaining doughnuts.

209. Mind-Blowing Vegan Chocolate Pie

Total time: 45 minutes
Serving: 2
Nutrient per serving: Calories: 290, Fats: 28g, Carbohydrates: 67g, Proteins: 26g, Sodium: 4.9mg, Calcium: 15mg, Iron: 19mg
Ingredients:
- 12 ounces of chocolate chips
- sea salt for topping
- 12 ounces of firm silken firm tofu
- 1/2 cup of Almond Breeze Chocolate Almond milk
- 1/2 cup of almond butter

Directions:
1. To make the chocolate pie filling, combine the soy, almond milk, and nut butter in a blender and blend until smooth. Melt the white chocolate in a double boiler. In a blender, combine all of the ingredients and mix until smooth — it will be rather thick, so you may need to assist with a spoon between blends.

2. Assembly of the Chocolate Pie: Pour the filling into the pie crust, garnish with salt if desired, and place in the refrigerator for 12-24 hours. It's time to cut and serve!

210. Easy Healthy Peanut Butter Cups

Total time: 1hour 15 minutes
Serving: 6
Nutrient per serving: Calories: 380, Fats: 21g, Carbohydrates: 43g, Proteins: 2.4g, Sodium: 2.1mg, Calcium: 23mg, Iron: 43.1mg

Ingredients:
- 1-2 teaspoons Nature's Way Primadophilus Children's Probiotic
- Sea salt to garnish
- 1 heaping cup of dark chocolate chips
- ½ cup of natural peanut butter
- 2 tablespoons of pure maple syrup

Directions:
1. Prepare a muffin tray by lining it with 10 plastic muffin liners.

2. In a large mixing bowl, add the peanuts butter, syrup, and probiotic powder (if using) and whisk until everything combines in a soft mound and thoroughly blended, then put it away to cool completely.

3. Melt the chocolate chips in a small saucepan over low heat until completely melted.

4. Fill the base of each cup liner with 1/2 spoonful of the molten dark chocolate and set aside.

5. To make a thin coating of chocolate around the inside border of the muffin liner approximately 1 cm thick, use your fingers or a small spoon to swirl the chocolate about in each cup until it is evenly distributed.

6. Set 1 tablespoon of the peanut filling in your palm and form it into a tiny ball. Flatten it to approximately 1 cm thick and nearly the entire circumference of the muffin lining and place on top of the cocoa layer in each muffin liner. Repeat with the remaining peanut butter filling.

7. Repeat the process for all ten cups.

8. Add the mixture of melted chocolate into each muffin cup to fully cover the butter layer, trying to make sure that no visible peanut butter layer can be seen in the finished product.

9. Once everything is finished, put the muffin tray in the refrigerator for 20 minutes or when the chocolate is totally firm.

10. Refrigerate or freeze the cereal bars once they have been made.

211. Vegan Peanut Butter Cookies

Total time: 1 hour 20 minutes
Serving: 4
Nutrient per serving: Calories: 125, Fats: 13g, Carbohydrates: 34g, Proteins: 12g, Sodium: 22.8mg, Calcium: 12.1mg, Iron: 34mg
Ingredients:

- 6 tablespoons of almond milk,
- 1 teaspoon of baking soda
- pinch of mineral salt
- 1 cup of natural peanut butter
- 1 cup of coconut sugar or pure cane sugar
- 2 teaspoons of vanilla extract
- 1 cup of flour spelt unbleached all-purpose, almond flour

Directions:

1. Preheat oven to 350 ° degrees Fahrenheit (180 degrees Celsius). Prepare a cookie sheet by lining it with a silicone mat, parchment paper or by leaving it uncoated.
2. To make the dough, combine the peanuts, butter, and sugar in a large mixing bowl until well combined and creamy. Mix in the coconut milk and vanilla extract until well combined. Next, flour mixture, bicarbonate of soda, and salt in a large mixing bowl. It will be difficult to stir the dough; but utilizing your hands to combine it will be less difficult.
3. Form and flatten the dough: Using a 1.5 tablespoon scooper, take out the pastry and roll it into balls around 1 14 inches in diameter. Place the dough balls on a baking sheet, spacing them about 2 12 inches apart. Flatten the mixture with the edge of a spoon in a diagonal direction. Garnish with honey or coarse salt, if desired, before serving.
4. Bake: Place the cookie sheet in the oven to bake for 12 − 13 minutes (13 minutes would result in a crispier biscuit that is still delicate on the inside). Allow for a few minutes of cooling before transferring the cookies to a wire rack. Repeat with the remaining dough.
5. This recipe makes 20–24 cookies.

212. Vegan Lemon Bars

Total time: 1 hour 3 mins
Serving: 3
Nutrient per serving: Calories: 360, Fats: 44g, Carbohydrates: 23.1g, Proteins: 34g, Sodium: 51.2mg, Calcium: 13mg, Iron: 12.1mg
Ingredients:

- ¼ cup of Maple Syrup
- ¼ teaspoon of Salt
- Vegan Powdered Sugar
- 2 cups of Cashews
- ½ cup of Lemon Juice
- 2 tablespoons of Arrowroot Powder
- ⅛ teaspoon of Turmeric
- Zest of 1 Lemon
- 1 teaspoon of Vanilla Extract

Directions:

1. Preheat oven to 350 ° degrees Fahrenheit. In a small mixing bowl, whisk the Powder Flax, Milk, and Maple Syrup until thoroughly combined. Set aside for 5 minutes to thicken.
2. Then, using a high-speed blender, pulse the other crust ingredients until they are finely ground. Using a food processor, pulse in the thickened Flax "Egg" until a thick consistency form.
3. Using your fingers, spread the topping into the bottom of a 9-by-9-inch baking sheet until it is firmly and evenly distributed throughout the pan. 10 minutes in the oven should be enough.
4. To make the Lemon Bar filling, combine all components in an elevated blender and mix until thick and creamy. Set aside. Using a spatula, evenly distribute this mix over the base of the Lemon Bars, and then return them to the oven for another 18-20 minutes to bake. The borders of the bars will be somewhat hard and will begin to peel from the tin; the middle of the bar may seem a little runny at first but take

into consideration that the mix will thicken as the bar cools.

5. Allow the bars to cool slightly in the baking pan before carefully removing them with the parchment paper and transferring them to a level surface to cut into squares. If desired, sprinkle with powdered sugar before serving and enjoying. It is possible to store leftovers at room temp for up to three days or in the refrigerator for up to 1 week.

213. Salted Caramel Tahini Cups

Total time: 1 hour 10 minutes
Serving: 3
Nutrient per serving: Calories: 23.1, Fats: 43g, Carbohydrates: 42g, Proteins: 25g, Sodium: 34mg, Calcium: 1.1mg, Iron: 5.1mg
Ingredients:
- 1 cup packed, pitted dates
- 1/4 teaspoon sea salt
- 1/3 cup melted coconut oil
- 1/2 cup smooth, drippy tahini

Directions:
1. Drain and put aside the pitted dates after soaking them in boiling water for 15 minutes.
2. While the dates are soaked, gently whisk together the heated coconut oil, tahini, and syrup (if using) in a bowl and mix until smooth and creamy, about 2 minutes.
3. 9 muffin cups or baking pans cups should be prepared, and 1 tablespoon of the batter should be placed in each. Refrigerate or freeze them until they are firm. It should take around 10 minutes for them to solidify fully.
4. Mix the soaked date with sea salt in a stick blender until they are smooth and creamy, like a thick paste, and set aside. It's possible that you'll have to pause just a few times to wipe down the edges.
5. Remove the firm muffin tins from the freezer and pour the date mixture into each one, one spoonful at a time. Pour the leftover tahini mixture over each one in an

even layer. They're spreading out a little bit so that they're more or less flat.

6. Place the pan back in the fridge for 20-30 minutes, or until it has firm.
7. Keep in the refrigerator in a well-closed bag for up to two days and eat whenever you like.

214. Healthy Almond Pistachio Frozen Yogurt

Total time: 1 hour 10 minutes
Serving: 3
Nutrient per serving: Calories: 660, Fats: 23g, Carbohydrates: 32g, Proteins: 29.1g, Sodium: 3.1mg, Calcium: 4mg, Iron: 10mg
Ingredients:
- 1/4 teaspoon of xanthan gum
- 2 tablespoons of shelled raw pistachios
- 1 1/2 cups of unsweetened coconut yogurt
- 2 medium bananas
- 1/4 cup of raw honey
- 3/4 teaspoon of pure almond extract
- 2 small nuggets frozen spinach
- 1 cup of raw spinach
- 1/2 medium avocado

Directions:
1. Blend the yogurt, thawed banana, greens, avocados, sugar, vanilla essence, xanthan gum, and two tablespoons of the pistachios in a high-speed food processor or blender until fully smooth and thick.
2. Prepare a loaf pan by lining it with baking parchment and pouring the mixture into it.
3. Remove from the oven and sprinkle the other 2 tablespoons of crushed pistachio nuts on the cake.
4. You can just put this mix into your equipment and process it according to the manufacturer's directions for those of you who have an electric mixer.
5. Place the loaf pan in the freezer for 3-4 hours, or until the mixture is solid enough to scrape with only an ice cream cone before serving. Enjoy!

215. Vegan Double Chocolate Cake

Total time: 40 minutes
Serving: 10
Nutrient per serving: Calories: 420, Fats: 12g, Carbohydrates: 28g, Proteins: 21g, Sodium: 5.8mg, Calcium: 20mg, Iron: 51mg
Ingredients:

- ½ teaspoon of sea salt
- Half cup of Coconut flour
- 1 teaspoon of baking soda
- 2 tablespoons of non-dairy milk
- ¾ cups of Date Sugar
- Half cup of cocoa powder
- 3 teaspoons of peanut butter
- 1 cup of brown rice flour
- Cooked blended beets
- 1 cup of fresh water
- 1 teaspoon of apple cedar vinegar.
- For Icing, maple syrup
- Cocoa powder
- Avocado

Directions:

1. Preheat your oven at 350 degrees Fahrenheit and let it warm up for some time.
2. Your first step would be to mix all of your wet ingredients together. To be exact you would have to take 1 cup (or more) of Water and mix it with 2 tablespoons of non-dairy milk, 3 tablespoons of Peanut butter and 1 teaspoon of Apple cedar vinegar.
3. After you are done with your wet ingredients, now you will take all your dry ingredients and add them to create a dry mixture. As far as quantities of these ingredients is concerned, you will have to add 1 cup of brown rice flour, Half cup of coconut flour and Cocoa powder. After it, add ¾ cup of date sugar, ½ teaspoon of sea salt, and ½ cup of cooked blended beets to your cake dough under formation.
4. Now, pour your wet ingredient mixture and dry-ingredient mixture together in a bowl and keep stirring until it is finely blended. Initially it would be in paste form but with time and continuous stirring, it will turn into dough like structure.
5. Line the insides of your baking pan with parchment paper and pour the entire mixture into the pan.
6. Bake for 25 mins at 350 degrees Fahrenheit.
7. Your cake would be ready in 25-30 mins after which you can top it with your icing.
8. For making your cake's icing, you would have to take icing ingredients in desired proportions and mix them up together until it looks even and feels smooth. You would have to mix 1 sliced/chopped Avocado and quarter cup of both cocoa powder and Date/ Maple syrup.

216. Raspberry Nice Cream

Total time: 5-10 mins
Serving: 2 people
Nutrient per serving: Calories: 270, Fats: 35g, Carbohydrates: 21g, Proteins: 43g, Sodium: 0.8mg, Calcium: 40mg, Iron: 29mg
Ingredients:

- 1 cup of Frozen Raspberries
- 1 Frozen Banana
- 1 cup of Water

Directions:

1. Fill your blender's jug with 3 evenly sliced frozen bananas and 2 Tablespoon of Water. Blend these two ingredients until they adopt a smooth paste-like form.
2. Add raspberries according to your taste and pulse rhythmically until it gets mixed thoroughly, resulting in evenly distributed raspberry chunks throughout your desert.
3. Finally, top it with raspberries to give your desert a better look and an improved taste. You can add some other berries too if you want.

217. Gluten-free Blueberry Crisps

Total time: 50 minutes
Serving: 10
Nutrient per serving: Calories: 300, Fats: 42g, Carbohydrates: 23g, Proteins: 21.5g, Sodium: 4.5mg, Calcium: 12mg, Iron: 3.2mg
Ingredients:

- Oats
- 1 cup of Frozen/Free blueberries
- 2-3 Lemon
- 1 cup of Flax Seeds
- Cinnamon
- 1 cup of Water
- Pinch of Sea salt
- Maple Syrup
- ½ cup of Almonds

Directions:

1. Make sure to turn your oven on so that it is preheated to 375°F.
2. Use a zester or a fine cheese grater to zest the lemon for experiencing a unique flavor.
3. At first you should take 7 cups blueberries and empty it in a large baking dish.
4. Pour the lemon juice over the blueberries and distribute it evenly.
5. After that, 1 cup oats, flax seed, 1 teaspoon sea salt, 12 cup almonds and 2 tablespoons cinnamon are blended in a food processor.
6. To prepare the baking mixture, combine 1 cup oats, 12 cup almonds, 12 teaspoon salt, 12 tablespoons lemon zest (about 2 TBS), 12 cup maple syrup (or agave nectar), and 14 cup water in a mixing bowl by hand until well combined.
7. Drizzle over the berries in the baking dish the remaining maple syrup (1/2 cup).
8. Blended oat mixture, wet oat mixture, 14 cup water, remaining lemon zest, and 2 tablespoons cinnamon are sprinkled over the berries (in this sequence).
9. For 35 minutes, bake the crisp. Before taking it out of oven, make sure that the blueberries in your desert are bubbling.

This measure is to enjoy your plant-based dish to the best of its flavor. Enjoy your desert with your friends or family

218. Fudgy Vegan Brownie

Total time: 40 minutes
Serving: 9
Nutrient per serving: Calories: 230, Fats: 54g, Carbohydrates: 39g, Proteins: 27g, Sodium: 0.3mg, Calcium: 16mg, Iron: 2mg
Ingredients:

- 2 tbs of Maple Syrup or Date Syrup
- 1 cup of Black beans
- 1 cup of Dates (soaked plus pitted)
- Natural peanut butter
- 1 tbs of Cocoa Powder
- 1 cup of Coconut flakes or Minced walnuts.

Directions:

1. Turn on your Oven to preheat it to 350-degree Fahrenheit.
2. Meanwhile your oven is getting preheated, you should utilize that time for blending the ingredients until they form a smooth paste. The list of ingredients to blend together includes 2 cups of cooked sweet potato, 1 cup of black beans, 6 Tablespoon Cocoa Powder, Quarter cup of Maple syrup and 8 dates.
3. Use a scrapper to empty your mixture onto a baking sheet, spread it evenly and use walnuts/ coconut flakes to top your plant-based desert.
4. Let it bake for about 25-30 minutes.
5. After you are sure that its properly cooked, take it out of oven and wait for a few hours for it to cool down. You can also put it in fridge if you like your desert chilled.

219. No-Bake Pumpkin Pie

Total time: 15 minutes
Serving: 5
Nutrient per serving: Calories: 450, Fats: 23g, Carbohydrates: 43.1g, Proteins: 29g, Sodium: 3.8mg, Calcium: 50mg, Iron: 5.2mg
Ingredients:

- Pecans
- Walnuts

- Dates
- Pinch of Sea Salt
- Pumpkin
- 1 tablespoon of cinnamon
- 1 tablespoon of pumpkin spice
- 1 cup of chia seed
- 1 tablespoon of Maple Syrup

Directions:

1. Combine the walnuts, pecans, dates, and a sprinkle of sea salt in a food processor and pulse until smooth (you can substitute any nut you like)
2. Line a pie plate with the crumble and press it into the bottom of the dish to form a crust.
3. Blend the coconut milk, maple syrup, pumpkin puree, ground chia seed, cinnamon, pumpkin spice, and a sprinkle of sea salt in a blender or food processor until it becomes smooth and creamy.
4. In a pie crust, pour the pumpkin mixture in a circular motion.
5. Refrigerate overnight and serve cold.

220. Chocolate Peanut Butter Shake

Total time: 5 minutes
Serving: 2
Nutrient per serving: Calories: 470, Fats: 32g, Carbohydrates: 29g, Proteins: 43g, Sodium: 0.8mg, Calcium: 9mg, Iron: 23mg
Ingredients:

- 1-2 Frozen Bananas
- 1 cup of Non-Dairy milk
- 1 tbs of Raw Cacao powder
- 1 teaspoon of Natural Peanut Butter

Directions:

1. Add 1 cup of non-dairy milk, 3 tablespoons of Natural Peanut Butter, 3 Tablespoons Raw Cacao Powder and 2 Frozen Bananas in your blender and blend it until it forms a smooth paste.
2. Make sure to blend until no chunks of unprocessed ingredients are left in your smoothie. Enjoy your plant-based desert.
3.

221. Raw Vegan Chickpea Cookie Dough

Total time: 5-10 minutes.
Serving: 2
Nutrient per serving: Calories: 430, Fats: 53g, Carbohydrates: 7g, Proteins: 12g, Sodium: 18mg, Calcium: 34mg, Iron: 6.2mg
Ingredients:

- 1 tablespoons of Vanilla Extract
- Pinch of Sea Salt
- 1 cup of fresh water
- 1 tablespoon of natural peanut butter
- 1 teaspoon of maple syrup/date syrup
- ½ cup of Dark chocolate chips
- 1 cup of Chickpeas

Directions:

1. Combine all of the ingredients in fixed proportions in a blender until smooth. Your ingredient to mix will include 1 can chickpeas, 1 Tablespoon Vanilla Extract, A dash of sea salt, 3 Tablespoons of Maple Syrup, some Tablespoons of water and 1 Tablespoon of Vanilla extract.
2. In order to guarantee consistent mixing, use a rubber spatula to compress the cookie dough in the blender.
3. Once the mixture is smooth, fold in the chocolate chips/raisins using a spoon.
4. Use this easy-to-cook plant-based cookie dough whenever you crave for dessert.

222. Nutty Cookies

Total time: 15 minutes
Serving: 2
Nutrient per serving: Calories: 343, Fats: 54g, Carbohydrates: 51g, Proteins: 29g, Sodium: 4.8mg, Calcium: 12.1mg, Iron: 7.3mg
Ingredients:

- ½ cup of Walnuts
- 1 cup of Pecans
- ½ cup of Pitted dates
- 1 tablespoon of Lemon Juice
- Pinch of Sea salt

Directions:

1. Pulse the ingredients in a food processor until the mixture resembles a crumbled cookie. For cooking 6 cookies, you would

have to mix a cup of walnuts and Pecans each, a spritz of Lemon Juice, 13-15 dates (pitted) and a dash of sea salt.

2. Cookie shaped should be firmly pressed in else your cookie would become deformed during baking process.

3. Preheat the oven to 350 degrees, and let the cookies in there for 10-15 minutes, or until the top is golden brown.

223. Pumpkin Spice Shake

Total time: 5 mins
Serving: 1
Nutrient per serving: Calories: 430, Fats: 23g, Carbohydrates: 43.1g, Proteins: 2g, Sodium: 6mg, Calcium: 1mg, Iron: 3.8mg
Ingredients:
- Pumpkin
- 1 teaspoon of Pumpkin Spice Mix
- 1-2 Frozen Bananas
- 1 cup of Soft Dates (soaked overnight)
- 1 cup of Coconut Milk/ Soy milk
- Cinnamon

Directions:
1. For preparing one large glass of shake and satisfying your belly, you would have to
5. mix ¾ cup of Chopped or Canned Pumpkins, 3 Dates (soft and drained), 1 Teaspoon of Pumpkin Spice Mix, half Teaspoon of Natural Vanilla Extract and 1 cup of Soy Milk/ Coconut Milk (optional).
2. Put the mixture in a blender and blend it until it is perfectly smooth.
3. Sprinkle Cinnamon on top for additional taste.

224. Apple Crisp

Total time: 60 mins
Serving: 8
Nutrient per serving: Calories: 280, Fats: 32g, Carbohydrates: 21g, Proteins: 42g, Sodium: 0.8mg, Calcium: 9mg, Iron: 2.8mg
Ingredients:
- Thin slices of apple
- 1 cup of Water
- Cinnamon
- 1-2 Lemon Juice

- Pinch of Sea salt
- Date Syrup/ Maple Syrup

Directions:
1. Preheat oven to 350 °Fahrenheit. Not Preheating your oven beforehand will not only fail your cake to rise evenly but also deform your cake's shape so it is important.
2. Pour over apples in a microwave-safe baking dish after mixing up the ingredients for Apple base together (excluding the apples).
3. Turn your Microwave's heat setting to High and leave the apple mixture inside for 5 minutes
4. 1 cup of oats should be processed in a food processor until it resembles fine coarse flour.
5. Add the other ingredients for the crumble and pulse until the walnuts are broken up and the ingredients are well combined.
6. Bake for 35-40 minutes, or until the crumble mixture has been spread over the apples in the microwave. Whether hot or cold, this dish is delicious.

225. Chocolate and Vanilla

Total time: 5 minutes
Serving: 4
Nutrient per serving: Calories: 480, Fats: 12g, Carbohydrates: 54g, Proteins: 21g, Sodium: 0mg, Calcium: 7.1mg, Iron: 19mg
Ingredients:
- 8 dates
- Pinch of sea salt
- Some raw cashews
- ½ cup of Cacao Powder (raw form of Cocoa)

Directions:
1. First thing is to fill a bowl with water, soak dates and cashews in it and leave overnight. However, if making this vegan desert was a sudden plan. You can soak the nuts in hot water for 15 mins to soft them up.

2. Fill your blender with 8 Dates, half cup of cashews and 1/8 Teaspoon of Sea salt and blend the ingredients until they form a sort of mixture.

3. You can also mix 1 Tablespoon of Cacao Powder if you feel like adding another flavor to your desert.

4. Refrigerate the mixture for 10 minutes and after that, it would be ready to be topped on cakes, waffles, coffee, or shakes. If you don't have any of the aforementioned item available instantly, you can simply grab a spoon and eat it from the bowl, just like the Pudding.

226. Peanut Butter Cookies

Total time: 35 minutes
Serving: 9
Nutrient per serving: Calories: 400, Fats: 28g, Carbohydrates: 10g, Proteins: 2g, Sodium: 22mg, Calcium: 6.8mg, Iron: 9mg
Ingredients:
- ½ cup of Coconut Oil
- Peanut Butter
- 2 tbs of Maple Syrup
- 1 tbs of Cocoa Powder
- Rolled Oats
- Pinch of Kosher salt
- 2 teaspoons of Vanilla Extract

Directions:
1. Fill a tiny muffin tray with 9 muffin liners and set aside (or for 18 mini bites).

2. Cook 5 tablespoons coconut oil in a small saucepan over low heat, stirring constantly, until it is completely melted. Stir in 2 tablespoons peanut butter, 14 cup maple syrup, 14 cup cocoa powder, extract, 1 teaspoon vanilla and a dash of kosher salt.

3. Remove the pan from the heat and toss in 1 cup of rolled oats until everything is well incorporated.

4. Fill cupcake liners halfway with the mixture. While preparing the peanut butter topping, place the container in the refrigerator.

5. In a small saucepan set over low heat, combine 14 cup peanut butter, 1 TABLESPOON maple syrup, and 1 TABLESPOON coconut oil, stirring constantly until smooth. Pour the heated peanut butter mixture over the chocolate oat mixture and stir until well combined.

6. Let the mixture freeze for 15-20 mins until firm, or chill until ready to serve. Keep the desert in refrigerated environment for better results and improved taste.

227. Chocolate Vegan Ice-cream

Total time: 1 hour (+ freezing time)
Serving: 2
Nutrient per serving: Calories: 230, Fats: 19.7g, Carbohydrates: 56g, Proteins: 41g, Sodium: 8mg, Calcium: 5g, Iron: 8.4mg
Ingredients:
- 1 cup of Cornstarch
- 2 tablespoons of Coconut Sugar
- ½ cup of melted Dark chocolate
- 1 cup of Cocoa Powder
- 2 tablespoon of Full-fat coconut milk
- 2 teaspoons of Vanilla Extract
- ½ cup of Crushed Pistachios (optional)

Directions:
1. Overnight, place the ice cream machine base in the freezer.

2. 12 cup coconut milk and 2 teaspoons cornstarch should be combined in a small dish and put away.

3. In a medium-sized saucepan, bring the remaining coconut milk to a boil. For 1-2 mins, heat the coconut milk over medium low heat, stirring constantly to ensure that all of the solids are included.

4. Then, combine the agave syrup and coconut sugar in a separate bowl.

5. Break the chocolate into bits and add it to the coconut milk, stirring constantly until it is completely incorporated. Whisk in the cocoa powder and then the cornstarch mixture until well combined.

6. Heat the chocolate mixture for 6 to 8 minutes, or until it has thickened (do not

boil). Remove the pan from the heat and mix in the vanilla extract.

7. Using a fine-mesh strainer, strain the mixture into a Ziplock bag.

8. Refrigerate for 4 hours or overnight if you are churning immediately. If you are churning the next day, throw the bag in an ice bath for 30 minutes until cool.

9. Using an ice cream machine, churn the ice cream until it thickens itself to the standards of soft serve, which should take around 10 to 15 minutes. As the mixture is churning, slowly include the chopped pistachios and sea salt, if using.

10. If you like a soft serve consistency, eat it right away; if you prefer a firm ice cream texture, freeze it according to the following instructions: To scrape the ice cream into the container, insert a piece of parchment or wax paper into the container's sealable lid and scrape the ice cream into the container with a spatula, being careful not to scrape in the portions frozen around the base edges ice cream maker. For a firm ice cream texture, place

5.25 Chewy Pumpkin Oatmeal Cookies

Total time: 55 minutes

Serving: 3

Nutrient per serving: Calories: 338, Fats: 14g, Carbohydrates: 67g, Proteins: 42g, Sodium: 8g, Calcium: 34mg, Iron: 54mg

Ingredients:

- 1 teaspoon of baking soda
- 2 cups of Flour
- Ground ginger
- Ground Cinnamon
- Rolled Oats
- Nutmeg
- 1 teaspoon of Coconut Oil
- Vanilla
- `1/2 cup of Granulated Sugar
- 1 cup of Brown Sugar
- ¾ cup of Confectioners' Sugar
- 2 tbs of Almond milk
- Pinch of Kosher Salt

Directions:

1. In a medium-sized mixing bowl, whisk together the rolled oats, all-purpose flour, nutmeg, kosher salt, baking soda, cinnamon, and ginger until well combined.

2. Using a stand mixer fitted with a paddle attachment, whip the coconut oil with brown and granulated sugar on medium high speed for approximately 30 seconds, scraping down the sides of the bowl as needed, until thoroughly incorporated. Add in the pumpkin and vanilla and blend on low for a few seconds, or until everything is completely blended. Gradually incorporate the wet components into the dry ingredients in a low-speed mixer until the dough is formed.

3. Refrigerate the bowl for 30 minutes to let the flavors to blend.

4. The oven should be preheated to 375°F. Prepare two baking sheets by lining them with parchment paper. Take the dough-filled bowl out of the refrigerator and set it aside. Make 24 1 12 tablespoon-sized balls (or use a size 40 cookie scoop if you have one) and lay them on a baking sheet lined with parchment paper. Make a little flattening motion with your palm on the top of each cookie.

5. Preheat the oven to 350°F and bake for 11 minutes, until the bottom is gently browned.

6. Remove from the oven and let to cool for 2 minutes on the baking sheet before transferring to a wire rack to cool completely. Bake in two batches for the best results; this will provide the most uniform baking outcomes. Allow the glaze to cool to room temp. (approximately 30 minutes) if you are creating it.

7. To prepare the powdered sugar frosting, combine the confectioners' sugar and almond milk in a large mixing bowl until a thick sauce develops, and all lumps have been dissolved.

8. Using a fork, dip the cookies into the glaze and pour in a zigzag pattern over the

parchment paper-covered baking sheet. Allow the cookies to set at room temperature for approximately 20 minutes or until the glaze has dried completely.

9. Allow the cookies to set at room temperature for approximately 20 minutes or until the glaze has dried completely.

10. Refrigerate for up to 3 days after storing in an airtight container at room temperature. If you want to store the cookies for long time period, you can freeze them in the same container and keep them fresh for up to 3 months.

228. Tahini no-bake cookies

Total time: 30 minutes
Serving: 2
Nutrient per serving: Calories: 560, Fats: 32g, Carbohydrates: 63g, Proteins: 19g, Sodium: 23mg, Calcium: 9mg, Iron: 4mg
Ingredients:

- 1 cup of Tahini
- 2 teaspoons of Cocoa Powder
- ½ cup of Coconut Oil
- 1 tbs of Maple Syrup
- Cinnamon
- Vanilla Extract
- Rolled Oats
- Pinch of Kosher Salt
- Pinch of Sea salt
- Sesame seeds

Directions:

1. Prepare a 12-cup muffin tray by lining it with cupcake liners.
2. Use a glass-measuring cup to measure 3 Tablespoons of tahini, Quarter cup of cocoa powder, 5 Tablespoons of coconut oil and maple syrup each, 1 Teaspoon of vanilla extract, Half Teaspoon of cinnamon, and a bit of kosher salt, and stir till the point when the mixture is uniformly combined.
3. Microwave for 20 seconds, then whisk until everything is fully blended and smooth, but not too hot to touch. Add in the rolled oats and mix well.

4. Spoon approximately 2 teaspoons of each into the cupcake liners and press down firmly if required to form flat cookies in the bottoms of the cupcake cups. Sesame seeds and flakes sea salt are sprinkled over top.
5. Freeze for 20 minutes at a time. Keep refrigerated or frozen until ready to use. Keep it chilled as near as possible to when you're going to serve it.

229. Double Chocolate Mug Cakes

Total time: 4-5 minutes
Serving: 2
Nutrient per serving: Calories: 230, Fats: 52g, Carbohydrates: 34.6g, Proteins: 4.8g, Sodium: 31mg, Calcium: 12mg, Iron: 2.1mg
Ingredients:

- 1 cup of Cocoa Powder
- 2 cups of All-purpose Flour
- 1 teaspoon of Baking Soda
- Pinch of Kosher Salt
- Oat Milk
- 2 tbs of Neutral Oil
- ½ cup of Granulated Sugar
- ½ cup of Dark-chocolate chips

Directions:

1. Mix 2 Tablespoons of flour, 2 Tablespoons of Sugar and granulated cocoa powder each, ¼ Teaspoon of baking soda, and a pinch of salt in a microwave-safe cup until well combined. Combine the dairy-free milk and oil in a separate bowl. Stir in the chocolate chunks until they are evenly distributed.
2. Use a paper towel to protect the bottom of the cup while cooking in the microwave on high for 60 seconds. Examine the finished product: if it's still sticky and moist on top, microwave it for another 20 seconds, followed by another 10 seconds.
3. When the top seems to be cooked and bounces back when you touch it, it is done. The precise duration may vary depending on your microwave; ours works nicely with

60 seconds followed by another 30 seconds on high power.

4. It is extremely vital to allow the cake for to cool down for 2 to 3 from piping hot to warm before cutting into it.

5. You shouldn't taste it straight away since it doesn't taste properly. However, a few minutes of cooling will do the work!

6. Serve while still warm, topped with whipped cream or any other form of toping you prefer in your deserts.

230. Chocolate Chip Cookies

Total time: 25 minutes
Serving: 2-3 person.
Nutrient per serving: Calories: 343, Fats: 39g, Carbohydrates: 49g, Proteins: 2g, Sodium: 21mg, Calcium: 42mg, Iron: 32mg

Ingredients:

- ½ cup of Brown Sugar
- 1 cup of Almond Butter
- 1 teaspoon of Vanilla extract
- 2 cups of Water
- 1 cup of Flaxseed
- 1 teaspoon of baking soda
- Pinch of Sea Salt
- 1 cup of Almond flour
- Vegan Chocolate Chips

Directions:

1. Preheat your oven to 350 degrees Fahrenheit and prepare your baking pan by lining its inside walls with parchment paper before starting.

2. Allow for 5 minutes thickening time in the bottom of a big mixing bowl after whisking water together with the ground flaxseed.

3. Add half cup of coconut oil, quarter cup of almond butter, and 1 Teaspoon of Vanilla extract to the same mixing bowl. Whisk until everything is well-combined.

4. Whisk until everything is well-combined. Pour the baking soda and salt uniformly over the almond flour mixture once it has been combined. Stir with a spatula until the ingredients are well blended, adding 1-2 TBSN water if the mixture formed is too

dry to stir. Blend in the chocolate chips until well combined.

5. To scoop the dough onto the baking sheet, use a 2-tablespoon cookie scoop to scoop the dough. If desired, softly press each ball down and sprinkle with flaky sea salt, if using. Bake for 10 to 13 minutes, or until the edges are just beginning to brown around the edges.

6. Allow cooling it down for 5 minutes of time on the pan before transferring to a wire rack to complete the cooling process.

7. As soon as the cookies have cooled fully, they may be kept in an airtight container or frozen until needed. To reheat frozen cookies, bake them for 5 minutes at 350 degrees Fahrenheit or until they are warmed through.

231. Apple Crumble

Total time: 1 hour 20 minutes
Serving: 2
Nutrient per serving: Calories: 420, Fats: 28g, Carbohydrates: 37g, Proteins: 26g, Sodium: 4.3mg, Calcium: 18mg, Iron: 23mg

Ingredients:

- Cooking Apple
- 1-2 teaspoon of Lemon Juice
- Fresh Grated Ginger
- 1-2 Lemon zest
- Cinnamon
- Nutmeg
- Cornstarch
- Pinch of Kosher Salt
- ½ cup of Sugar
- 1 cup of Almond Flour
- 1 cup of Brown Sugar
- 1 cup of Gluten-free Oats
- Walnuts(optional)
- Vanilla
- 2 tablespoons of Coconut Oil

Directions:

1. In baking, the first step always is to preheat the oven to 350 degrees Fahrenheit equivalent to 180 degrees Celsius.

2. Apples should be cored, peeled, and thinly sliced. Grate the ginger once it has been peeled.
3. In a large mixing bowl or dish, combine the apple slices and the filling ingredients and toss well with your hands until fully covered.
4. Make the crumble topping in a separate bowl by combining the flour, brown sugar, oats, walnuts, and kosher salt in a large mixing bowl.
5. Stir in the vanilla extract until well incorporated. Small dollops of coconut oil should be added at a time. Crumble the topping together using a pastry cutter or fork to create a crumbly texture.
6. Coconut oil should be used to lubricate the baking dish. Make sure to place the apple filling in the bottom of the pan, and then equally spread the crumble on top of the apple filling in the pan.
7. Bake for 45-50 minutes, or until the top is golden and bubbling. Allow for a little cooling period before serving Plant-based Gluten free Whipped Cream. You can also add any other topping as per your choice.

232. Chocolate Pudding

Total time: 10-15 minutes
Serving: 3
Nutrient per serving: Calories: 230, Fats: 67g, Carbohydrates: 49g, Proteins: 22g, Sodium: 6mg, Calcium: 0.7mg, Iron: 2.9mg
Ingredients:
- Cornstarch
- 1 cup of Cocoa Powder
- ½ cup of Granulated Sugar
- 1 cup of Oat Milk/Almond Milk
- Pinch of Salt
- Vegan Choco chips
- 2 teaspoons of Vanilla Extract

Directions:
1. To make the cocoa powder mixture, place it in a medium pot and turn off the heat. Whisk vigorously to ensure that there are no lumps. Pour in the milk in little

quantities at a time, whisking after each addition, until the mixture is completely smooth.
2. At first, increase the heat to medium and bring the mixture to a simmer, stirring constantly. You will witness its edges to start bubbling.
3. Reduce the heat to low until the sides of the pan are just beginning to boil. Cook for 2 mins while stirring constantly, until the sauce has thickened, approximately 2 minutes.
4. Cook for 2 mins while stirring constantly, until the sauce has thickened, approximately 2 minutes. Because of pudding continuing to thicken and solidify as it cools, it is not necessary to make it completely thick at this time.
5. Remove the pan from the heat and whisk in the vegan Choco chips as well as vanilla until the chocolate chips are completely melted. It can be done efficiently if you keep on stirring while cooking.
6. Fill a container halfway with plastic wrap or wax paper and press it down on the surface.
7. Refrigerate for 2 hours or until the mixture is cool and firm. In the refrigerator, it can keep for up to 1 week.

233. Banana Blueberry Crumble

Total time: 50 minutes
Serving: 6
Nutrient per serving: Calories: 430, Fats: 13g, Carbohydrates: 43g, Proteins: 9g, Sodium: 4.9mg, Calcium: 2mg, Iron: 0mg
Ingredients:
- 1/2 teaspoon of vanilla powder or extract
- 1/4 cup of coconut oil
- 4 cups of blueberries
- 1/4 cup of maple syrup divided
- 3 cups of rolled oats
- 1/2 teaspoon of cinnamon
- 1 teaspoon of lemon juice
- 1 tablespoon of tapioca starch

- 1 medium banana

Directions:

1. Preheat oven to 350 degrees Fahrenheit.
2. In a large mixing bowl, combine the blueberries, 2 tablespoons maple syrup, lemon juice, and tapioca starch to make a thick, creamy sauce. Combine all ingredients in a mixing bowl until well incorporated, then move to a pie pan
3. Make a smooth banana puree by mashing it in the same bowl as before, aiming to eliminate as many stones as possible. Combine the oats, seasonings, remaining maple syrup, and coconut oil in a large mixing bowl. Stir together until well blended, then spoon the topping over the blueberries, spreading it out evenly over the top with your hands.
4. Bake the crumble for 40 - 45 mins on the middle rack of the oven, covering it for the final 10 minutes if necessary. The raspberries should be bubbling at the edges, and the oats must be golden brown on the bottom.
5. Remove the pan from the heat and cool for ten minutes before serving. Hot or warm, top with ice cream, Greek yogurt, or cocoa whipped cream and enjoy!

234. Easy Chocolate Avocado Pudding

Total time: 10 minutes
Serving: 4
Nutrient per serving: Calories: 200, Fats: 85g, Carbohydrates: 61g, Proteins: 2.8g, Sodium: 7.1mg, Calcium: 1mg, Iron: 43mg
Ingredients:

- 2 tablespoons of pure maple syrup
- 1 teaspoon of vanilla extract
- 2 ripe avocados
- 4 tablespoons of cacao powder
- 1 tablespoon of hemp seeds

Directions:

1. Blend or process all components in a food processor or blender until smooth, brushing down the sides as needed. If necessary, add more almond butter to aid in the blending process.
2. Taste it to determine whether you like more chocolate taste add extra cacao powder, 1 tablespoon at a time, extra sweet add a splash of maple syrup), or more vanilla flavor add more vanilla extract. Blend until the mixture is smooth.
3. Transfer the mixture to a sealed jar for archival purposes. Freeze for up to four days before serving. Chill before serving and top with coco creamy or your favorite garnishes.

235. Vegan Snickerdoodles Soft and Chewy

Total time: 30 minutes
Serving: 18
Nutrient per serving: Calories: 340, Fats: 12g, Carbohydrates: 65g, Proteins: 2g, Sodium: 45mg, Calcium: 9mg, Iron: 3.4mg
Ingredients:

- ½ teaspoon of cream of tartar
- 1 ¼ cup of white whole wheat flour
- ½ cup of vegan butter
- ½ cup of pure organic cane sugar
- 2 ½ tablespoon of water
- ½ teaspoon of baking soda
- 1 teaspoon of pure vanilla extract
- 1 tablespoon of flax

Directions:

1. Preheat the oven to 375 degrees Fahrenheit. Prepare a flax egg. In a small mixing dish, combine the flaxseed and the water. Allow for 5 minutes of resting time.
2. Using a handheld or stand mixer, beat together room temp vegan butter and sugar for about 2 minutes, or until smooth. Combine the flax egg and vanilla extract in a separate bowl until fully blended.
3. Combine the flour, cream of vinegar, and baking soda in a small mixing dish.
4. Pour in three parts, slowly mixing at moderate speed until the dry components are well incorporated with the wet ingredients. Scrape the edges of the bowl

to ensure complete incorporation. The dough will be rather thick.

5. Combine the cinnamon and 3 tablespoons of cane sugar in a small mixing bowl.

6. A biscuit scoop or spoon may scoop two tablespoons of batter and roll it into a ball. Roll the balls in the cinnamon-sugar coating and lay them on a cookie sheet lined with parchment paper.

7. 10 minutes in the oven should be enough. Immediately after you get the cookies out of the oven, gently flatten them with the wooden spoon to make them a little more uniform. Allow for 10 minutes of cooking time on the cookie sheet before transferring to a cooling rack entirely, if possible.

236. Dairy Free Chocolate Chip Cookies

Total time: 25 minutes
Serving: 18
Nutrient per serving: Calories: 433, Fats: 54g, Carbohydrates: 43g, Proteins: 62g, Sodium: 4.3mg, Calcium: 0.5mg, Iron: 19mg
Ingredients:
- 2 ½ tablespoon of fresh water
- ½ teaspoon of almond extract
- ½ cup of dairy free chocolate chips
- ½ cup of chopped pecans
- ½ cup of vegan butter
- ½ cup of muscovado sugar
- ½ teaspoon of baking soda
- ¼ teaspoon of salt
- 1 tablespoon of free milk
- 1 tablespoon of ground flax

Directions:
1. Preheat the oven to 350 degrees Fahrenheit. In a small mixing bowl, whisk together the flax and water until well combined. Allow for a 5-minute resting period.

2. In a large bowl, cream together the butter, sugar, and milk until smooth. Combine the flax egg and almond extract in a mixing bowl. Mix until everything is well-combined.

3. Sift together all the flour, bicarbonate of soda, and salt in a medium mixing bowl until well combined.

4. Combine flour mixture and butter mixture, mixing in one-third of the wheat at a time until well combined.

5. Fold in the white chocolate and pecans until well combined.

6. Prepare a baking sheet by lining it with parchment paper. Scoop the dough into little balls using a biscuit scoop or a tablespoon. Gently flatten the dough with the flat of a wooden spoon.

7. In a preheated oven, bake for ten min at 350°F. Allow for 5 minutes of cooking time on the baking sheet before transferring to a cooling rack entirely.

237. Vegan Cookie Dough Balls

Total time: 35 minutes
Serving: 18
Nutrient per serving: Calories: 540, Fats: 12g, Carbohydrates: 32g, Proteins: 19g, Sodium: 4mg, Calcium: 7.6mg, Iron: 32mg
Ingredients:
- 1 teaspoon of vanilla extract
- 3 tablespoon of chocolate chips
- 1 cup of almond flour blanched
- 2 tablespoon of maple syrup
- 3 tablespoons of almond butter

Directions:
1. Pour the almond flour into a mixing dish and stir well. Combine the maple syrup, nut butter, and vanilla in a mixing bowl.

2. Stir until everything is well-combined. When you roll it into balls, it will have a crumbly quality, but it will hold together when you bake it.

3. Toss in the chocolate chunks until evenly distributed.

4. 1 spoonful of dough should be scooped and rolled into a ball. Repeat the process with the remaining balls.

5. Freeze for thirty min in a sealed jar to firm up and establish the texture of the sauce.

238. Chocolate Coconut Date Balls

Total time: 20 minutes
Serving: 18
Nutrient per serving: Calories: 200, Fats: 32g, Carbohydrates: 43g, Proteins: 0.2g, Sodium: 11.6mg, Calcium: 7.1mg, Iron: 34mg
Ingredients:

- 1 teaspoon of vanilla extract
- 1 tablespoon of maple syrup optional
- 15 pitted dates
- 1 cup of blanched almond flour
- 6 tablespoons of cocoa powder
- ¼ cup of dairy free chocolate chips
- ½ cup of desiccated coconut flakes unsweetened

Directions:

1. Toss pitted dates into the food processor and pulse until smooth. Continue to process
until they are crumbly.
2. Combine the almond flour, cocoa, coconut, white chocolate, and vanilla in a large mixing bowl. Mix until everything is well-combined. The result will be a crumbly mixture.
3. If the mixture needs more moisture, 1 tablespoon of maple syrup may be added.
4. Make small scoops of dough using a tablespoon cookie scoop and push firmly into the scoop before releasing it into your hand. Form a ball out of the dough. Roll the ball into the coconut coating in a uniform layer in the bowl. Continue until all of the dough has been utilized. You must have between 16 and 18 balls in your possession.

239. Vegan Strawberry Cake

Total time: 1 hour
Serving: 12
Nutrient per serving: Calories: 230, Fats: 32g, Carbohydrates: 69.1g, Proteins: 42g, Sodium: 3.9mg, Calcium: 0mg, Iron: 2.4mg
Ingredients:

- 1 teaspoon of vanilla extract
- 1 cup of strawberries diced
- 6-8 additional strawberries to decorate the cake
- 1 cup of soy milk
- 1 teaspoon of apple cider vinegar
- ¾ cup of organic cane sugar
- ⅓ cup of vegetable oil
- 2 cups of all-purpose flour
- 1 teaspoon of baking powder
- ½ teaspoon of baking soda
- ¼ teaspoon of salt

Directions:

1. Preheat the oven to 350 degrees Fahrenheit. Combine soy milk and apple cider
vinegar in a mixing bowl. Set aside for a total of 10 minutes. 1 cup of sliced strawberries should be chopped.
2. In a blender or food processor bowl, sift together the wheat, rising powder, bicarbonate of soda, and salt. Make a mental note to put it away.
3. Nondairy milk and cider vinegar, together with cinnamon, sugar, and coconut oil, are combined in a medium-sized mixing bowl. Whisk the ingredients together until the sugar is completely dissolved.
4. Pour the wet ingredients into the bowl with the dry ingredients and mix well. Fold gently until everything is well combined. Take care not to over-mix the ingredients. Strawberries should be included in the batter.
5. Prepare a baking pan by lining it with parchment paper. Grease the inside and outside of the pan. Pour the batter into the pan. Shake or dump the pan onto the counter just a few times to distribute the batter evenly. Preheat the oven to 200°F and bake for 20-25 minutes, or until a toothpick inserted in the middle comes out clean.

240. Vegan Choco-Cakes

Total time: 30 minutes
Serving: 2
Nutrient per serving: Calories: 300, Fats: 12g, Carbohydrates: 7g, Proteins: 32g, Sodium: 62mg, Calcium: 12mg, Iron: 1.4mg

Ingredients:
- Nondairy milk
- Wheat Flour
- Baking Soda
- Brown Coconut sugar
- Vanilla extract
- Cider Vinegar
- Cocoa Powder
- Unsweetened Apple Sauce

Directions:
1. Preheat the oven to 350 degrees Fahrenheit. In a mixing dish, combine non-dairy milk and vinegar. Make a mental note to put it away. You will observe that the milk curdles and turns into buttermilk if left alone.
2. In a medium-sized mixing bowl, whisk together the whole wheat flour, cocoa powder, baking soda, baking powder, and salt. Mix everything together with a whisk.
3. In a large mixing bowl, combine the Vanilla extract, applesauce, and coconut sugar. Mix everything together with a whisk. Combine non-dairy milk and vinegar in a mixing bowl. Using a whisk, blend the ingredients until they are thoroughly incorporated.
4. Pour the dry ingredients into the mixing bowl with the liquid ingredients and stir until well combined.
5. Pour the dry ingredients into the mixing bowl with the liquid ingredients and stir until well combined. Stir until the ingredients are barely blended. The mixture will be lighter and thinner than other batters because of the use of baking soda.
6. Cupcake liners should be used to line a muffin tray. Distribute the batter evenly among the 12 muffin liners. They should be around three-quarters of the way filled. Bake your mixture for about 18-20 mins at 350 degrees Fahrenheit in a preheated oven, or until a toothpick put in the middle comes out completely clean. Allow the muffins to cool in the muffin tray for 10 mins before shifting to a wire rack to finish cooling.
7. Use your favorite coconut cream chocolate icing to finish off the cake.

241. Pumpkin Mug Cake

Total time: 3-4 minutes
Serving: 1
Nutrient per serving: Calories: 230, Fats: 76g, Carbohydrates: 45g, Proteins: 39.6g, Sodium: 34.1mg, Calcium: 32mg, Iron: 9.6mg

Ingredients:
- Date Sugar
- Pumpkin pie spice
- Whole wheat Four
- Pumpkin puree
- Oat Milk
- Vanilla extract
- Baking Powder

Directions:
1. In a cup, whisk together all of the dry ingredients until well combined 4 Tablespoons of flour, 2 Tablespoons of sugar, 1 Tablespoons of baking powder, and Half Tablespoons of pumpkin pie spice.
2. Combine the wet ingredients in a separate bowl 2 Tablespoons of pumpkin puree, 3 Tablespoons of dairy free milk, and Half Teaspoon of vanilla.
3. Combine the wet ingredients in a separate bowl. 2 Tablespoons of pumpkin puree, 3 Tablespoons of dairy free milk, and Half Teaspoon of vanilla. Stir until everything is well-combined, being careful to include the dry ingredients to the bottom of the cup.
4. Microwave on high for 2 minutes or until hot.

5. Remove the dish from the microwave. Finish with a dollop of coconut whipped cream and a pinch of pumpkin pie spice on top.

242. Vanilla Pudding with Fresh Berries

Total time: 2 hours 15 minutes
Serving: 4
Nutrient per serving: Calories: 250, Fats: 16.9g, Carbohydrates: 7.6, Proteins: 24.1g, Sodium: 6.1mg, Calcium: 5mg, Iron: 54.1mg
Ingredients:
- Vanilla Extract
- Salt
- Strawberries
- Blueberries
- Maple Syrup
- Cornstarch
- Coconut Milk
- Almond Milk (Unsweetened)

Directions:
1. In a small mixing dish, combine 12 cup almond milk. Corn starch should also be added in ratio of about 3 TBSN. Whisk the ingredients together until they are well blended. Make a mental note to put it away.
2. Melt the coconut milk in a small saucepan over medium heat, stirring constantly to blend the flavors. Add the maple syrup and salt and mix well. To blend, whisk the ingredients together.
3. Pour in 1/2 cup of almond milk and 3 TBSN of corn starch and whisk frequently until there are no lumps.
4. Bring the mixture to a boil above medium heat until it starts to bubble. Reduce the heat to low and continue to cook for another 5 minutes.
5. Put plastic wrap on top of the pudding so that it rests on top of the dessert. This will get rid of the topmost skin that develops on the pudding when it is baked.
6. Allow pudding to set in the refrigerator for 1 12-2 hours, or until it is hard and fully cold.

7. Remove strawberries from the pudding while it is cooling and cut into thin pieces.
8. Remove the pudding from the refrigerator after it has firmed up. Create a star shape with the strawberry's slices, and then arrange the strawberries and blueberries on alternate locations to complete the star pattern. Keep the dish refrigerated until you're ready to serve it.

243. Chocolate Chia Pudding

Total time: 2 hours 10 minutes
Serving: 2
Nutrient per serving: Calories: 533, Fats: 21g, Carbohydrates: 34.1g, Proteins: 54g, Sodium: 9.9mg, Calcium: 0mg, Iron: 44mg
Ingredients:
- Chia Seeds
- Cocoa Powder
- Almond Milk
- Vanilla Extract
- Banana
- Maple Syrup

Directions:
1. In a high-speed blender, mix together about 1 cup of almond milk, 4 TBSN of chia seeds, a banana, 2 TBSN of maple syrup, 2 TBSN of chocolate powder, and 1 Teaspoon of vanilla extract until it gets smooth.
2. Start with a slow speed and gradually raise it to a high one. Toss the chia seeds in the blender until they are thoroughly blended and invisible. It may be necessary to scrape the edges of the bowl in order to fully absorb every one of the chia seeds.
3. Pour the mixture into two short jars. Enjoy immediately from the blender, or chill for up to 2-3 hours to solidify and cool down even more.
4. To finish, add your favorite fruits, garnished nuts, flavored toppings, or seeds to the top of your plant-based desert.

244. Halloween Graveyards Pudding Cups

Total time: 40 minutes
Serving: 8
Nutrient per serving: Calories: 434, Fats: 32g, Carbohydrates: 86g, Proteins: 2.3g, Sodium: 5.8mg, Calcium: 12mg, Iron: 34mg

Ingredients:
- Water
- Cornstarch
- Vanilla Extract
- Raw Organic Sugar
- Cacao Powder
- Soy Milk

Directions:
1. In a small mixing bowl, whisk together the water and half cup of cornstarch to produce a paste.
2. In a large saucepan, boil the cornstarch paste after adding 4.5 cups of soy milk, 1 Teaspoon of vanilla extract, 3/4 cup of both sugar and cacao powder over medium heat until the mixture is smooth. Continue to stir constantly until the mixture comes to a boil.
3. Reduce the heat to low and continue to simmer, stirring constantly, until the pudding thickens.
4. Remove the pan from the heat. As the pudding cools, the consistency will continue to thicken. Allow for 5 minutes of cooling at ambient temperature before transferring to the refrigerator to chill entirely, if desired.
5. Meanwhile, separate the cream fillings from the cookies and set them aside to cool. Place all of the ingredients in a food processor and pulse until they turn crumbly.
6. Each big vegan graham cracker should be broken into four individual halves. To round the edges, use a butter knife to shave off the top of the cake. Write the letters RIP or any other message you like with care using a black gel decoration pen.
7. Transfer the pudding to separate serving cups after it has cooled. Decorate the top of the cake with chocolate cookie soil, a graham cracker gravestone, and any other extra decorations you choose.

245. Aquafaba Chocolate Mousse

Total time: 3 hours 20 minutes
Serving: 4
Nutrient per serving: Calories: 600, Fats: 36g, Carbohydrates: 52g, Proteins: 39g, Sodium: 6.5mg, Calcium: 32mg, Iron: 5mg

Ingredients:
- Dairy free milk
- Cocoa Powder
- Coconut Sugar/Cane sugar
- Aquafaba
- Dairy-free chocolate

Directions:
1. Using a metal strainer, drain the liquid from the chickpeas into a mixing dish.
Chickpeas should be set aside to be used in another dish. Refrigerate the liquid and the bowl for 10-15 minutes after they have been combined.
2. Raise 1-2 inches of water to a boil in a double boiler, following the directions on the package. Place a glass dish on top of the stove and fill it with 100 grammes of dairy-free chocolate chips or dairy-free chopped chocolate.
3. Allow the unsweetened chocolate to melt while you stir it every few minutes. Remove the melted chocolate from the double boiler and set it aside to cool. 1 TBSN of dairy milk chocolate may be used as an optional ingredient to make the chocolate melt more smoothly.
4. Take the aquafaba out from the fridge and set it aside. By making use of stand mixer, beat the aquafaba until it forms firm peaks. Put 1 spoonful of organic cane sugar at a time, stirring constantly. When you are able to invert the dish, the aquafaba has whipped to firm peaks.
5. While beating, gradually incorporate sifted cocoa powder into the foam. Pour in the melted chocolate. Make certain that the chocolate has fully cooled to room temperature before using it. In addition, if

you add the chocolate before it cools down, it will harden as it comes into contact with the foam, resulting in a gritty mousse texture. Adding the chocolate, a little at a time, mix until everything is properly blended. After you add the chocolate, the foam will begin to deflate. This is quite normal.

6. Pour into four individual serving glasses.
7. If you want the best results, keep it in the fridge for a minimum of 3 hours or overnight. Finish with some fresh raspberries and chocolate shavings on top.

246. Vegan Blondies

Total time: 35 minutes
Serving: 3
Nutrient per serving: Calories: 430, Fats: 12g, Carbohydrates: 34g, Proteins: 21g, Sodium: 3.1mg, Calcium: 38mg, Iron: 32mg
Ingredients:
- Chickpeas
- Almond Flour
- Maple syrup
- Baking powder
- Almond Butter
- Salt
- Vanilla extract
- Dairy free Choco chips

Directions:
1. Preheat the oven to 350 degrees Fahrenheit. In some kind of a food processor, pulse together 1 can of chickpeas, 1/3 cup of almond butter, half cup of almond flour, 1/3 cup of maple syrup, 1 Teaspoon of vanilla essence and baking powder respectively, and 2 pinches of salt until well combined.
2. Pulse until the batter becomes smooth and all of the chickpeas are evenly distributed.
3. Remove the blade from the food processor. Remove any additional dough that has accumulated on the blade. Pour the chocolate chips into the container of the food processor. Using a spatula, mix in the chocolate chips until well combined.

4. Prepare an 8-inch baking pan by lining it with parchment paper. Pour the batter into the baking pan. Using a spatula, distribute the batter evenly on the baking sheet. The batter will be sticky, and you may need to spread it with your clean hands to get it evenly distributed. Add an extra 2 TBSN of chocolate chips on top to finish it off. Using your fingers, lightly push them into the batter to include them.
5. Bake for 25-30 minutes at 350 degrees Fahrenheit in a preheated oven. The top will be a golden-brown color. Allow the pan to cool fully before removing it from the oven. Remove from the baking pan and slice it into 9 equal pieces using a sharp knife. Don't forget to Enjoy.

247. Watermelon Popsicles

Total time: 3 hours 15 minutes
Serving: 4
Nutrient per serving: Calories: 220, Fats: 32g, Carbohydrates: 39.1g, Proteins: 51g, Sodium: 32.1mg, Calcium: 2.3g, Iron: 21mg
Ingredients:
- Watermelon
- Vegan Chocolate Chips/Raisons
- Strawberries
- Coconut milk
- Kiwi

Directions:
1. Firstly, 2 cups of Watermelon should be cut and transformed into cube shaped pieces.
2. Remove the stems from the strawberries and chop them into quarters. The watermelon and strawberries should be blended together until smooth in a food processor or blender before serving in the ratio of 2:1.
3. Pour the mixture into four popsicle molds, filling them approximately three-quarters of the way.
4. Chocolate chips should be distributed equally throughout the four molds. Using a popsicle stick, carefully press the chocolate

chips right into the molds, ensuring that they are equally distributed. You may also use raisins in this recipe.

5. Put your Popsicle molds in freezer and let it freeze for at least an hour or until the chocolate has set.

6. While the first portion is freezing, combine 14 cup coconut milk and 1 teaspoon maple syrup in a separate bowl. After the initial layer has hardened, equally distribute the coconut milk among the four molds, using approximately 1 tablespoon for each mold.

7. After that, put it back in and continue to let it freeze for one more hour or until the mixture has set.

8. Meanwhile, peel the outer surface of the kiwi in half and slice it into tiny bits while your 2nd layer is still in the freezer. Two TBSN coconut milk should be added to the blender.

9. Spread the kiwi layer above the surface of the coconut layer after it has hardened. Freeze for a further hour, or until the mixture is set. Serve and take pleasure in it!

248. Spinach-Mango Popsicles

Total time: 3 hours 5 minutes
Serving: 4
Nutrient per serving: Calories: 553, Fats: 42g, Carbohydrates: 87g, Proteins: 31g, Sodium: 12mg, Calcium: 0mg, Iron: 51mg
Ingredients:
- Fresh Spinach
- Frozen Mango
- Almond Milk
- Coconut Milk
- Maple Syrup
- Frozen Bananas

Directions:
1. Blend 1 cup of almond milk, 1.5 cups of spinach, and a bit of salt in a blender until a uniform mixture is formed.
2. Pulse on medium speed, escalating to high speed as needed, until spinach is thoroughly broken down and mixed.

3. Combine 1/3 cup of coconut milk, half cup of mango and banana each, & 2 Tablespoons of maple syrup in a blender. Blend until the mixture is smooth.

4. Pour the mixture into popsicle molds. Popsicle sticks should be used. If they aren't standing up straight in the molds, freeze them for an hour before inserting them.

5. For obtaining optimal results, let your popsicles freeze for three hours at least. However, overnight freezing time would give you more ideal results.

249. Vegan Pumpkin Brownies

Total time: 1 hour 10 minutes
Serving: 9
Nutrient per serving: Calories: 322, Fats: 31g, Carbohydrates: 53g, Proteins: 64g, Sodium: 53mg, Calcium: 5mg, Iron: 4mg
Ingredients:
- Whole Wheat Flour
- Pumpkin Pie Spice
- Pumpkin Puree
- Applesauce (unsweetened)
- Cane Sugar
- Vanilla Extract
- Brown Sugar
- Cacao Powder
- Salt
- Baking Powder

Directions:
1. Preheat the oven to 350 degrees Fahrenheit.
2. Add 15 oz of pumpkin purée and quarter cup of applesauce, to 2 Tablespoon of pumpkin pie spice in a large mixing bowl. Combine all of the ingredients in a separate bowl and put aside.
3. Combine all of the ingredients in a separate bowl and put aside. Take 3/4 cup of both almond milk and applesauce with 1 Teaspoon of vanilla extract, 1 cup of cane sugar, and half cup of brown sugar. Place

all of this mixture in a mixing bowl until well combined. Whisk the ingredients together until they are well blended.

4. Take a separate bowl for mixing the recipe's dry ingredients in proportions as follow: 1.5 cups of Whole wheat flour, 1 Teaspoon of Baking Powder. 1/2 cup of cacao powder, and half teaspoon of salt.

5. Whole wheat flour, 1 Teaspoon of Baking Powder. 1/2 cup of cacao powder, and half teaspoon of salt. To blend, whisk the ingredients together.

6. Combine wet and dry ingredients in a separate bowl. Using a whisk, mix all of the ingredients.

7. Pour the brownie batter into an 8-inch square baking cookie sheet and bake for 20 minutes.

8. Pour the brownie batter into an 8-inch square baking cookie sheet and bake for 20 minutes. The pumpkin pie filling should be spread on top of the brownie batter.

9. Preheat the oven to 45-55 degrees. To check if they are thoroughly cooked, insert a toothpick in the middle. Prior to removing your brownies from the baking pan and slicing into 9 squares, allow the cake to cool fully

250. Lemon sorbet

Total time: 20 minutes
Serving: 6
Nutrient per serving: Calories: 430, Fats: 21g, Carbohydrates: 54g, Proteins: 75g, Sodium: 15mg, Calcium: 2.5mg, Iron: 21mg
Ingredients:
- juice of 2-3 lemons
- 2 tablespoons of vodka
- 250g of white caster sugar
- thick strip of lemon peel

Directions:
1. In a small saucepan, heat 250 ml beaker water, the sugar, and the fresh lemon over medium heat until the carbohydrate has dissolved, then bring the liquid to a boil.

(Optional) Cook for 3 minutes before turning off the fire and allowing the dish to cool. Remove the lemon peel from the dish and set it aside. Take out 100ml of lime juice and stir it into the sugar mixture, along with the alcohol if you're using it. Set aside.

2. After 1 hour and 30 minutes of freezing, remove from the freezer and whisk together to end things and integrate the ice (which will have begun to form around the edges) before putting in the freezer for another hour and 30 minutes.

3. Continue to stir the sherbet once hourly for the next 4 hours in order to split the ice. Mix until the mixture is solid but still scoopable, then place in the fridge for up to 1 month. Serve the sorbet in scoops. Each one is topped with just a few curls of lime juice.

251. Rhubarb & Star Anise Sorbet

Total time: 40 minutes
Serving: 2
Nutrient per serving: Calories: 433, Fats: 26g, Carbohydrates: 50g, Proteins: 0.7g, Sodium: 3.7mg, Calcium: 12mg, Iron: 2.9mg
Ingredients:
- 3 tablespoons of liquid glucose
- 1 lemon juice
- 1 tablespoon of vodka
- 700g of thin forced rhubarb
- 140g of golden caster sugar
- 1 vanilla pod
- 2-star anise

Directions:
1. Place the raspberries in a saucepan with the sugar, 75 mL water, and the fluid glucose and bring to a boil. Remove the beans from the juice and zest and put them in the pan (together with the pod and star anise) to cook for another minute.

2. Stirring periodically, bring the mixture to a boil over a medium-high flame. Reduce the heat to a low setting and cook for fifteen min, or until the honey has completely

dissolved as well as the fruit is mushy and beginning to break down. Remove the remove from heat and carefully remove the pea pod and allspice from the mixture. Blend everything in a blender.

3. Pour the liquid through a small mesh strainer to remove any stringy pieces of rhubarb that may have remained after straining.

4. Transfer the mixture to a jug and toss in the lemons and vodka, if desired. After covering with plastic wrap and placing it in the refrigerator until completely cooled, churn it in an ice cream maker according to the manufacturer's directions. Fill an airtight container halfway with the sorbet, then freeze for at least three hours before serving. It will keep for up to a month if kept frozen.

252. Almond Jam Dot Cookies

Total time: 1 hour 10 minutes
Serving: 4
Nutrient per serving: Calories: 320, Fats: 12g, Carbohydrates: 43g, Proteins: 5g, Sodium: 5.8mg, Calcium: 10mg, Iron: 0.8mg
Ingredients:
- ⅓ cup of coconut oil
- 1/2 teaspoon of Ceylon cinnamon
- 1/2 teaspoon of sea salt
- 1 ½ cup of almond meal
- 1 ¼ cup of oat flour
- ⅓ cup of maple syrup
- ½ cup of fruit preserves

Directions:
1. Heat the oven to degrees Fahrenheit.
2. Combine all of the dry ingredients.
3. Combine the coconut and maple syrup in a separate bowl before incorporating it into the dry ingredients.
4. Using a tiny scoop, place it on a baking sheet lined with parchment paper.
5. Make a hole in each biscuit for the jam by using a teaspoon.

6. 15 minutes in the oven should be enough. After 8 minutes, rotate the baking sheet. Take the baking sheet out of the oven.

7. Bake for 2-3 minutes, or until the jam is golden brown, in the middle of the pan.

253. No-Bake Cookies

"**Preparation time:** 30 minutes."
"**Cooking time:** 0 minutes."
"**Servings:** 9"
"**Ingredients:**"
- "1 cup rolled oats"
- "¼ cup of cocoa powder"
- "⅛ teaspoon salt"
- "1 teaspoon vanilla extract, unsweetened"
- "¼ cup and 2 tablespoons peanut butter, divided"
- "6 tablespoons coconut oil, divided"
- "¼ cup and 1 tablespoon maple syrup, divided"

"**Directions:**"
1. Put five tbsps. of coconut oil into a little pot, put the pot at low flame, and allow the oil to dissolve.
2. Mix in a quarter cup of cocoa powder and a quarter cup of maple syrup, along with two tbsps. of peanut butter, a pinch of salt, and one tsp. of vanilla essence. Stir till everything is thoroughly blended.
3. Take the pot away from the flame. After stirring in the oats, divide the batter equally among the nine cups of a muffin pan.
4. After cleaning the skillet, place it back over a low temperature setting. Stirring in the remainder amount of peanut butter, maple syrup, and coconut oil should bring everything together. Heat it completely by giving it another min in the oven.
5. After drizzling the peanut butter sauce across the oat mixture that is already contained within the muffin tin, place it into the freezer for around twenty mins so that it can solidify.
6. Serve straight away.

137

Per serving: Calories: 213kcal; Fat: 14.8g; Carbs: 17.3g; Protein: 4g

254. Lemon Cake

"**Preparation time:** 10 minutes"
"**Cooking time:** 50 minutes"
"**Servings:** 9"
"**Ingredients:**"

- "½ cup white whole-wheat flour"
- "½ teaspoon baking powder"
- "2 tablespoons almond flour"
- "1 lemon, zested"
- "¼ teaspoon baking soda"
- "⅛ teaspoon turmeric powder"
- "⅓ teaspoon salt"
- "¼ teaspoon vanilla extract, unsweetened"
- "⅓ cup lemon juice"
- "½ cup maple syrup"
- "¼ cup olive oil"
- "¼ cup of water"

"For the frosting:"

- "1 tablespoon lemon juice"
- "⅛ teaspoon salt"
- "¼ cup maple syrup"
- "2 tablespoons powdered sugar"
- "6 ounces vegan cream cheese, softened"

"**Directions:**"

1. "Switch on the oven. Set it to 350°F and let it preheat."
2. Grab a big container and add water, lemon juice, and oil to it. Stir to combine. Add vanilla extract and maple syrup and whisk until blended.
3. Whisk in flour, ¼ cup at a time, until smooth. Then whisk in almond flour, salt, turmeric, lemon zest, baking soda, and powder until well combined.
4. Take a loaf pan. Grease it with oil, spoon the prepared batt, and then bake for 50 minutes.
5. In the meantime, make the icing by grabbing a little container and placing each of the necessary components inside of it. After you have whisked it till it is

homogeneous, place it in the refrigerator until it's needed.
6. "When the cake has cooked, let it cool for 10 mins in its pan, then let it cool totally on the wire rack."
7. "Spread the prepared frosting on top of the cake. Slice the cake and then serve."

Per serving: Calories: 275kcal; Fat: 12g; Carbs: 38g; Protein: 3g

255. Chocolate Clusters

"**Preparation time:** 15 minutes"
"**Cooking time:** 0 minutes"
"**Servings:** 12"
"**Ingredients:**"

- "1 cup chopped dark chocolate, vegan"
- "1 cup cashews, roasted"
- "1 teaspoon sea salt flakes"

Directions:

1. "Take a large baking sheet, line it with wax paper, and then set aside until required."
2. "Take a medium bowl, place chocolate in it, and then microwave for 1 minute."
3. After giving the chocolate a stir, place it in the microwave for one min at a time and maintain to mix it throughout each break till the chocolate is fully melted.
4. When melted, stir the chocolate to bring it to 90°F, and then stir in cashews.
5. Scoop the walnut-chocolate mixture on the prepared baking sheet, ½ tablespoon per cluster. Then sprinkle with sea salt.
6. "Let the clusters stand at room temperature until harden, and then serve."

"**Per serving:** Calories: 79.4kcal; Fat: 6.6g; Carbs: 5.8g; Protein: 1g"

256. Banana Coconut Cookies

"**Preparation time:** 40 minutes"
"**Cooking time:** 20 minutes"
"**Servings:** 8"
"**Ingredients:**"

- "½ cup shredded coconut, unsweetened"
- "1 cup mashed banana"

"**Directions:**"

1. "Switch on the oven. Set it to 350°F and let it preheat."
2. "Take a medium bowl, place the mashed banana in it, and stir in coconut until well combined."
3. Take a large baking sheet, line it with a parchment sheet, and then scoop the prepared mixture on it, 2 tablespoons of mixture per cookie.
4. "Place the baking sheet into the refrigerator and let it cool for 30 minutes or more until it hardens."
5. Serve straight away.

Per serving: Calories: 51kcal; Fat: 3g; Carbs: 4g; Protein: 0.2g

257. Maple Syrup and Tahini Fudge

"**Preparation time:** 2 hours"
"**Cooking time:** 3 minutes"
"**Servings:** 15"
"**Ingredients:**"
- "1 cup dark chocolate chips, vegan"
- "¼ cup maple syrup"
- "½ cup tahini"

"**Directions:**"
1. Put the chocolate chips inside a container that can withstand temperature, put the container inside the oven for two to three mins while mixing them per min, and then they should be fully dissolved.
2. After the chocolate has dissolved, retrieve the container from the oven and immediately begin whisking in the tahini and maple syrup till they are completely combined.
3. Get a cookie sheet that's four inches by eight inches and coat it using parchment paper. Spoon the chocolate mixture and then press it into the baking dish.
4. Cover another sheet with wax paper. Press it down until smooth, and let the fudge rest for 1 hour in the freezer until set.
5. Then cut the fudge into 15 squares and serve.

Per serving: Calories: 110.7kcal; Fat: 5.3g; Carbs: 15.1g; Protein: 2.2g

258. Banana Muffins

"**Preparation time:** 10 minutes"
"**Cooking time:** 30 minutes"
"**Servings:** 12"
"**Ingredients:**"
- "½ cup mashed banana"
- "½ cup and 2 tablespoons white whole-wheat flour, divided"
- "¼ cup of coconut sugar"
- "¾ cup rolled oats, divided"
- "1 teaspoon ginger powder"
- "1 tablespoon ground cinnamon, divided"
- "2 teaspoons baking powder"
- "½ teaspoon salt"
- "1 teaspoon baking soda"
- "1 tablespoon vanilla extract, unsweetened"
- "½ cup maple syrup"
- "1 tablespoon rum"
- "½ cup of coconut oil"

"**Directions:**"
1. "Switch on the oven. Then set it to 350°F and let it preheat."
2. In the meantime, get a container around this size. Put a half cup of flour inside it, as well as a half cup of oats, ginger, baking powder, soda, salt, and two tsps. of cinnamon. Mix everything together thoroughly. Whisk till blended.
3. Put a quarter cup of coconut oil inside a basin that can withstand burning. In the oven, dissolve it, and afterwards mix in the maple syrup till it is completely incorporated.
4. Combine the chopped banana with the rum and vanilla extract. Shake till all the ingredients are incorporated, and afterwards swirl the wet ingredients into the dry ingredients till a homogeneous dough is formed.
5. Prepare a distinct moderate container. Put all of the leftover flour and oats into the container. After that, incorporate cinnamon, coconut sugar, and coconut oil into the mixture.

6. "Then stir with a fork until a crumbly mixture comes together."
7. Take a 12-cup muffin pan and fill it evenly with the prepared batter. "Top with oats mixture, and then bake for 30 minutes until firm and the top turns golden brown."
8. "When done, let the muffins cool for 5 minutes in their pan, then cool them completely before serving."

Per serving: Calories: 240kcal; Fat: 9.3g; Carbs: 35.4g; Protein: 2.6g

259. Juicy Brussel Sprouts

"**Preparation time:** 10 minutes"
"**Cooking time:** 10 minutes"
"**Servings:** 4"
"**Ingredients:**"
- "1-pound Brussels sprouts, trimmed"
- "¼ cup green onions, chopped"
- "6 cherry tomatoes, halved"
- "1 tablespoon olive oil"
- "Salt and black pepper to taste"

"**Directions:**"
1. Take a baking dish suitable to fit in your air fryer. "Toss Brussels sprouts with salt and black pepper in the dish. Place this dish in the air fryer and seal the fryer. Cook the sprouts for 10 minutes at 350ºF on air fryer mode."
2. "Toss these sprouts with green onions, tomatoes, olive oil, salt, and pepper in a salad bowl."

Per serving: Calories: 120kcal; Fat: 3g; Carbs: 23g; Protein: 4g

260. Balsamic Artichokes

"**Preparation time:** 10 minutes"
"**Cooking time:** 7 minutes"
"**Servings:** 4"
"**Ingredients:**"
- "4 big artichokes, trimmed"
- "¼ cup olive oil"
- "2 garlic cloves, minced"
- "2 tablespoons lemon juice"
- "2 teaspoons balsamic vinegar"
- "1 teaspoon oregano, dried"
- "Salt and black pepper to taste"

"**Directions:**"
1. "Season artichokes liberally with salt and pepper, then rub them with half of the lemon juice and oil."
2. "Add the artichokes to a baking dish that fits in the air fryer."
3. "Place the artichoke dish in the air fryer basket and seal it."
4. Cook them for 7 minutes at 360°F on air fryer mode.
5. "Whisk the remaining lemon juice, oil, vinegar, oregano, garlic, salt, and pepper in a bowl."
6. "Pour this mixture over the artichokes and mix them well. Enjoy."

Per serving: Calories: 310kcal; Fat: 10g; Carbs: 25g; Protein: 4g

261. Tomato Kebabs

"**Preparation time:** 10 minutes"
"**Cooking time:** 6 minutes"
"**Servings:** 4"
"**Ingredients:**"
- "3 tablespoons balsamic vinegar"
- "24 cherry tomatoes"
- "2 cups vegan feta cheese, sliced"
- "2 tablespoons olive oil"
- "3 garlic cloves, minced"
- "1 tablespoon thyme, chopped"
- "Salt and black pepper to taste"

"For the Dressing:"
- "2 tablespoons balsamic vinegar"
- "4 tablespoons olive oil"
- "Salt and black pepper to taste"

"**Directions:**"
1. "In a medium bowl, combine oil, garlic cloves, thyme, salt, vinegar, and black pepper."
2. "Mix well, then add the tomatoes and coat them liberally."
3. Thread 6 tomatoes and cheese slices on each skewer alternatively.

4. "Place these skewers in the air fryer basket and seal them."
5. "Cook them for 6 minutes at 360F on air fryer mode."
6. Meanwhile, whisk together the dressing ingredients.
7. Place the cooked skewers on the serving plates.
8. Pour the vinegar dressing over them.
9. Enjoy.

Per serving: Calories: 190kcal; Fat: 6g; Carbs: 18g; Protein: 8g

262. Parsley Potatoes

"**Preparation time:** 10 minutes"
"**Cooking time:** 10 minutes"
"**Servings:** 4"
"**Ingredients:**"
- "1 pound of gold potatoes, sliced"
- "2 tablespoons olive oil"
- "¼ cup parsley leaves, chopped"
- "Juice from ½ lemon"
- "Salt and black pepper to taste"

"**Directions:**"
1. "Take a baking dish suitable to fit in your air fryer."
2. "Place the potatoes and season them liberally with salt, pepper, olive oil, and lemon juice."
3. "Place the baking dish in the air fryer basket and seal it."
4. "Cook the potatoes for 10 minutes at 350°F on air fryer mode."
5. Serve warm with parsley garnishing.

Per serving: Calories: 280kcal; Fat: 5g; Carbs: 36g; Protein: 4g

263. Eggplant and Zucchini Snack

"**Preparation time:** 10 minutes"
"**Cooking time:** 8 minutes"
"**Servings:** 4"
"**Ingredients:**"
- "1 eggplant, cubed"
- "3 zucchinis, cubed"
- "2 tablespoons lemon juice"
- "1 teaspoon oregano, dried"
- "3 tablespoons olive oil"
- "1 teaspoon thyme, dried"
- "Salt and black pepper to taste"

Directions:
1. Take a baking dish suitable to fit in your air fryer.
2. Combine all ingredients in the baking dish.
3. "Place the eggplant dish in the air fryer basket and seal it."
4. "Cook them for 8 minutes at 360°F on air fryer mode."
5. Enjoy warm.

Per serving: Calories: 210kcal; Fat: 4g; Carbs: 16g; Protein: 3g

264. Artichokes with Mayo Sauce

"**Preparation time:** 10 minutes"
"**Cooking time:** 6 minutes"
"**Servings:** 4"
"**Ingredients:**"
- "2 artichokes, trimmed"
- "1 tablespoon lemon juice"
- "2 garlic cloves, minced"
- "A drizzle of olive oil"

"For the Sauce:"
- "1 cup vegan mayonnaise"
- "¼ cup olive oil"
- "¼ cup coconut oil"
- "3 garlic cloves"

Directions:
1. "Toss artichokes with lemon juice, oil, and 2 garlic cloves in a large bowl."
2. "Place the seasoned artichokes in the air fryer basket and seal it."
3. "Cook the artichokes for 6 minutes at 350º on air fryer mode."
4. "Blend coconut oil with olive oil, mayonnaise, and 3 garlic cloves in a food processor."
5. Place the artichokes on the serving plates.
6. Pour the mayonnaise mixture over the artichokes.
7. Enjoy fresh.

Per serving: Calories: 230kcal; Fat: 11g; Carbs: 24g; Protein: 6g

265. Cashew Oat Muffins

"**Preparation time:** 10 minutes"
"**Cooking time:** 22 minutes"
"**Servings:** 12"
"**Ingredients:**"

- "3 cups rolled oats"
- "¾ cup raw cashews"
- "¼ cup maple syrup"
- "¼ cup sugar"
- "1 teaspoon vanilla extract"
- "½ teaspoon salt"
- "1½ teaspoon baking soda"
- "2 cups water"

"**Directions:**"

1. "Preheat your oven to 375°F."
2. "Separately, whisk together the dry ingredients in one bowl and the wet ingredients in another."
3. Beat the two mixtures together until smooth.
4. Fold in cashews and give it a gentle stir.
5. "Line a muffin tray with muffin cups and evenly divide the muffin batter among the cups."
6. "Bake for 22 minutes and serve."

Per serving: Calories: 520kcal; Fat: 4g; Carbs: 54g; Protein: 9g

266. Fried Asparagus

"**Preparation time:** 10 minutes"
"**Cooking time:** 8 minutes"
"**Servings:** 4"
"**Ingredients:**"

- "2 pounds fresh asparagus, trimmed"
- "½ teaspoon oregano, dried"
- "4 ounces vegan feta cheese, crumbled"
- "4 garlic cloves, minced"
- "2 tablespoons parsley, chopped"
- "¼ teaspoon red pepper flakes"
- "¼ cup olive oil"
- "Salt and black pepper to the taste"
- "1 teaspoon lemon zest"
- "1 lemon, juiced"

"**Directions:**"

1. "In a large bowl, combine lemon zest with oregano, pepper flakes, garlic, and oil."
2. Add asparagus, salt, pepper, and cheese to the bowl.
3. "Toss well to coat, then place the asparagus in the air fryer basket."
4. "Seal the fryer and cook them for 8 minutes at 350ºF on air fryer mode."
5. Garnish with parsley and lemon juice.
6. Enjoy warm.

Per serving: Calories: 310kcal; Fat: 10g; Carbs: 32g; Protein: 6g

267. Carrot Flaxseed Muffins

"**Preparation time:** 10 minutes"
"**Cooking time:** 20 minutes"
"**Servings:** 12"
"**Ingredients:**"

- "2 tablespoons ground flax"
- "5 tablespoons water"
- "¾ cup almond milk"
- "¾ cup applesauce"
- "½ cup maple syrup"
- "1 teaspoon vanilla extract"
- "1 ½ cups whole wheat flour"
- "½ cup rolled oats"
- "1 cup grated carrot"

Directions:

1. In a container, mix the ground flaxseed with the water, then set it aside for ten mins. Now, inside one dish, mix all of the dried components, and in a second one, stir all of the moist components.
2. Beat the two mixtures together until smooth. Next, fold in flaxseed and carrots, and give it a gentle stir.
3. "Line a muffin tray with muffin cups and evenly divide the muffin batter among the cups."
4. "Bake for 20 minutes and serve."

Per serving: Calories: 320kcal; Fat: 4g; Carbs: 50g; Protein: 4g

268. Chocolate Peanut Fat Bombs

"**Preparation time:** 10 minutes"
"**Cooking time:** 1 hour 1 minute"
"**Servings:** 12"
"**Ingredients:**"

- "½ cup coconut butter"
- "1 cup plus 2 tablespoons peanut butter"
- "5 tablespoons cocoa powder"
- "2 teaspoons maple syrup"

"**Directions:**"

1. "In a bowl, combine all the ingredients. Melt them in the microwave for 1 minute."
2. Mix well, then divide the mixture into silicone molds. Freeze them for 1 hour to set.

Per serving: Calories: 350kcal; Fat: 15g; Carbs: 45g; Protein: 8g

269. Chocolate Raspberry Brownies

"**Preparation time:** 15 minutes + 8 hours"
"**Cooking time:** 15 minutes"
"**Servings:** 4"
"**Ingredients:**"
"For the Chocolate Brownie Base:"

- "12 Medjool Dates, pitted"
- "¾ cup oat flour"
- "¾ cup almond meal"
- "3 tablespoons cacao"
- "1 teaspoon vanilla extract, unsweetened"
- "⅛ teaspoon sea salt"
- "3 tablespoons water"
- "½ cup pecans, chopped"

"For the Raspberry Cheesecake:"

- "¾ cup cashews, soaked, drained"
- "6 tablespoons agave nectar"
- "½ cup raspberries"
- "1 teaspoon vanilla extract, unsweetened"
- "1 lemon, juiced"
- "6 tablespoons liquid coconut oil"

"For the Chocolate Coating:"

- "2 ½ tablespoons cacao powder"
- "3 ¾ tablespoons coconut oil"
- "2 tablespoons maple syrup"
- "⅛ teaspoon sea salt"

"**Directions:**"

1. Make the base by placing all of the crust's components in a mixing bowl and pulsing it for three to five mins, or till the components mix to form a firm mixture.
2. Grab a springform pot with a diameter of six inches and coat it using oil. After spreading and pressing the crust solution uniformly on the lower part and around the edges of the pan, put the crust solution inside the saucepan. Refrigerate unless needed.
3. To make the covering for the cheesecake, put all of the topping's components within a mixing bowl and process for two mins, or till the mixture is homogeneous.
4. "Pour the filling into the prepared pan. Smooth the top and freeze for 8 hours until solid."
5. Create the chocolate covering by combining each of its components in a bowl with a beater till the mixture is well-combined. Sprinkle it over the cake, and afterwards offer.

"**Per serving:** Calories: 340kcal; Fat: 7g; Carbs: 50g; Protein: 4g"

Conclusion

A vegetarian diet is beneficial to one's health. Reduced cholesterol levels, weight loss, decreased blood hypertension, and a reduced chance of developing cardiovascular illnesses are all benefits of exercising. It also aids in the prevention of life-threatening chronic illnesses such as diabetes and cancer. It may also aid in the extension of one's life span. Nevertheless, if the meal is not correctly planned, it may be detrimental to one's health and wellbeing. Therefore, further research should be undertaken in order to demonstrate the favorable impacts of a vegetarian diet. Considering a vegetarian diet as an alternative to adjuvant treatment, I believe that anybody at risk of acquiring any of the illnesses such as diabetes, cardiovascular disease, kidney stones, hyperlipidemia, and cataracts, or who is suffering from depression, should seriously consider it.

Several scientific studies have been published in recent years suggesting that a nutritious vegetarian diet has considerable health benefits compared to diets that include meat and other items derived from animals (such as eggs and dairy). A variety of health advantages may be obtained by consuming fewer calories from saturated fats and animal proteins while increasing dietary fiber, Vit C and E, carotene, magnesium, folic acid, and other phytochemical intakes. Despite the fact that vegetarian diets are sometimes criticized for being deficient in nutrients such as vitamin B12 and proteins as well as zinc and calcium, a well-planned "Appropriate diet with good planning" containing supplements would ensure that these shortages never occur.

30-Day Meal Plan

Day	Breakfast	Lunch	Dinner	Dessert
1	Chewy Oatmeal Banana Pancakes	Brown Rice with Vegetables and Tofu	Chard Wraps with Millet	Vegan Double Chocolate Cake
2	Banana Almond Granola	Balsamic Arugula and Beets	Grilled Eggplant Steaks	Raw Vegan Chickpea Cookie Dough
3	Apple-Lemon Breakfast Bowl	Tex-Mex Pita Pizzas	Grilled Cauliflower Steaks	Chocolate Peanut Butter Shake
4	Black Bean and Sweet Potato Hash	Creamy Wild Rice Soup	Adzuki Bean Bowls	Apple Crumble
5	Smokey Tempeh Bacon	Avocado & White Bean Salad Wraps	Macro Veggie Bowl	Easy Chocolate Avocado Pudding
6	Low Fat Cinnamon Nut Granola	The Best Oil-Free Hummus	Radish Salad	Chocolate Chia Pudding
7	Cornmeal Waffles	Black Bean and Sweet Potato Quesadillas	Stuffed Poblano Peppers	Lemon sorbet
8	Cinnamon Semolina Porridge	Potato-Cauliflower Curry	Portobello Mushroom Burger	Maple Syrup and Tahini Fudge
9	Date and Oat Flour Waffles	Potato Salad with Avocado and Dill	Stuffed Acorn Squash	Cashew Oat Muffins
10	Crunchy Almond Cereal Breakfast	Vegan Mashed Potatoes and Gravy	Twice Baked Sweet Potatoes	Chocolate Raspberry Brownies
11	Sweet Potato Hash Browns	Veggie Olive Wraps with Mustard Vinaigrette	Butternut Squash Soup	Eggplant and Zucchini Snack
12	Baked Corn Casserole	Easy Healthy Falafels	Stuffed Zucchini with Freekeh Pilaf and Currants	Double Chocolate Mug Cakes
13	Vegan Huevos Ranchero Case roll	Smoky Spiced Veggie Rice	White Bean Soup with Garlic and Parsley	Healthy Almond Pistachio Frozen Yogurt
14	Oatmeal with Berries and Nuts	Vegan Kebabs with Avocado Dressing	Vegan Black Bean Burgers	Halloween Graveyards Pudding Cups
15	Easy Breakfast Chia Pudding	Lentil Lasagna	Rutabaga Laksa	Vegan Snickerdoodles Soft and Chewy
16	Apple-Walnut Breakfast Bread	Kidney Bean Curry	Vegetarian Thai Pineapple Forbidden Fried Rice	Vanilla Pudding with Fresh Berries
17	Gluten-free Breakfast Muffin	Vegan Shepherd's Pie	One-Pot Skinny Pasta Primavera	Dairy Free Chocolate Chip Cookies

18	Vegan Breakfast Benedict	Sesame Parsnip & Wild Rice Tabbouleh	Instant Pot No-Soak Black Bean Soup	Chocolate Vegan Ice-cream
19	Healthy Oatmeal with Fruit and Nuts	Fennel, roast lemon & tomato salad	Spicy Miso Eggplant & Broccoli Salad	Gluten-free Blueberry Crisps
20	Brown Rice Breakfast Pudding	Butternut Squash and Chickpea Curry	Zucchini Verde Vegan Enchiladas	Healthy Cookie Dough Blizzard Recipe
21	Vegan Kale Caesar Salad	Grain Dishes Cranberry and Walnut Brown Rice	Spaghetti Squash w/ Chickpeas & Kale	Easy Healthy Peanut Butter Cups
22	Banana Bread with Maple Glaze	Spicy Hummus Quesadillas	Easy Coconut Curry	Easy Vegan Paleo Chocolate Cupcakes
23	Baked Pears with Cardamom	Cilantro and Avocado Lime Rice	Kale Salad with Carrot Ginger Dressing	Salted Caramel Tahini Cups
24	Sweet Potatoes with a Twist	Brown Rice Pilaf	Best Buddha Bowl	Chocolate and Vanilla
25	Vegan Breakfast Potatoes	Lentil Vegetable Soup	Cauliflower Rice Kimchi Bowls	Vegan Peanut Butter Cookies
26	Simple Avocado Toast	Quick and Easy Noodle Soup	Freekeh Bowl with Dried Figs	Tahini no-bake cookies
27	Pumpkin Griddle Cakes	Corn and Black Bean Cakes	Portobello Burritos	Chocolate Coconut Date Balls
28	Baked Bean Toast	Stove-Top Vegan Macaroni and Cheese	Sweet Potato Quesadillas	Aquafaba Chocolate Mousse
29	Blueberry Lemon French Toast	Spicy French Fries	Grilled Veggie Kabobs	Chocolate Clusters
30	Buckwheat Pancakes	Black Beans & Avocado on Toast	Cream of Mushroom Soup	Spinach-Mango Popsicles

Index

"Nacho" Vegan Baked Potato, 52
"No-Tuna" Salad Sandwich, 53
8-Ingredient Slow-Cooker Chili, 59
Acai Bowl, 73
Adzuki Bean Bowls, 83
Almond Jam Dot Cookies, 137
Antioxidant Blueberry Smoothie, 17
Apple Crisp, 122
Apple Crumble, 126
Apple-Lemon Breakfast Bowl, 22
Apple-Walnut Breakfast Bread, 24
Aquafaba Chocolate Mousse, 133
Artichoke & Aubergine Rice, 65
Artichokes with Mayo Sauce, 141
Avocado & White Bean Salad Wraps, 54
Baked Bean Toast, 19
Baked Corn Casserole, 36
Baked Mushroom Polenta Bowls, 15
Baked Pears with Cardamom, 35
Balsamic Artichokes, 140
Balsamic Arugula and Beets, 48
Banana Almond Granola, 20
Banana Baked Oatmeal, 18
Banana Blueberry Crumble, 127
Banana Bread with Maple Glaze, 31
Banana Coconut Cookies, 138
Banana Muffins, 139
Banana Sandwich, 16
Banana Split Deluxe, 114
Barley and Mushrooms with Beans, 49
Bartha, 107
Best Buddha Bowl, 82
Best Lentil Soup, 94
Best Veggie Burger, 85
Black Bean and Sweet Potato Hash, 23
Black Bean and Sweet Potato Quesadillas, 57
Black Bean Burgers, 55
Black Beans & Avocado on Toast, 66
Blueberry Lemon Bars, 32
Blueberry Lemon French Toast, 17
Boiled Potato on Rye Bread, aka Potato Salad on Toast, 100
Breakfast Scramble, 22

Broccoli and Rice Stir Fry, 80
Broccoli Casserole with Beans and Walnuts, 82
Brown Rice Breakfast Pudding, 22
Brown Rice Pilaf, 48
Brown Rice with Vegetables and Tofu, 44
Buckwheat Pancakes, 32
Burritos with Spanish Rice and Black Beans, 55
Butternut Squash and Chickpea Curry, 43
Butternut Squash Soup, 93
Carrot Chia Pudding, 33
Carrot Flaxseed Muffins, 142
Cashew Oat Muffins, 142
Cauliflower and Chickpeas Casserole, 43
Cauliflower and Potato Curry, 79
Cauliflower Lentil Bowl, 71
Cauliflower Rice Kimchi Bowls, 84
Cauliflower Steaks with Roasted Red Pepper & Olive Salsa, 73
Celeriac, Hazelnut & Truffle Soup, 64
Chard Wraps with Millet, 77
Chewy Oatmeal Banana Pancakes, 17
Chickpea Omelet, 20
Chickpeas and Sweet Potato Curry, 48
Chocolate and Vanilla, 122
Chocolate Buttermilk Pancakes, 23
Chocolate Chia Pudding, 132
Chocolate Chip Cookies, 126
Chocolate Clusters, 138
Chocolate Coconut Date Balls, 130
Chocolate Peanut Butter Shake, 121
Chocolate Peanut Fat Bombs, 143
Chocolate Pudding, 127
Chocolate Raspberry Brownies, 143
Chocolate Vegan Ice-cream, 123
Cilantro and Avocado Lime Rice, 47
Cinnamon Semolina Porridge, 41
Coconut Rice, 48
Coconut Sorghum Porridge, 49
Corn and Black Bean Cakes, 58
Cornmeal Waffles, 31
Country Hash Browns with Sausage Gravy, 27
Cream of Mushroom Soup, 96
Creamy Porridge with Almonds, 41

Creamy Wild Rice Soup, 51
Crispy Baked Falafel, 86
Crispy Roasted Shallot and Lentil Sheet-Pan Mujadara, 103
Crunchy Almond Cereal Breakfast, 37
Crustless Broccoli Sun-Dried Tomato Quiche, 30
Curried Rice, 45
Dairy Free Chocolate Chip Cookies, 129
Date & Coconut Ice Cream, 114
Date and Oat Flour Waffles, 41
Double Chocolate Mug Cakes, 125
Easy Breakfast Chia Pudding, 29
Easy Chocolate Avocado Pudding, 128
Easy Coconut Curry, 95
Easy Healthy Falafels, 69
Easy Healthy Peanut Butter Cups, 116
Easy Overnight Oats with Chia, 24
Easy Vegan Corn Chowder, 51
Easy Vegan Paleo Chocolate Cupcakes, 114
Easy Vegetarian Chili, 95
Eggplant and Zucchini Snack, 141
Egyptian Breakfast Beans, 21
Fennel, roast lemon & tomato salad, 74
Freekeh Bowl with Dried Figs, 76
Fresh Avocado Toast With Pesto, 37
Fried Asparagus, 142
Fudgy Vegan Brownie, 120
Full Flour Chock Veggies Chickpea Pizza Crust, 50
Garlic-Jalapeño Naan, 24
Gingery Noodle Salad, 98
Gluten-free Blueberry Crisps, 120
Gluten-free Breakfast Muffin, 16
Gluten-Free Chocolate Chip Muffins, 38
Gluten-Free Chocolate Chip Pancakes, 19
Grain Dishes Cranberry and Walnut Brown Rice, 45
Grilled Cauliflower Steaks, 81
Grilled Eggplant Steaks, 80
Grilled Vegetable Sandwich, 112
Grilled Veggie Kabobs, 80
Guacamole & Mango Salad with Black Beans, 65
Halloween Graveyards Pudding Cups, 133
Healthy Almond Pistachio Frozen Yogurt, 118
Healthy Cinnamon Apples, 39
Healthy Cookie Dough Blizzard Recipe, 115
Healthy Oatmeal with Fruit and Nuts, 21

Healthy Taco Salad, 92
Hibiscus Tea, 34
Indian Peanutty Noodles, 101
Instant Pot No-Soak Black Bean Soup, 106
Italian-Style Zucchini and Chickpea Sauté, 63
Juicy Brussel Sprouts, 140
Kale Salad with Carrot Ginger Dressing, 92
Kidney Bean Curry, 67
Kimchi Brown Rice Bliss Bowls, 82
Lemon Cake, 138
Lemon sorbet, 136
Lentil Lasagna, 70
Lentil Oats Power Porridge, 34
Lentil Ragu with Courgetti, 69
Lentil Sloppy Joes, 57
Lentil Vegetable Loaf, 77
Lentil Vegetable Soup, 50
Low Fat Cinnamon Nut Granola, 28
Macro Veggie Bowl, 85
Maki Sushi Recipe, 91
Mango Madness, 42
Maple Glazed Tempeh with Quinoa and Kale, 44
Maple Syrup and Tahini Fudge, 139
Millet Fritters, 76
Mind-Blowing Vegan Chocolate Pie, 116
Mint Chocolate Smoothie, 30
Mixed Berry Bowl, 40
Mushroom Veggie Tacos, 35
No-Bake Cookies, 137
No-Bake Pumpkin Pie, 120
No-Fry Fried Rice, 61
Nutty Cookies, 121
Oatmeal with Berries and Nuts, 33
Oil-Free Blueberry Scones, 26
Oil-Free Roasted Potatoes, 29
One-Pot Skinny Pasta Primavera, 108
Orange French Toast, 15
Parsley Potatoes, 141
Peanut Butter Cookies, 123
Peanut Soup with Veggies, 46
Pears and Cranberries, 21
Penne with Tomato-Mushroom Sauce, 53
Pineapple and Mango Oatmeal, 41
Plant-Strong Power Bowl, 75
Portobello Burritos, 75
Portobello Mushroom Burger, 86

Potato Salad with Avocado and Dill, 62
Potato-Cauliflower Curry, 60
Pumpkin Griddle Cakes, 40
Pumpkin Mug Cake, 131
Pumpkin Pie Cake, 27
Pumpkin Spice Shake, 122
Quick and Easy Noodle Soup, 52
Quinoa & Breakfast Patties, 40
Quinoa Lentil Burger, 45
Radish Salad, 91
Raspberry Nice Cream, 119
Raw Vegan Chickpea Cookie Dough, 121
Rhubarb & Star Anise Sorbet, 136
Rice Bowls with Kidney Beans, Spinach, and Mixed Veggies, 60
Roasted Cauli-Broc Bowl with Tahini Hummus, 67
Roasted Veggie Grain Bowl, 83
Rutabaga Laksa, 105
Salted Caramel Tahini Cups, 118
Satay Tempeh with Cauliflower Rice, 76
Sesame Parsnip & Wild Rice Tabbouleh, 72
Sesame Soba Noodles, 90
Simple Avocado Toast, 39
Smokey Tempeh Bacon, 26
Smoky Spiced Veggie Rice, 71
Spaghetti Squash w/ Chickpeas & Kale, 90
Spiced Peanut Sweet Potato Salad, 101
Spicy French Fries, 63
Spicy Hummus Quesadillas, 46
Spicy Miso Eggplant & Broccoli Salad, 101
Spicy Tuna Poke Bowls, 108
Spinach, Sweet Potato & Lentil Dhal, 66
Spinach-Mango Popsicles, 135
Spinach-Potato Tacos, 56
Spiralized Zucchini, Quinoa and Turkey Sausage Stuffed Peppers, 109
Squash & Spinach Fusilli with Pecans, 64
Stove-Top Vegan Macaroni and Cheese, 52
Stuffed Acorn Squash, 88
Stuffed Indian Eggplant, 78
Stuffed Poblano Peppers, 89
Stuffed Zucchini with Freekeh Pilaf and Currants, 99
Sushi Salad, 97
Sweet Oatmeal "Grits", 47
Sweet Polenta with Pears, 42

Sweet Potato & Cauliflower Lentil Bowl, 70
Sweet Potato Chili with Kale, 59
Sweet Potato Hash Browns, 34
Sweet Potato Quesadillas, 78
Sweet Potatoes With A Twist, 37
Taco-Spiced Tortilla Chips, 58
Tahini no-bake cookies, 125
Tex-Mex Pita Pizzas, 49
The Best Oil-Free Hummus, 59
Tofu Scramble, 18
Tomato Basil Soup, 96
Tomato Kebabs, 140
Turmeric-Roasted Cauliflower with Pistachio Gremolata, 102
Twice Baked Sweet Potatoes, 88
Twice-Baked Potatoes with Creamy Chive Pesto, 99
Vanilla Pudding with Fresh Berries, 132
Vegan Apple Cider Donuts, 115
Vegan Bacon, 87
Vegan Black Bean Burgers, 109
Vegan Blondies, 134
Vegan Breakfast Benedict, 18
Vegan Breakfast Potatoes, 38
Vegan Broccoli Soup, 93
Vegan Cauliflower Alfredo Bake, 104
Vegan Chicken Phở, 106
Vegan Choco-Cakes, 131
Vegan Cookie Dough Balls, 129
Vegan Curried Rice, 79
Vegan Double Chocolate Cake, 119
Vegan Huevos Ranchero Case roll, 29
Vegan Kale Caesar Salad, 25
Vegan Kebabs with Avocado Dressing, 73
Vegan Lemon Bars, 117
Vegan Mashed Potatoes and Gravy, 61
Vegan Peanut Butter Cookies, 117
Vegan Pumpkin Brownies, 135
Vegan Shepherd's Pie, 68
Vegan Snickerdoodles Soft and Chewy, 128
Vegan Strawberry Cake, 130
Vegan Whole Wheat Waffles, 39
Vegan Yogurt Parfait with Berries & Granola, 28
Vegetable Hash with White Beans, 81
Vegetable Lasagna with Butternut Squash and Shiitake Mushroom, 110

Vegetable Stir-fry, 46
Vegetarian Thai Pineapple Forbidden Fried Rice, 111
Veggie And Apple Slaw, 62
Veggie Olive Wraps with Mustard Vinaigrette, 65

Watermelon Popsicles, 134
White Bean Soup with Garlic and Parsley, 104
Yummy Jelly & Peanut Butter Oatmeal, 36
Zucchini Cakes, 35
Zucchini Verde Vegan Enchiladas, 97